ABOUT STOPPARD: The Playwright and the Work

Jim Hunter is the author of two previous studies of Stoppard (including *The Faber Critical Guide to Rosencrantz and Guildenstern Are Dead, Jumpers, Travesties and Arcadia*) as well as of other critical works and novels. A former teacher and headmaster, he is now an associate lecturer with the Open University.

Series Editor: Emeritus Professor Philip Roberts was Professor of Drama and Theatre Studies and Director of the Workshop Theatre in the University of Leeds from 1998 to 2004. Educated at Oxford and Edinburgh, he held posts in the Universities of Newcastle and Sheffield before arriving in Leeds. His publications include: *Absalom and Achitophel and Other Poems* (Collins, 1973), *The Diary of Sir David Hamilton, 1709–1714* (Clarendon Press, 1975), *Edward Bond: A Companion to the Plays* (Theatre Quarterly Pubs, 1978), *Edward Bond: Theatre Poems and Songs* (Methuen, 1978), *Bond on File* (Methuen, 1985), *The Royal Court Theatre, 1965–1972* (Routledge, 1986), *Plays without Wires* (Sheffield Academic Press, 1989), *The Royal Court Theatre and the Modern Stage* (CUP, 1999).

Series Editor: Richard Boon is Professor of Performance Studies at the University of Leeds. He is the author of a number of studies of modern British political theatre, including *Brenton the Playwright* (Methuen, 1991), and is co-editor of *Theatre Matters: Performance and Culture on the World Stage* (CUP, 1998). He is also author of *About Hare: The Playwright and the Work* (Faber and Faber, 2003).

in the same series

ABOUT BECKETT
The Playwright and the Work

ABOUT FRIEL
The Playwright and the Work

ABOUT HARE
The Playwright and the Work

ABOUT O'CASEY
The Playwright and the Work

ABOUT PINTER
The Playwright and the Work

ABOUT STOPPARD

The Playwright and the Work

Jim Hunter

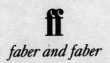

faber and faber

First published in 2005
by Faber and Faber Limited
3 Queen Square London WC1N 3AU

Typeset by Faber and Faber Limited
Printed in England by Bookmarque Ltd, Croydon

A CIP record for this book
is available from the British Library

ISBN 0-571-22023-1

2 4 6 8 10 9 7 5 3 1

In memory of Gay Firth

Contents

Editors' Note ix
A Chronology of Stoppard's Work xi
Preface xv

1 Stoppard's Life and Views 1
2 Contexts of Uncertainty 25
3 Stoppard's Development 45
4 Stoppard on Stoppard 109
5 Working with Stoppard 179

Select Bibliography 265
Acknowledgements 271
Index 273

Editors' Note

There are few theatre books which allow direct access to the playwright or to those whose business it is to translate the script into performance. These volumes aim to deal directly with the writer and with other theatre workers (directors, actors, designers and similar figures) who realise in performance the words on the page.

The subjects of the series are some of the most important and influential writers from post-war British and Irish theatre. Each volume contains an introduction which sets the work of the writer in the relevant historical, social and political context, followed by a digest of interviews and other material which allows the writer, in his own words, to trace his evolution as a dramatist. Some of this material is new, as is, in large part, the material especially gathered from the writers' collaborators and fellow theatre workers. The volumes conclude with annotated bibliographies. In all, we hope the books will provide a wealth of information in accessible form, and real insight into some of the major dramatists of our day.

A Chronology of Stoppard's Work

All theatres are in London unless otherwise stated.

1963 *A Walk on the Water*, Rediffusion Television
1964 *The Dissolution of Dominic Boot*, BBC Radio
 –   *'M' is for Moon Among Other Things*, BBC Radio
 –   Short stories ('Reunion', 'Life, Times: Fragments', and 'The Story') in *Introduction Two*, Faber and Faber
1966 *If You're Glad I'll Be Frank*, BBC Radio
 –   *Tango* (revision of Nicholas Bethell's translation of Slawomir Mrozek's play), the Royal Shakespeare Company, Aldwych Theatre
 –   *A Separate Peace*, BBC Television
 –   *Lord Malquist and Mr Moon* (novel), Faber and Faber
 –   *Rosencrantz and Guildenstern Are Dead*, Oxford Theatre Group (amateur), Cranston Street Hall, Edinburgh
1967 *Teeth*, BBC Television
 –   *Another Moon Called Earth*, BBC Television
 –   *Albert's Bridge*, BBC Radio
 –   *Enter A Free Man* (adaptation of *A Walk on the Water*), St Martin's Theatre
1968 *The Real Inspector Hound,* Criterion Theatre
 –   *Neutral Ground*, Thames Television
1970 *After Magritte*, Ambiance Lunch-hour Theatre Club
 –   *Where are They Now?* BBC Schools Radio
1971 *Dogg's Our Pet*, Almost Free Theatre
1972 *Jumpers*, National Theatre Company, Old Vic Theatre
 –   *Artist Descending A Staircase*, BBC Radio

1973   *The House of Bernarda Alba* (adaptation of Federico Garcia Lorca's play), Greenwich Theatre

1974   *Travesties*, the Royal Shakespeare Company, Aldwych Theatre

1975   *The Romantic Englishwoman* (screenplay, with the novel's author, Thomas Wiseman)

  –   *Three Men in a Boat* (adaptation of Jerome K. Jerome's novel), BBC Television

  –   *The Boundary* (with Clive Exton), BBC Television. This play was scripted from scratch, rehearsed, and performed live, within a week.

1976   *Dirty Linen* and *New-Found-Land*, Almost Free Theatre, transferring to Arts Theatre

1977   *Every Good Boy Deserves Favour* (with André Previn), Royal Festival Hall

  –   *Professional Foul*, BBC Television

1978   *Night and Day*, Phoenix Theatre

1979   *Dogg's Hamlet, Cahoot's Macbeth*, University of Warwick, Coventry, transferring to the Collegiate Theatre

  –   *Despair* (screenplay of Vladimir Nabokov's novel)

  –   *Undiscovered Country* (adaptation of Arthur Schnitzler's *Das weite Land*), National Theatre

1980   *The Human Factor* (screenplay of Graham Greene's novel)

1981   *On the Razzle* (adaptation of Johann Nestroy's *Einen Jux will er sich machen*), National Theatre

1982   *The Real Thing*, Strand Theatre

  –   *The Dog It Was That Died*, BBC Radio

1983   *The Love for Three Oranges* (translation of Prokofiev libretto), Glyndebourne Touring Opera

1984   *Squaring the Circle*, Television South

  –   *Rough Crossing* (adaptation of Ferenc Molnar's *Play at the Castle*), National Theatre

1985   *Brazil* (screenplay, with Terry Gilliam)

1986   *Dalliance* (adaptation of Arthur Schnitzler's *Liebelei*), National Theatre

–   *Largo Desolato* (adaptation of Vaclav Havel's play), Bristol Old Vic

1987   *Empire of the Sun* (screenplay of J. G. Ballard's novel)

1988   *Hapgood*, Aldwych Theatre

1990   *The Russia House* (screenplay of John Le Carré's novel)

–   *Rosencrantz and Guildenstern Are Dead*, screenplay and direction

1991   *In the Native State*, BBC Radio

–   *Billy Bathgate* (screenplay from E. L. Doctorow's novel)

1993   *Arcadia*, National Theatre

–   *The Merry Widow* (narration for Glyndebourne concert version of Lehar's operetta)

1994   *Three Men in a Boat* (adaptation of Jerome K. Jerome's novel), BBC Radio

1995   *Indian Ink* (adaptation of *In the Native State*), Yvonne Arnaud Theatre, Guildford, transferring to Aldwych Theatre

1997   *The Seagull* (version of Anton Chekhov's play), Old Vic Theatre

–   *The Invention of Love*, National Theatre

1999   *Shakespeare in Love* (screenplay, with Marc Norman)

2000   *Vatel* (screenplay for French costume film)

2001   *Enigma* (screenplay of Robert Harris's novel)

2002   *The Coast of Utopia* (*Voyage, Shipwreck, Salvage*), National Theatre

2004   *Henry IV* (adaptation of Luigi Pirandello's play), Donmar Warehouse

Preface

About Stoppard offers insights into the work of a leading living dramatist who has brought delight to the world's theatres for more than forty years. My own first book on Tom Stoppard appeared in 1982, only halfway through his career; here I hope to show how richly his work has developed, and how he has always been ready to accept new challenges. Starting as a writer of a sort of intellectual farce, he gradually allowed himself to engage much more deeply and seriously with our human condition – which doesn't mean we should ever forget to laugh.

The first chapter summarises Stoppard's life and apparent views, quoting him directly when possible. The second locates his writing within its intellectual context, and the third offers a commentary on his forty years of development. The playwright's own voice is then heard in interviews and articles, including some not previously available. The final chapter consists entirely of new interviews: I was fortunate to be able to talk about Stoppard with people who have worked most often with him, and with others who have helped to create original productions or revivals.

Page numbers on their own here refer to this book, usually to an interview printed later. All named sources quoted are listed in the bibliography at the end; 'Delaney' refers to Paul Delaney's invaluable collection of Stoppard interviews, and 'Nadel' to Ira Nadel's 600-page unauthorised biography.

Jim Hunter.

Stoppard's Life and Views

Tom Stoppard's one-act play *After Magritte* opens with a ludicrous tableau, vaguely domestic yet altogether grotesque. The characters, however, treat it as commonplace, and as it gradually unravels, each element proves to have a rational explanation. The characters are much more puzzled by a different grotesqueness which they glimpsed while out driving. Halfway through the play the room looks entirely normal – whereupon a police inspector bursts in with the line: 'What is the meaning of this bizarre spectacle?' Comic interrogations follow, during which it emerges that the absurdity seen while driving was also logically explicable – and, as it happens, featured the inspector himself. Meanwhile onstage a second weird tableau is gradually taking shape, but for reasons which this time are known.

In such controlled craziness the play resembles the Theatre of the Absurd, and also alludes to the surrealist painter René Magritte. But whereas the Absurdists and Magritte were challenging the conventional, this brilliant, jollier entertainment is basically reassuring: life is logical even when it doesn't look it. Though *After Magritte* doesn't claim to be more than theatrical fun, a similar instinct tends to underpin Stoppard's more serious material. He seems to relish the intellectual shocks of the twentieth century and yet to resist much of the resultant thinking; in a time when all knowledge and value systems have been questioned, he seeks to reassert traditional absolutes of goodness and moral justice.

Such faith is both caricatured and celebrated in the character of George in *Jumpers*. George's philosophy is intuitionist – not ultimately subject to rational argument: it is an intuition of the good. A few years later, when Stoppard's children were young, he wrote several times of a small child's direct intuition of natural justice. In the TV play *Professional Foul*, 'there is a sense of right and wrong which precedes utterance', as opposed to the untrustworthiness of those grown-ups who are 'clever' and can therefore be persuaded 'to believe almost anything'. This in context, opposing the lies of a Communist police state, carries an Orwellian simplicity and strength.

In Stoppard's view, a person's attitudes and opinions are partly formed by temperament. As we shall see, his own life began harshly, yet the general impression he gives is of warmth, fun and generosity, of being a man who anywhere in any circumstances might find some way to be upbeat. Even where all former certainties have been demolished, the young mathematician Valentine in *Arcadia* can say: 'It makes me so happy. To be at the beginning again, knowing almost nothing . . . It's the best possible time to be alive, when almost everything you thought you knew is wrong.'

Valentine, who seems to carry Stoppard's voice, is excited by the order within apparent orderlessness, which somehow produces the elegant patterns of a leaf, a waterfall, a snowflake. Valentine believes not that life is shapeless, only that we have previously misunderstood its shape; and this is where Stoppard seems to put his own faith.

But that faith too, on his own argument, may be a matter of temperament. One element of Stoppard's good humour, as reported by friends over the years, is an apparent insouciance, a reluctance to let anything upset him too much. Several examples of this will be mentioned later, and were shocking to himself in hindsight. At nearly sixty-five he could tell an interviewer: 'What people tend to underestimate is my capacity for not bothering, not caring, not minding, not being that interested. It's pretty awful actually, when I think about it myself.'

Yet this is clearly not an insensitive man. What he might call his 'temperament' seems to me a mode of behaviour – indeed a mode of *thinking* – learned very early because it had to be: a mode, in short, of survival.

'Everything can be all right'

Sung by the child Sacha, these are the final words of *Every Good Boy Deserves Favour*, the play for actors and orchestra which Stoppard wrote with André Previn.

Here, 'Everything is going to be all right' is the insistent message of the Soviet state. As a political dissident, Sacha's father is locked up in a mental hospital (in the boy's shrewd perception, 'the lunatics' prison'). He cannot be released until the 'Colonel-Doctor' can save face by a cynical fudge, which Sacha himself half-suggests, pleading with both his father and the hospital doctor not to be 'rigid'. As the play ends, father and son walk free, while everyone else joins the orchestra as the state demands. The boy runs ahead and sings 'Papa, don't be crazy!' – as if fearful that his father will resume his dissident actions – and then 'Everything can be all right', which partly and poignantly echoes the state's lies, yet also, in the modulation to 'can be', challenges the audience to work for ultimate real freedom.

There are deep resonances here with Tom Stoppard's own life. In his earliest years he survived a succession of twentieth-century extremities. Twice his family fled for their lives: first from the Nazis, whose concentration camps brought death to all four of his grandparents and three of his aunts; and three years later from the Japanese, who killed his father. He put together his own account[1] when he was sixty-two, using parts of a memoir (in italics below) by his mother, Martha:

> When I was born, in July 1937 in Zlin, a small town in Moravia, my name was Tomas Straussler, Tomik to my mother and father. We left Czechoslovakia – my parents, my brother Petr and I – when the German army moved in. By the time I understood that there was a connection between these two events I was an English schoolboy, Stoppard Two at prep school (Peter being Stoppard One), Tommy at home.

1 'Another Country', *Sunday Telegraph*, 10 October 1999.

So were we Jewish? My mother would give a little frown and go 'Tsk!' in her way and say, 'Oh, if anyone had a Jewish grandparent at that time . . .'

I believe I understand her 'Tsk!' It was less to do with denial than irritation. To ask the question was to accept the estimation put on it not by her but by the Germans. She had no sense of racial identity and no religious beliefs. Of course there were Jews in Zlin, she said, but they were proper Jews who wore black hats and went to the synagogue and the rest of it, Jews who were Jewish . . . Zlin was the world headquarters of the Bata shoe company, and my father was a doctor at the company hospital . . .

As I understand it, if I do, 'being Jewish' didn't figure in her life until it disrupted it, and then it set her on a course of displacement, chaos, bereavement and – finally – sanctuary in a foreign country, England, thankful at least that her boys were now safe. Hitler made her Jewish in 1939. By the spring, in good time before the European war started, all that was behind her, literally; we embarked at Genoa for Singapore, in good time for the Japanese onslaught.

For the Japanese were a different story. They killed my father and did their best to sink the ship which got the rest of us to India, but it wasn't personal, we weren't on a list, it was simply the war and being in the wrong place at the wrong time.

By the end of [January, 1942] *all women and children were evacuated. I stayed as long as I could, specially as I did not want to go on my own to Australia. Hoping that we might all go eventually. It just did not work out and the last few days were chaotic, boats, days and times always being changed. The journey from Singapore was pretty dreadful. We were bombed just about everywhere. In the harbour, standing three days just off Singapore, then on the way to Australia, then turned back to Singapore and finally to India.*

All the time we were so worried about the men left

4

behind in Singapore we did not really notice or mind any-
thing. Cabins were over-crowded and mattresses on decks
preferable. Children were always getting lost (not mine!)
but I cried myself silly one night because I lost two silver
medallions engraved with your names my best friend gave
you. Hung them on a hook in the bathroom instead of
putting them into my pocket – will I never learn?

I remember this. I remember the medallions, and the loss,
and most of all my mother crying.

Bata, who had facilitated the Strausslers' original escape
from Nazism, appointed Martha as manager of their
Darjeeling shop. When 'Tommy' was five he and his brother
were sent to boarding school, visited there by their mother on
Sundays. In her memoir:

Personally I did not like being in India . . . The four years
seem even now like a lifetime and a nightmare. I have no
idea how and why I came to Darjeeling. By that time I was
feeling rather ill, depressed, and it was all getting too much.
Darjeeling was the change I needed. Otherwise it was just a
matter of waiting and waiting. Once I was asked to go to
Calcutta, only to be told that after the people were account-
ed for, your father was amongst those missing, presumed
lost, and as they were all listed as civilians, it was all they
could do.

I returned the next day to Darjeeling but did not tell you.
Rightly or wrongly. Rightly, I think. You had enough to
cope with.

But one day in Darjeeling, a woman friend, at my mother's request, took Peter and me for a walk and told us that
our father was dead. Then she walked us back to the house
where my mother was waiting for us, teary-eyed and anxious about how we had taken it. For my own part, I took it
well, or not well, depending on how you look at it. I felt
almost nothing. I felt the significance of the occasion but
not the loss.

Not until the 1990s could he ascertain that the ship carrying his father, 'trying to make it to Australia', had been sunk by the Japanese. In 1946 Martha married an English major, Kenneth Stoppard, and her sons were uprooted yet again, then to settle finally in England.

Psychologists tend to be gloomy about people whose infancy has been so disturbed. But the adult Stoppard has little time for such determinism, and in his own personality contrives to refute it. Persistently he and his work are inclined to sing that 'everything can be all right'. I believe that this sequence, of sharp disturbance overlaid by security gratefully cherished, is a key to the man and his work.

Sometimes it can look like disturbance *denied*, or at least suppressed. Peter Wood, who directed most of his new plays over two decades, recalls that 'for all his radiant, cultivated, dazzling personality . . . there was always a glimmer of rage on the horizon'. What Stoppard seems to have done, from a very early age, is to pack suffering away in the basement – as do we all to some degree, though few have had so much to pack away. He has admitted: 'my memory is very good at erasing things I'd rather not remember' – something he learned from his mother. In his recollection of being told of his father's death, the words 'I felt almost nothing' don't quite exclude, even if they intend to, the subtext *couldn't permit myself to feel*: the image of a white-faced five-year-old, clenched in his resistance to being hurt any further. Then, aged seven, 'at prep. school – I remember walking down one of the corridors, trailing my finger along a raised edge along the wall, and I was suddenly totally happy . . . everywhere I looked, in my mind, *nothing was wrong*.'

The poignancy of this moment of white light lies in its revelation of darkness elsewhere, its glimpse of a seven-year-old only too accustomed to checking around ('everywhere I looked, in my mind') and to finding things that *were* wrong. The child Stoppard had every reason to look very warily about him, defending his own emotional security. Such wariness may partly account for his lifelong conservatism, and also for the frivolous manner of his early writing – where a good listener can detect barrels of pain bumping around in the basement, even though they are locked away. The quotation above is from the character Gale in the early radio play *Where Are They Now?*, but Stoppard repeated it in his own voice twenty years later, after revisiting Darjeeling:

> When Bengal was replaced by Derbyshire, India misted over, a lost domain of uninterrupted happiness. Of course, it couldn't have been that. What I was remembering was a particular day which became all my days at Mount Hermon, a day when I was walking along the corridor which led from the door to the playground, trailing a finger along a raised edge on the wall, and it suddenly came upon me that *everything was all right*, and would always be all right.[2]

A moment when *nothing was wrong* has now become an infinity where *everything is all right*. Not a hint of pain is allowed into this piece, which ends: 'My childhood was a different place . . . Life was familiar and safe and didn't change, and there were no decisions to be made, a long time ago when we lived in Darjeeling.'

The cadence seems quite deliberately sentimental: *this is how I choose to remember*. His mother's memory was altogether different: 'like a lifetime and a nightmare'.

Embracing England

> My stepfather, formerly Major Kenneth Stoppard in the British Army in India, believed with Cecil Rhodes that to be born an Englishman was to have drawn first prize in the lottery of life, and I doubt that even Rhodes, the Empire builder who lent his name to Rhodesia, believed it as utterly as Ken . . . 'Don't you realise,' he once reproached me

2 *Independent*, 23 March 1991.

7

when, aged nine, I innocently referred to my 'real father', 'don't you realise *that I made you British*?[3]

Major Stoppard may have influenced his wife's decision to hide from her sons their full Jewishness. Even in her memoir of 1981, Stoppard found, 'the word Jew or Jewish does not occur'. She writes there:

The move to England had been so sudden, unplanned and drastic that I – perhaps subconsciously – decided the only thing to make it possible to live and truly settle down (I mean the three of us) was to draw a blind over my past life and start so to speak from scratch. Whether this was realistic or possible I don't know. I mean whether it was the right thing to do.

Her sons learned to collude in her reticence: 'Rightly or wrongly, we've always felt that she might want to keep the past under a protective covering,' Stoppard told Kenneth Tynan in the 1970s, saying then of his father's death, 'we've never delved into it'. He was quite happy to be turned into a young Englishman. 'As soon as we all landed up in England, I knew I had found a home. I embraced the language and the landscape.' The brothers were sent to board at a preparatory school, which Stoppard remembers warmly, and then at Pocklington, in Yorkshire, which he doesn't. There he studied classics, played cricket, and debated, with reasonable success but without being much noticed. Above all, he was bored:

We just sat around the class doing The Merchant of Venice and all having to read a part. All you did was look ahead to see when it was Nerissa's turn and then you said your line . . . I didn't like being there at all, I'm afraid; and the idea of, you know, carrying on with books and exams and lectures didn't appeal to me . . .[4]

3 'Another Country'.
4 *Platform*, National Theatre, 1993, quoted Nadel, p. 49.

I left school totally bored by the idea of anything intellectual and gladly sold all my Greek and Latin classics to George's bookshop in Park Street.[5]

I didn't know what I wanted to do for a while, but the moment the thought of journalism came into my head I became passionate to be a journalist, and I joined a newspaper in Bristol when I was 17, and I have to say I loved every moment of it, unless I've forgotten the moments I didn't love . . .[6]

Come 1956, when the British and French went into Suez and the Russians went into Budapest, then I wanted to be Noel Barber on the *Daily Mail* or Sefton Delmer on the *Daily Express* – that kind of big-name, roving reporter. Noel Barber actually got shot in the head in Budapest, which put him slightly ahead of Delmer as far as I was concerned.

'At seventeen,' according to his older brother Peter, 'Tom was more like twenty.' Asked long afterwards whether he regretted not having gone to university, Stoppard replied: 'I came to regret it, years later. I realised when I was thirty-ish that I would probably have become part of a kind of network of interesting people . . . I felt that I'd gone along a different road and probably missed a lot of education in the best possible sense of the word. I may have got a bad Third, but I think I would have learned a great deal.'[6]

The decision to leave school after O Levels wasn't exceptional at that time, when only about 5 or 6 per cent of British young people went to university. But it did require him to work his way up from the bottom, whereas in those days to have been to a leading university meant a head start in many careers, as it were by-passing several qualifying rounds. It assisted many theatre people, whereas Stoppard had to serve a twelve-year apprenticeship, first as journalist and later as freelance

5 To *Theatre Quarterly* 14, May–July 1974.
6 To John Tusa, BBC Radio, June 2002.

jobbing writer. Yet if he had gone to university we might never have had his plays as we know them. His political perspectives might have been extended, but on the other hand he might have turned out as a more conventional artist – if indeed an artist at all, since he had no such intention at the time.

Where the Stoppard brothers were really unusual was in not being made to waste two years in the armed forces, as was then compulsory for all young males not just in Britain but in most of the developed world. For all Major Stoppard's claims to have made the boys British, they found that actually he hadn't: they were still 'aliens'. Peter Stoppard explained to me: 'I had to register with the police and was issued with an "identity card". In about 1957, I think, I obtained British nationality, and presume that Tom's situation was similar . . . I know that becoming British did not cancel Czech nationality, as a document warned me that I could not rely on protection if I entered Czechoslovakia: as far as I am aware, neither of us has formally renounced Czech nationality.'

Significantly, the *Western Daily Press* in Bristol included pieces by both 'Tom Stoppard' and 'Tomik Straussler'.

During those Bristol years theatre in England was developing excitingly (see p. 34 below). In 1955 the young actor Peter O'Toole joined the Bristol Old Vic, later attracting national attention as Hamlet; he became friendly with Stoppard, who in 1960, after six years of full-time journalism, went part-time in order to write his first play. In 1962 he moved to London, to work as theatre critic for the short-lived *Scene* magazine, while trying to write another play and also fiction. In 1964 a Faber anthology included three short stories, and plays were broadcast on both radio and TV; he did other jobbing scriptwriting for the BBC, was commissioned to write a novel, and enjoyed an extraordinary summer-long freebie for young writers in Berlin, during which he produced a first knockabout attempt at a play about Rosencrantz and Guildenstern. By early 1965 this had developed more seriously, and interested the Royal Shakespeare Company. In March 1965 Stoppard married Jose

Ingle, a consumer researcher, and in August he finished his novel. Early in 1966 another radio play was broadcast and Trevor Nunn at the RSC asked Stoppard to work on the English version of Slawomir Mrozek's *Tango*, which was performed in May. Then, within a few days in August, a TV play was broadcast, the novel was published, and *Rosencrantz and Guildenstern Are Dead* opened in a student production on the Edinburgh Festival fringe. Three paragraphs by Ronald Bryden in the *Observer*, plus a snapshot captioned 'The most brilliant debut since Arden's', were seen overnight by Kenneth Tynan, who instantly demanded the play for the National Theatre. It was a breakthrough of startling suddenness, twelve long years after the boy journalist started in Bristol.

After that slow start, Stoppard's success has been extraordinarily sustained, over getting on for forty years. Audiences and critics have found a few plays hard to chew and swallow, but even the toughest of those, *Hapgood*, has its defenders. He startled me by saying of his output: 'It doesn't seem that much to me, when you think how many years have gone by. I mean there are people who write a play every eighteen months, and I don't.'

On the contrary, it's a large and rich body of work, remarkable for its consistent quality. Script after script, when revisited, still cries out for performance, and indeed one revival or another is usually running in London. What is more, in between his own new plays Stoppard has kept constantly busy with commissioned work, stage translations more or less Stoppardian in character and screenplays which are usually not.

When *Rosencrantz* opened in New York in 1967 Stoppard was asked what it was about and in an off-the-cuff pun replied: 'It's about to make me rich.' The seventeen-year-old who wanted to be famous, if only for being shot in the head, grew up into a writer who was thrilled by show business, kept wicket for Harold Pinter's showbiz cricket team, enjoyed spending money (flying by Concorde to see a son's school football match) and giving it away (setting up two charitable trusts and also supporting human-rights movements) and threw occasional glittering parties for stars of the entertainment industry. The Queen's sister, Princess Margaret, regarded herself as a friend; Prime Ministers Thatcher, Major and Blair invited him to functions at 10 Downing Street. In 1997 he was knighted, becoming officially 'Sir Tom', and in 2000 he received the Order of Merit, which is rarely offered to an artist. Yet this is a man who describes himself as shy[7] and for whom privacy is vital. Always generous in giving interviews, particularly to promote a new production, he has nevertheless steered well clear of chat-show circuits and the cult of celebrity – his second wife, Miriam, a TV doctor and health adviser, became more widely known to the British public.

During the childhood of his four sons Stoppard's priority was fatherhood. It needed to be, since his first marriage foundered early. An unnamed source is quoted by Stephen Schiff, writing in *Vanity Fair*:

> In her cups [Jose] would tell Tom's friends how she had really written *Rosencrantz and Guildenstern* ... And all the time Tom was behaving with a kind of chivalric constancy. His friends were throwing up their hands because he was spending all his time looking after the children and doing the washing up. Then came the time when he decided it was over, at which point [December 1969] he behaved with a kind of frightening clarity, taking the two kids with him and setting up a new home with Miriam.[8]

At the divorce in 1972 Stoppard was awarded custody of his children, Oliver and Barnaby. Two further sons, William and Edmund, were born to Miriam, within what was for many years a deeply successful second marriage. In 1979 the family moved spectacularly upmarket, from a substantial Victorian house to an eighteenth-century mansion, Iver Grove, standing

7 p. 160.
8 Delaney, p. 220.

in seventeen acres of Buckinghamshire. The boys were sent to independent schools, and family holidays included traditional pursuits of the upper-class English: shooting and fishing – almost as if to placate Stoppard's stepfather. Ten years later, visiting Iver Grove in February 1989, Stephen Schiff was entranced not only by the ambience but by the marriage itself: 'It's Love on Mount Olympus . . . Watching the Stoppards now, in their living room, one realises how much the works of his new, "serious" period have been, amongst other things, valentines to Miriam.'[9]

Ouch. God-like in their success Tom and Miriam Stoppard may have seemed, but Mount Olympus was never noted for marital concord, and what Schiff's piece also shows is two extremely busy individuals whose work is beginning to push their lives apart. Stoppard already had his own flat in London, and was soon seen keeping company with the actor for whom he has written most, Felicity Kendal. The Stoppards announced their amicable separation late in 1990 and divorce followed in 1992. Miriam later married Christopher Hogg, with whom Stoppard sat on the Board of the National Theatre. He himself has not remarried, and although he and Kendal remained very close till 1998, they never shared a home together.

For this book Kendal talks to me about her many Stoppard roles, between 1981 and 1997. It emerges that she has never thought of him as English; nor are his characters – startlingly, she suggests: 'Even in *Jumpers*, they could be Bengali'. All this she evidently approves, adding of herself, 'I don't feel remotely English.' Her parents certainly were, but her childhood and adolescence were spent in India, acting in the family troupe which performed Shakespeare around the subcontinent – all vividly recalled in her autobiography *White Cargo*. Stoppard's radio play *In the Native State* was clearly written for her with love (dedicated to her; its stage successor, *Indian Ink*, is dedicated to the memory of her mother).

9 Delaney, p. 218.

Another thread appears – that of Jewishness. Stoppard always knew that he was at least partly Jewish; Miriam was also Jewish, and Felicity Kendal had converted to Judaism for her marriage in 1983 to Michael Rudman. Though these are varied kinds of Jewishness, they share a quality of *difference*, within the 'embrace' of England, and one which – particularly in the twentieth century – stood always in some relationship to *danger*.

'Another Country'

Remembering his mother's determination to 'draw a blind' over her past, Stoppard writes in 'Another Country':

> All my life I have been told that I 'take after my mother', whatever that was supposed to mean, and now it does appear to mean more than a compliment. In August 1968 when the armies of the Warsaw Pact put down the movement for reform in Czechoslovakia, my then wife was firstly incredulous and secondly infuriated that I didn't get worked up about it as a Czech. It was true. I had no special feeling other than the general English one of impotent condemnation, tinged with that complacency felt when the ogres of one's personal demonology behave true to form. I knew I was – used to be – Czech but I didn't feel Czech.

'Another Country' was not only a family memoir but also to some extent a self-reproach, the more painful because 'it's all too late'. In 1968 the embracing of England seems to have gone too far: any response was now 'the general English one' (assumed to be 'impotent') from someone who merely 'used to be' Czech. Yet ten years after the Warsaw Pact invasion, Stoppard could insist: 'I'm as Czech as Czech can be.'[10]

John Tusa asked in 2002 whether his admiration for the absurdist protest plays of his Czech contemporary, Vaclav

10 Delaney, p. 110.

Havel (later the first President of Czechoslovakia after Communism) had first led him to get involved with Czech human rights. Or was it 'because of politics or a sense of Czech-ness? Was it words that took you into politics?' To which he replied: 'No. So far as I recall I was active, if that's the word, earlier in Russian dissidents rather than Czech dissidents; and the one led to the other . . . It was certainly something to do with being Czech, but not entirely.'

The political shift appears in attacks on Lenin in 1974, both in *Travesties* and in interview (p. 122ff.). Soviet totalitarianism and abuses of human rights excited Stoppard to a cold and eloquent anger. Already he was an active supporter of Amnesty International and *Index on Censorship*, writing letters on behalf of Soviet dissidents, and in 1976 he addressed a Trafalgar Square rally organised by the Committee Against Psychological Abuse. Early in 1977 he visited the Soviet Union with the assistant director of Amnesty (which had dedicated the year to 'Prisoners of Conscience').

Meanwhile in Czechoslovakia Havel had been arrested on 6 January for attempting to publish Charter 77, a document of political protest. In April Stoppard, petitioning on his behalf, was refused admission to the Czech Embassy in London. Havel was, however, released in May, and in June Stoppard, who had not previously risked revisiting his country of birth, did so in order to meet him. He also met another banned playwright, Pavel Kohout, and a banned actor, Pavel Landovsky, and from that new friendship grew the later play *Cahoot's Macbeth*. Through the following years Stoppard persisted, through newspaper articles, letters and other protest campaigns, in reminding the Western public of the treatment of Soviet and Czech dissidents. As a result he was three times refused permission to visit Czechoslovakia again.

When Communist rule there collapsed late in 1989, Havel was elected President of the new republic. The dissidents and literary intellectuals became the holders of power, with the bizarre result that when Stoppard visited in 1991, for a production of *Travesties*, he found that several of the dignitaries he met had translated his own work.

In 1993 Martha Stoppard received a letter from a niece, Sarka, proposing to visit her in Devon. From 'Another Country':

> My mother (I can see it all) had slightly panicked because Ken would not have been receptive to this sort of thing and could not be relied on to behave gracefully. So we met in London, in the restaurant of the National Theatre where I was working that day – my mother, my sister (half-sister, but I never call her that), my sister's little girl and Sarka and I, who was Sarka's father's cousin. After a while, at one end of a long table cluttered with the remains of the meal, I got into a tête-à-tête with Sarka. She wrote down the family tree of my mother's generation, on a sheet of foolscap which she turned sideways to get them all in.

Sarka revealed that Stoppard was 'completely Jewish', and that not only all four of his grandparents but three of his aunts had died in Nazi concentration camps.

Years earlier he had organised in London an event about the imprisonment in psychiatric hospitals of Russian Jews who applied for exit visas to Israel.

> As a result I received letters thanking me as a Jew, and I remember once or twice – feeling obscurely that I was receiving credit under false pretences – I replied that I was not Jewish or at any rate not really Jewish. I had become habituated to the unexamined idea that although – obvious- ly – there was some Jewish blood in me (my father's father's?), enough to make me more interesting to myself, and to have risked attention from the Nazis, it was not real- ly enough to connect me with the Jews who died in the camps and those who didn't.
>
> This almost wilful purblindness, a rarely disturbed absence of curiosity combined with an endless willingness

not to disturb my mother by questioning her, even after – no, especially after – our meeting with Sarka, comes back to me now in the form of self-reproach, not helped by my current state of mind now that I'm Jewish. I feel no more Jewish than I felt Czech when, 22 years ago, I went to Prague to do my bit for Charter 77 . . . and now I have the odd sense of its being too late. I don't want to be claimed as if I've turned into someone else. This is why I think I understand my mother going 'Tsk!' . . .

In 1994 he revisited Czechoslovakia, and again in 1998, with his brother Peter, travelling to Zlin, their birthplace. In 1999 he went once more.

In April this year the 96-year-old widow of Dr Albert, chief of the Bata hospital, receives me in her flat in Prague, with her two daughters, Senta and Zaria . . . All three remember Dr Straussler. The two 'girls' tell me he was considered the nicest of the young doctors, the one they asked to have when they had measles and other childhood illnesses. 'When Dr Straussler talked to us we knew everything would be all right.' . . .

When Zaria was young she put her hand through a glass pane and cut it. Dr Straussler stitched the cut. Zaria holds out her hand, which still shows the mark. I touch it. In that moment, I am surprised by grief, a small catching-up of all the grief I owe. I have nothing which came from my father, nothing he owned or touched, but here is his trace, a small scar . . .

'Another Country' ends with a sad recollection of his stepfather:

A few days after my mother died, Ken, whom from England onwards I had called 'Daddy' or 'Father' or 'Dad' (though he objected to 'Dad' which he thought was lower class) wrote to me to say that he had been concerned for some time about my 'tribalization', by which he meant mainly my association, ten years earlier, with the cause of Russian Jews, and he asked me to stop using 'Stoppard' as my name. I wrote back that this was not practical . . .

Until I went to the bad, and the first sign of that was when I turned out to be arty, I was coming on well as an honorary Englishman. He taught me to fish, to love the countryside, to speak properly, to respect the Monarchy. In the end I disappointed him. And yet, did he but know it, it's all too late, this going back, these photographs, that small scar on Zaria's hand. They have the power to move, but not to reclaim. I was eight-and-a-half . . . when Ken gave me his name; and long before he asked for it back Englishness had won and Czechoslovakia had lost.

The pain and regret in that 'all too late' are clear. But Stoppard's mixed identity is in no way neurotic. Neither, of course, is it self-invented – it's quite unlike the masks and personae of some other artists. If anything, he has too amiably colluded with other people's expectations: at eight, embracing Englishness and learning to keep quiet about his origins; in his thirties, allowing himself to be Czech; in his fifties, 'turning out to be Jewish'. Similar acquiescence appears at times in interviews: you want the wit, I'll give you wit; you want moral seriousness, I can do that too. What he doesn't do, in public, is insecurity. He may voice craftsman's anxieties, about finding the next idea, guiding the coming production, postponing the next deadline; but any deeper, more personal doubts are excluded from discussion. The subtext in interviews is always: however you care to label me – Czech, Jewish, tomfool, conservative – it won't alter who I am, what I believe, or what I create. Of elements thought to be under-represented in his work – such as character delineation, or political or social 'commitment' – he will say, 'They don't interest me.' In moral argument he tends to reach a sticking-point, not susceptible to change: 'Well, that's what I think.' This firmness may have originated in the small boy's defensive carapace; but it grew fast into a convincing self-confidence, already apparent to those who knew him when he was young, hard up, but always somehow on the way to eventual success.

'I think of myself as a reactionary'

In these words the self-confidence is pre-emptive. They are Stoppard's when he was only thirty – and looking scarcely eighteen, in the accompanying *Sunday Times* photographs. The piece, 'Something to Declare' – alas without the pictures – is reproduced later, on p. 109ff. What the young playwright 'declares' is non-commitment. 'I burn with no causes. I cannot say that I write with any social objective.' In context, that was courageous; it isn't a genuinely reactionary position but he knew that in 1968, a time when artists were particularly required to be 'committed', it might be so caricatured.

Yet the point of the title metaphor is that the writer who walks through the green exit thinking he has nothing to declare, no baggage of commitment, may be carrying contraband in his subconscious. A decade or so later this became a routine idea of deconstructionist theory; it's typical of Stoppard's independent acuteness that he's already there, and his image of going through Customs is far easier to grasp than most critical theory: 'One is the beneficiary and victim of one's subconscious: that is, of one's personal history, experience and environment . . . A concrete example. My mother married again and my name was changed to my stepfather's when I was about eight years old.'

He promptly starts to walk through the green exit: 'This I didn't care one way or another about.'

Nothing to declare: we may recall 'I felt almost nothing' (his father presumed dead) and 'no special feeling' (the invasion of Czechoslovakia). But this time he calls himself to open his baggage: 'Then it occurred to me that in practically everything I had written there was something about people getting each others' names wrong.'

The article is partly about the new possibilities of theatre, paying homage to Beckett. Yet within its baggage lie distinctly unprogressive elements: 'language as an end in itself', 'I'd like to cold-bloodedly kill them' (admittedly referring to racist murderers), 'that lovely group' of refugee Russian aristocrats, and a tart resistance to the fashion for 'theatrical experiences' which are not 'written plays'. Readers at the time would recognise *US*, the 'theatrical experience' praised for just one of its effects, as a polemic against American action in Vietnam.

'I'm a conservative in politics, literature, education and theatre,' he told Mel Gussow in 1979.[11] After early years as bruising as Stoppard's, many have understandably embraced and clung not only to England's stable democracy but also to the stock images which define it for a foreigner: cricket and country houses and, yes, even royalty. Long before he could dream of acquiring a country house of his own he refused to join a strike, causing himself at the age of twenty-two to be suspended for three months by the National Union of Journalists.[12] Much later he was one of very few artists to praise Prime Minister Margaret Thatcher, claiming that she spoke her mind and avoided politicians' fudge. In both cases he was prepared to isolate himself from the prevailing opinions in his workplace.

Stoppard's political views are reactionary in the best sense of the word – not pressing a right-wing message of his own, but vigorously resistant to false new orthodoxies; as he added to Gussow, 'My main objection is to ideology and dogma.' He has involved himself not with party politics but with the wider concerns of Amnesty International, which he has consistently supported.

In his 2002 trilogy *The Coast of Utopia*, which deals sympathetically with early Russian radicals, the writer Turgenev resembles Stoppard as he knows he is often seen.

11 Delaney, p. 133.
12 According to Nadel, p. 25. Stoppard to me: 'It rings a faint bell. But I'm certain I would have been one of a group of journalists, not a lone standout.'

HERZEN: What you mean by civilisation is your way of life
. . . as if life as evolved in the European upper classes is the
only life in tune with human development.

TURGENEV: Well, it is if you're one of them. It's not my fault.
If I were a Sandwich Islander I expect I'd speak up for navi-
gating by the stars and eighteen things you can do with a
coconut, but I'm not a Sandwich Islander. To value what is
relative to your circumstances, and let others value what's
relative to theirs – you agree with me. That's why despite
everything we're on the same side.

HERZEN: But I fought my way here with loss of blood,
because it matters to me and you're in my ditch, reposing
with your hat over your face, because nothing matters to
you very much – which is why despite everything we'll
never be on the same side.

Where Stoppard's views and tone always harden is on the
influence of Karl Marx. 'Marx got it wrong,' was his 1974 line,
and in *The Coast of Utopia* Marx, though rarely seen, is an
alarming caricature. In 1977 Stoppard wrote a book review[13]
applauding 'the defence of objective truth from Marxist relativism'. The book, *Enemies of Promise*, was by Paul Johnson, a
maverick intellectual who has ploughed his own provocative
course for many years after veering sharply away from the left
(when young, he edited the *New Statesman*, a socialist weekly).
Stoppard and Johnson lived near each other and had been
friends for some time (a year later, Johnson was the dedicatee
of *Night and Day*). The review mentions differences between
them, but Stoppard associates himself explicitly with the
book's overall position.

The society which Paul Johnson wishes to defend from its
enemies is the Western liberal democracy favouring an
intellectual elite and a progressive middle class and based
on a moral order derived from Christian absolutes . . .

13 'But for the Middle Classes', *Times Literary Supplement*, 3 June 1977.

[His] fundamental assertions are these. Truth is objective. Civilisation is the pursuit of truth in freedom. Freedom is the necessary condition of that pursuit. Political freedom and economic freedom are dependent on each other. Material and cultural progress (growth) is dependent on both together. The loss of freedom leads to civilisation's decline . . . One does not have to be an expert on anything to know that in one of his themes – the defence of objective truth from the attacks of Marxist relativism – Johnson has got hold of the right end of the right stick at the right time.

Stoppard gives examples of the 'unreason' he and Johnson detect in 1970s academia:

'The assumption that there exists a realm of facts independent of theories which establish their meaning is fundamentally unscientific' . . . 'all facts are theory-laden'. These are now the quite familiar teachings of well-educated men and women holding responsible positions in respectable universities, and the thing to say about such teaching is not that it is 'radical', but that it is not true. What it is, is false. To claim the contrary is not 'interesting', it is silly. Daft. Not very bright. Moreover, it is wicked.

Such anger may have been timely in 1977, but the slippage of tone is uncharacteristic: Stoppard here seems to abandon debate, preferring to storm out and slam the door. His attack on intellectual relativism is far more effective in *Jumpers*:

GEORGE: It occurred to you that belief in God and the conviction that God doesn't exist amount to much the same thing?
ARCHIE: It gains from careful phrasing.

or in *Professional Foul*: 'You can persuade a man to believe almost anything provided he is clever enough . . .'

On art, Stoppard finds Johnson excessively blinkered. A few years earlier, however, he had described his own views on art as 'square, conservative and traditional'. The topic is his play *Artist Descending a Staircase*; and because he is known for his own clever cut-ups the interviewer wrongly associates him with the cut-up artist Beauchamp. The playwright has to put him right: his sympathies lie with the conservative artist Donner. 'I absolutely think that Beauchamp's tapes *are* rubbish, and I think that what Donner says about them is *absolutely* true. I think that when Donner says that much of modern art is the mechanical expression of a very simple idea which might have occurred to an intelligent man in his bath and be forgotten in the business of drying between his toes, that is me.'[14]

Nearly thirty years later, in 2001, Stoppard caused a stir at the Royal Academy with after-dinner remarks about conceptual art, which he sees as hardly even 'mechanical' – all concept, no craft. 'An object can be a work of art just because the artist says it is.' In his subsequent article about the affair he asks: 'When did it stop being true that an artist is somebody who can do something more or less well which the rest of us can only do badly or not at all? . . . Conceptual art is exactly what it says it is. It is thought exhibited, thought bodied forth. ("Eureka! The plinth repeated upside down and transparent!") But so is a Turner, he of the prize. So is art itself. The thought varies in profundity. The rest, the making, is, or was, the hard part.'[15]

14 Delaney, p. 37.
15 'Making It', *Times Literary Supplement*, 15 June 2001.

2

Contexts of Uncertainty

All centuries are disturbed, but the twentieth century was the most disturbed yet. Stoppard was active in its last forty years, and addressed many of the upheavals of the whole hundred: in the arts, in philosophy, in politics, in physics, in mathematics. The century saw political and military violence on a grimmer scale than ever before, taking the lives of many of his family; that darkness lies behind his light, and his tone hardens when totalitarian regimes are in question. But to the wider range of modern uncertainty he responds with happier interest. He reads, he wants to know and understand, and always he is on the lookout for what might be the material of a *play*. This chapter briefly outlines some of the intellectual context for Stoppard's plays.

Modernism

Luigi Pirandello's *Six Characters in Search of an Author* (1922) walk into a theatre at rehearsal time, with bored actors and a director standing around. Each wears a face mask defining their identity, and they carry within them a powerful story, though their play has not yet been written. They persuade the actors to represent them on stage, but are then disappointed with the result: the performance is too stagey, blinkered by past convention. The 'characters' find themselves insisting that they are more real than the actors who try to imitate them, because their 'reality' in art doesn't change.

Pirandello's idea seems merely clever until we recall that Tom Stoppard's *Rosencrantz* depends on a basic knowledge of *Hamlet*. Shakespeare's characters turn out to be far better known worldwide than almost any figures from history, politics or even legend. (Joyce, in *Travesties*: 'What now of the Trojan War, if it had been passed over by the artist's touch? Dust.') An extra irony is that Hamlet himself, though known everywhere, is so little agreed on, so altogether *unfixed* in our knowledge; and that his play is itself intensely metatheatrical, compulsively self-conscious about the very genre that it uses. *Hamlet* contains not only a play within a play but also the protagonist's advice to the players on their delivery, even on what is 'the purpose of playing'.

Pirandello's play is even more explicit: its fictional reality may be longer-lasting than the life people actually lead. He was writing at the height of the movement now called Modernism, which ran roughly from 1900 to 1935 and whose works still seemed interestingly 'modern' when Stoppard and I were growing up in the 1950s. T. S. Eliot's 1911 poem 'Love-Song of J. Alfred Prufrock' is quoted frequently in Stoppard's only novel; *After Magritte* and *Artist Descending a Staircase* allude in their titles to Modernist painting, and *Travesties* is located in the heart of the Modernist disturbance, its hero James Joyce, its villain Lenin, its setting Switzerland, its date roughly 1917.

Much Modernist art tries, as does Stoppard's, to be both *new* and yet also *allusive*. Though often ironic and sportive with the past, it still sets a high value on canonical art and its lasting significance, taking a humanist long view. By others it may then be criticised as apolitical, 'formalist' or 'art for art's sake', and also for relying on the erudition of an educated elite, with aspirations to be international (Eliot's notes to *The Waste Land*, for example, show off to an imaginary reader competent in Latin, French, German and Italian).

Raymond Williams has claimed that Modernism could not have developed without the modern metropolis, such as London or Paris, where *émigré* intellectuals produced art which sought to synthesise and transcend their common experience of dislocation. And it's true that, of three key influences on Stoppard, the American-born Eliot chose London and the

Dubliners Joyce and Beckett chose Paris. Stoppard is also a child of twentieth-century dislocation, and however warmly he embraced England and English manners, his writing is not parochial: intellectually, its reach is indeed international.

The Modernist period saw the dismantling of recent assumptions – the all-knowing of the nineteenth-century psychological novel, the self-important expansiveness of vast symphonies and operas – together with the presumption which lay behind them. Genres and texts became self-conscious, unstable and ironic. And meanwhile even greater dismantlings were taking place in science. In quantum physics, which was puzzling scientists, a manifestation alters if it is observed; in Modernist art, from Cubism to *The Waste Land* and Virginia Woolf's *Mrs Dalloway*, there are many observers, multiple rather than single, secure viewpoints. Einstein's work on relativity coincided with the growth of that relativist thinking in the humanities which Stoppard would come to deplore.

Thus Modernism finds little to be cheerful about; the First World War alone was enough to shatter previous confidence. Modernist art can be superficially fun, in its novelty and iconoclasm, yet even there its emotional import is generally bleak. Typically, an individual consciousness is turned alarmingly in on itself, no longer trusting contact with others, uncertain even of external reality, let alone of any lasting value: Modernism and religious faith begin to seem incompatible, though the later Eliot attempted to combine them. Laughter (essentially something shared) tends to be in short supply, unless it is bitterly satirical, as in Tzara's Dadaism; the rich humanist comedy of Joyce's *Ulysses* is unusual.

Stoppard's writing brilliantly exploits the generic tricks of Modernism: instability of viewpoint and language, fragmentation of form, allusiveness, irony and subversion of expectation. It also deals habitually with the intellectual uncertainties of the Modernist period. But from the start his characters try to kick against that context, those uncertainties: they dream of escape out, away, up, and sometimes back. His early cartoon figures, their anxieties elegantly caricatured, repeatedly seek some sort of order, even if only existentially created by themselves against flux and meaninglessness.

'Almost everything you thought you knew is wrong'

Valentine in *Arcadia* thus explains why he feels that 1993 is 'the best possible time to be alive'. His scenes, however, alternate with others set in 1809 or 1812, where a bright pupil, Thomasina, can ask her tutor: 'Is God a Newtonian?' Her question is not quite just a joke: it sums up the Enlightenment impression that Newton's science can sort out the universe; everything may eventually prove capable of being explained, and even predicted. The play shows this confident edifice beginning to crumble, and in Valentine's modern era it has entirely collapsed: all the old certainties have gone. Twentieth century *physics* subverted some of our most basic assumptions: about time, dimension, and 'reality' itself. According to John Gribbin, who has worked hard to increase the popular understanding of science: 'What quantum physics says is that nothing is real and that we cannot say anything about what things are doing when we are not looking at them . . . Nothing is real unless it is observed.'

Quantum physics contradicts our common-sense view of the world, and yet we prove its practical working every day of our lives, for example (Gribbin again), 'when you buy a packet of cornflakes and have it scanned by a laser at the checkout'. Something we don't understand is nevertheless a great help to us.

In *Arcadia* Thomasina is beginning to grasp the coming significance of *thermodynamics* – not new science in Stoppard's day, but possibly still unfamiliar to some of his audience. Thirty years earlier the scientist and novelist C. P. Snow had lamented that most people hadn't yet grasped the second law of thermodynamics, and it's as if Stoppard is determined to ensure that, after *Arcadia*, they should. Everything is gradually running down: 'We're all going to end up at room temperature.'

What Thomasina also seems to be anticipating, though only in a fantasy, is the late twentieth-century *mathematics* known as 'chaos theory'. She dreams of being able to plot a leaf, deducing its 'equation'; by the time Stoppard wrote his play, computers were producing patterns of iterated algorithms some of which resemble leaves. Her modern relative Valentine is working on these algorithms; his constantly changing graphs of results show patterns of repetition which are nevertheless unpredictable – findings which, while perfectly deterministic, may always look 'chaotic'.

'How do I know what I know?'

Much of Stoppard's earlier work addresses different twentieth-century challenges, those of *philosophy*. In *Jumpers* the subject is not so much whether what one 'knows' may turn out to be wrong, but – even more basically – what we mean by knowledge. 'Tom Stoppard Doesn't Know' was the title of a verbal and visual statement he made for BBC TV in 1974; in the same year, to *Theatre Quarterly*, he recognised that in his plays 'conflicting statements . . . tend to play out a sort of infinite leapfrog' (p. 115). This 'not knowing' could seem like fence-sitting, but was intended as a basis of integrity: it's wrong to pretend to certainties you don't actually have.

In *Jumpers* George Moore (his name that of a real early twentieth-century philosopher) has failed to write his big book. His wife Dotty tells us it was to have been called *The Concept of Knowledge*, but unfortunately that title was bagged by someone else, and 'while you were still comparing knowledge in the sense of having-experience-of, with knowledge in the sense of being-acquainted-with, and knowledge in the sense of inferring facts with knowledge in the sense of comprehending truths, and all the time as you got more and more acquainted with, though no more comprehending of, the symbolic patterns on my Persian carpet, it was knowing in the biblical sense of screwing that you were learning about . . .'

George is at heart a moral philosopher, and his problem – with which Stoppard himself seems to identify – is that he has intuitive convictions, things he feels he 'knows', which he cannot justify by rational argument. Significantly in his final speech he refers not to 'the existence of God' but to 'a knowledge of God', a claim of personal private experience. Stoppard does allow George, who is comically confused for most of the play, one passage of effective argument (end of Act One). A relativist may crow over the fact that different codes of good conduct exist in different cultures, as if that made the concept of good meaningless; George argues that, on the contrary, this demonstrates that there is a common impulse to behave well: what should impress us is that every society has some concepts and instincts of goodness, honour and relative value. George's argument refuses to be hobbled by the problems of language.

Language

Those problems, however, were basic to much twentieth-century philosophy and critical theory. Round about the time that Stoppard's George was first saying on the London stage 'that language is an approximation of meaning and not a logical symbolism for it', post-structuralist academics were developing the point. Early twentieth-century structuralist analysis noted that a word is a sign carrying no inherent meaning; what it means depends on who is interpreting it (rather as, in quantum physics, nothing exists till it is observed). The interaction of the interpreter with the word helps to construct its meaning, which is therefore always relative and many-layered.

This was not a new perception, but post-structuralism argued that we had failed to grasp its full significance; we continued to overestimate the stability of words and therefore of all the texts, assumptions and institutions that words help to create. Even our *concepts*, since they are all constructs of language, are always provisional and shifting. Philosophy in the first half of the twentieth century was constantly wrestling with language, yet it could do so only by *means* of language, means increasingly seen as slippery and suspect.

The particular target for attack in *Jumpers* is the philosophical school called Logical Positivism, best known in Britain through the work of A. J. Ayer (who wrote a cheerful review of Stoppard's play). Dotty says that Archie 'knows not "seems"'(an ironic quotation from *Hamlet*, where 'seeming' is always suspect); things should be described only by their verifiable properties ('green, square, or Japanese'), not by unverifiable opinions such as 'good and bad, better or worse'. Whether or not this does justice to Ayer, it seemed to try to exclude from philosophy what others would see as its very life-blood: questions of ethics and metaphysics. Stoppard's satire depicts a university, a nation, indeed a moon surface, where moral considerations are regarded as outmoded; those who should be the guardians of such debate take pride instead in their intellectual jumping, their ability to 'persuade a man to believe almost anything' (*Professional Foul*). Stoppard clearly feels this is 'wicked' (p. 22). Archie is arguably the only villain in all Stoppard's work, unless one includes his predecessor, Lord Malquist.

George is often in difficulties with language himself (though experienced in guessing his wife's charades); but he knows that a word has no inherent meaning and is therefore unimpressed when its meaning turns out to vary: 'that the word "good" has also meant different things to different people at different times . . . is not a statement which anyone would dispute, and . . . nothing useful can be inferred from it. It is not in fact a statement about value at all; it is a statement about language and how it is used.'

Accepting that language is unstable, he is interested by the recurrence of moral principle – something beyond language – in societies whose languages and cultures are superficially very different. He believes this shows there is a good 'which is knowable but not nameable', just as the less caricatured philosopher Anderson, in *Professional Foul*, asserts that 'there is a sense of right and wrong which precedes utterance'.

Stoppard's own speaking voice is characteristically precise: this is not a man for sloppiness. His accent suggests a private-school education, with a faint hint of foreignness. His baby language was, of course, Czech, but while still in infancy he was exposed to the multilingualism of Singapore and its own dialect of English, which was then overlaid by Indian and American versions. A compulsive punster, he relishes the duplicity of language; yet he insists on the need to treat it carefully, precisely because it is so frail and fickle and because the quality of our thought depends on it so much. His regular mockery of cliché deepens into anguish when dead metaphors are mixed: 'He got hammered by an emotional backlash. / No, no, you *can't* – ' (*The Real Thing*, which also includes the famous cricket-bat speech). Protective concern for language is one way in which Stoppard attempts to ward off moral and intellectual anarchy.

Much of his comedy, of course, turns on language's potential absurdity. Play after play begins in a language – or a sound-language, or a mime, or a tableau – which the audience doesn't understand. The first ten speeches of *Dirty Linen* are in Latin, Spanish or French; the first English words, 'Bloody awkward though', are immediately followed by 'Pardon my French'. Linguistic misunderstanding is an age-old device of comedy, but Stoppard exploits it more frequently and ingeniously than most; George does not realise till late in *Jumpers* that Bones has come to investigate a murder rather than a complaint about late-night rowdiness, or that the 'him' whom Dotty pretends to be eating is supposed to be a jugged hare, not Professor McFee; and for a surreal moment in *Professional Foul* the language holds up when a footballer is mistaken for a philosopher: 'I hear you're doing some very interesting things at Newcastle. Great stuff. I still like to think of myself as a bit of a left-winger at Stoke.'

More grimly, in a white man's Africa (Francis is the black servant): 'We're Geoff and Ruth to everyone around here. (*He takes a beer off the tray.*) Isn't that right, Francis?' 'Yes, sir, Mr Carson.'

When the exuberance of language is entirely shut off, the air goes cold: 'You see all the trouble writers cause' (*Every Good Boy*; Ivanov's whole speech is devastatingly understated). 'It's only a couple of marriages and a child' (*The Real Thing*). 'Something went wrong. I forget what' (Nadya, Lenin's wife, in *Travesties*).

Postmodernism

Stoppard was famous before this term became current. Sometimes it's used merely chronologically: John Fletcher in *About Beckett* (Faber, 2003) sees Postmodernism as 'a second and final flowering' of Modernism between the 1950s and the 1970s, headed by Beckett and just about including Stoppard. More commonly today it refers to a kind of free-floating in intellectual space, having cast ourselves off from all past explanations and systems – whether of science, religion, Marxism, psychoanalysis, or even history. All such large-scale theories, being linguistic constructs and therefore suspect, are 'grand narratives' rather than truth: the only absolute is absolute relativism. Appropriate responses are therefore ironic and self-conscious, often taking the form of pastiche and parody or the creation of a 'virtual' reality in parallel with canonical landmarks of culture.

The voices here do resemble that of Sir Archibald Jumper, who already in 1972 runs a thoroughly postmodern university. Then, in 1974, *Travesties* caricatures several grand narratives and refuses the illusion of historical accuracy; it's also the most ingenious of Stoppard's dances within someone else's famous structure, in this case *The Importance of Being Earnest*. So when, in the 1980s, smart people began to talk of Postmodernism, he might reasonably have murmured that he'd already been there, showing the plays as his T-shirt.

He would certainly have added, however, that 'there' wasn't somewhere he would choose to live. Stoppard's lifelong response to the promulgators of uncertainty in the twentieth century is to take on their clothing, their material, their apparatus, yet then, as it were from within their walls, to fight for the old faiths – not, admittedly, for Newtonian physics, but for the notions of 'objective reality and absolute morality' and 'a moral order derived from Christian absolutes'.

Theatre

'After 1956 everybody of my age who wanted to write, wanted to write plays.' Stoppard's first years as a reporter saw the London premières of Beckett's *Waiting for Godot* (1955) and John Osborne's *Look Back in Anger* (1956), the visit of the Berliner Ensemble set up by Bertolt Brecht (also 1956), and in 1958 new plays by Harold Pinter, Arnold Wesker and John Arden. What many audiences, critics and young writers most noticed in this new writing was an aggressive social realism ('kitchen-sink' was one label). Pinter, Wesker and Arden dared to set plays within the working class, a rarity previously in England, and though Osborne's characters are graduates, they choose to live in a garret.

What attracted Stoppard was not the leftism or the social realism – which were not in fact new, since both were being done before he was born – but 'that you could do a lot more in the theatre than had previously been demonstrated' (p. 111, with Beckett most in mind). As Richard Eyre puts it to me (p. 222): 'Tom has sort of taken [Shakespeare and] Brecht . . . and Beckett, and has simply seen "Yeah, this medium: you can expand and contract, it's a poetic medium that is fantastically flexible."'

Beyond Realism

Since the mid-nineteenth century Western theatre had been dominated by stage realism. Curtains closed off the stage under a proscenium arch; when they were opened, it was the removal of the fourth wall of a room, fully furnished, where characters showed no awareness of being watched. Realism was also expected of dialogue, which made exposition harder and led to mechanisms such as that gleefully parodied in *The Real Inspector Hound*:

(*The phone rings.* MRS DRUDGE *seems to have been waiting for it to do so and for the last few seconds has been dusting it with an intense concentration. She snatches it up.*)

MRS DRUDGE: (*into phone*): Hello, the drawing room of Lady Muldoon's country residence one morning in early spring?

This realist stranglehold was a temporary aberration. Theatre is one of the oldest of art forms, and makes use of many means of presentation – verse, song, dance, masks, ritual, symbolism, as well as, at times, realistic speech and properties. If an audience can accept the first, basic convention of a play – knowing perfectly well that it's not real life happening in front of them – they have no great problem in accepting the others, from a character addressing them directly to a consumptive heroine singing her heart out. Theatrical realism (at its most dogmatic, 'naturalism': the eggs on stage must be properly boiled) regards such conventions as frivolous, compromising a play's fidelity to life; and some great plays, such as those of Henrik Ibsen and Anton Chekhov, were conceived within that earnest limitation. But Ibsen was a poetic dramatist first (and, to some extent, last) and one of the finest moments in Chekhov's *The Cherry Orchard* – 'a distant sound . . . out of the sky, like the sound of a string snapping' – belongs magically to theatre, but not to realism.

Some reaction against the stranglehold, back to older and freer forms, had begun as early as the 1920s, in early Brecht, Pirandello and some Modernist poet-dramatists. But mainstream theatre remained in the mode roughly of, say, 1880, and several young 1950s playwrights were content to accept realist conventions, often being more concerned with changing society than with changing theatre. Realist drama is of course alive and well today because it's the natural mode of the camera, which does it far better; but theatre has returned to what it can do best, gathering a live audience together for a *representation* which need not be a full *simulation*. Furniture, moods or vast spaces can be indicated by a gesture or two; exposition can be made direct to the audience; action may slide into dance, and song or poetry or lavishly heightened speech may replace plodding prosaic dialogue.

Samuel Beckett once spoke of realism as 'a grotesque fallacy', which was echoed by Stoppard to Kenneth Tynan: 'That sort of truth-telling writing is as big a lie as the deliberate fantasies I construct. It's based on the fallacy of naturalism. There's a direct line of descent from the naturalistic theatre which leads you straight down to the dregs of bad theatre, bad thinking, and bad feeling.'[16]

Richard Eyre again: 'It's essentially the thing about theatre that everything there is unreal, and the audience knows it's unreal. It's all metaphor ... Tom will always be that fantastic exemplary figure who demonstrates that the medium is capable of anything, and is so alive.' (p. 223)

Thus Stoppard could open *Jumpers* with a wild mixture of cabaret act, trapeze work, knockabout farce, gymnastics and murder mystery. Thus he took up with enthusiasm André Previn's challenge to write a play which required an entire symphony orchestra on stage. Thus he begins his mostly realist play *Night and Day* with a piece of, as it were, hyper-realism – a jeep driven on stage, its headlights blinding the audience – but very soon slips in a non-realist convention (we can hear some of Ruth's thoughts) and later an entire scene of fantasy. In another relatively realist play, *Arcadia*, he alternates scenes from two eras which then, in a great ultimate scene, take the stage together; and *The Invention of Love* turns on an extraordinary dialogue between the same man's older and younger self. Most recently Stoppard's trilogy *The Coast of Utopia* used

16 Tynan, p. 64.

William Dudley's video projections to create on a vast screen scenes from a country estate, Moscow, Paris, London, summer, winter, and a span of thirty-five years.

Utopia was directed by Trevor Nunn, who also directed *Every Good Boy* and *Arcadia*. It's a big, serious work; but both Stoppard and Nunn are also happy to work in showbiz, and their previous project together, just after the success of *Arcadia*, had been a screenplay for Steven Spielberg of Andrew Lloyd Webber's *Cats*, which Nunn had directed in the theatre. The film has not been made; but that, too, is show business.

Metatheatre

This is jargon, with overtones of postmodernist theory where every utterance is thought to allude in some way to previous utterances, and to be self-conscious about its own uttering. But the idea is age-old: the Latin phrase *theatrum mundi* was painted up in Shakespeare's Globe Theatre and translated by him as: 'All the world's a stage': God is a personnel trainer setting up role-plays. Yet even if real life is merely God's set-up, the playing on stage may teach us about reality – or at least, about our own roles. We are aware of our own situation as we watch actors playing others; so, too – of *theirs* – are the actors.

Some of this poignant interest enlivens film, but it's far stronger in the theatre, where actors and audience meet in one space 'live' (the word implies an intrinsic deadness in film). And theatre often teases both audience and actors, never more so than in the playwright whom Stoppard dubs 'World Champ' – in *Julius Caesar*: 'How many ages hence / Shall this our lofty scene be acted o'er' (here we are, ages *thence*, watching it); or in *Macbeth*: 'Life's a poor player, / That struts and frets his hour upon the stage.' Beckett often nudges his audience with the subtext that they are fools to sit and watch his play, yet maybe that's no more pointless than the rest of life: '*(He picks up the telescope, turns it on auditorium.)* I see a multitude . . . in transports of joy. *(Pause.)* That's what I call a magnifier'; and he pre-empts the would-be consolation of 'significance': 'We're not beginning to . . . to . . . mean something?' (both from *Endgame*).

Stoppard's *Rosencrantz* joins this club on its first page; after five coins are spun, correctly called 'Heads' each time by Ros, Guil is allowed to speak: 'There is an art to the building up of suspense.'

The audience laugh nervously, and in doing so are drawn into complicity with dramatist and actors, and each other, realising the possible absurdity of the way they have chosen to spend an evening. For a long time after this we are still not told who these characters are (it's possible that thus far they themselves don't know). Things become more reassuringly Shakespearean (we do, after all, know the play's *title*) on the entry of the Tragedians, and Ros and Guil turn out to know their names – except that Ros gets them the wrong way round:

ROS: My name is Guildenstern, and this is Rosencrantz. (GUIL *confers briefly with him.*)
(*Without embarrassment*) I'm sorry – *his* name's Guildenstern, and *I'm* Rosencrantz.

This is a metatheatrical in-joke, since everyone who knows *Hamlet* knows this pair, yet virtually no one can remember which is which; the joke is doubled because it originates in Shakespeare.

KING: Thanks, Rosencrantz and gentle Guildenstern.
QUEEN: Thanks, Guildenstern and gentle Rosencrantz.

(In Stoppard's version, the Queen is *correcting* her husband!)

The Real Inspector Hound is about people watching a play and their eventual interaction with the play's characters; it's also a parody of theatrical clichés and the country-house murder mystery. *Travesties* is constructed with even more ingenuity within and without the frame of Wilde's *The Importance of Being Earnest*, some knowledge of which is essential (but also likely, in most theatre audiences). *The Real Thing* opens with a two-hand scene which later proves to be from a stage play by a third character; two passages from John Ford's *'Tis Pity She's a Whore* are played out later, and we hear no less than three versions of an encounter on a train, the first scornfully read out from the script, the second parodied by the actors in their 'real life', and the third a fully performed rewrite. *The Real Thing* is a play about a playwright, and its levels of metatheatre are yet further complicated, in hindsight, by biographical irony: dedicated to Miriam Stoppard, it was first performed by Felicity Kendal.

Absurdist Comedy

The so-called Theatre of the Absurd was fashionable in Paris in the 1950s and reached London in translations of plays by Beckett and Eugène Ionesco. Absurdist theatre is a Modernist extension of metatheatre and a derisive repudiation of realism. All the world's a stage, and all the men and women merely clowns, not even aware whether their trousers are up or down; the attempt at rational reasoning (Lucky, in *Waiting for Godot*) belongs in 'the Acacacademy of Anthropopopometry'. Life is meaningless and futile; so therefore are plays, but they pass the time and they offer some consoling shape within the absolute shapelessness. How much of a consolation *laughter* is is doubtful; more often it seems savagely angry, an existentialist defiance.

Ionesco wrote the blackest of farce: ludicrous material intended, he claimed, to remind the spectator that one day he would be a corpse. As a young reporter Stoppard knew the plays of N. F. Simpson (such as *A Resounding Tinkle*, 1957, and *One-Way Pendulum*, 1959) which developed amiably the more farcical, less alarming elements of Ionesco, somewhat in the manner of the later and now better-known television series *Monty Python's Flying Circus* (1969–74). He was also soon struck by the much darker work of Harold Pinter, which has lasted better. Where Ionesco and Simpson specialised in obviously surreal juxtapositions, Pinter's plays seek no cheap laughs; his stage sets are mundane, his characters' dialogue apparently dully realistic; the absurdity comes in the inconsequences and disjunctions within that dialogue, and the darkness in the cruelty and fear – 'the theatre of menace' – below its surface.

Long before such names were known to Stoppard, however, he was a schoolboy fan of the BBC radio *Goon Show* (1951–9), which introduced absurdism to a mass audience and whose influence on the next generation of writers and performers was immense. The Goon scripts ruled out nothing as too grotesque, and also played havoc with the genre of radio, then the main provider of popular entertainment. They exploited the clichés of radio comedy, such as funny voices and the inclusion of catchphrases, and they specialised in a mighty mockery, by overkill, of radio sound effects. The blacked-out opening of Act Three of *Rosencrantz* is pure Goons:

(*... the sea. Ship timbers, wind in the rigging, and then sounds of sailors calling obscure but inescapably nautical instructions from all directions far and near ...*)
    Hard a larboard!
    Let go the stays! . . . [and so on]
(*When the point has been well made and more so*)
ROS: We're on a boat.

Beckett's own radio play *All That Fall* (1957) includes an equally mischievous parody:

The wind – (*brief wind*) – scarcely stirs the leaves and the birds – (*brief chirp*) – are tired singing. The cows – (*brief moo*) – and sheep – (*brief baa*) – ruminate in silence. The dogs – (*brief bark*) – are hushed and the hens – (*brief cackle*) – sprawl torpid in the dust. We are alone. There is no one to ask.

Practicalities

Beckett's play was commissioned for the BBC Third Programme.

When, five years later, Stoppard came to London, there were promising possibilities for young writers both in radio and in television, and he found work in both, whereas he had to wait years to see a play of his on the London stage.

Performance possibilities are the essential context for understanding a playwright: poets and novelists may cherish works that remain unpublished, but a play cannot exist until it has actors and audience. Born twenty years earlier, Stoppard might have written far more for radio; as it is, followers in America and elsewhere may be puzzled that he persisted at all with that genre, where the financial rewards are modest. When young he was glad to get the work; it included a series for overseas radio about an Arab student in London, and a week's episodes of the daily fifteen-minute soap *Mrs Dale's Diary*, about as un-Stoppardian a commission as can be imagined. (It would have secured his largest ever audience at one time if the scripts had been accepted: they weren't.) Later, as a famous dramatist, he still returned to radio at intervals, with works that – although later staged – were essentially conceived to be heard and not seen.

In Britain, BBC radio and television are subsidised by the tax-payer. In theatre, too, Kenneth Tynan's seizing of *Rosencrantz* for the fledgling National Theatre did much to shape Stoppard's future practice. Where other dramatists develop their skills within a small and usually struggling workshop, he was suddenly launched in the subsidised theatre, very much on his own, and was expected to produce more for it. His next full-length play, *Jumpers*, was therefore an extravaganza exploiting such resources, and two years later he could be reasonably confident that *Travesties* would be snapped up by one or other of the big British subsidised bodies, the National and the Royal Shakespeare.

On the other hand, by far the greater part of his work, particularly when screenplays are included, has been created for commercial expectations. In British theatre this means 'the West End', where plays are unlikely to have large casts and are less free to bewilder the audience – though *Hapgood*, than

41

which they don't come more bewildering, was written for the commercial producer Michael Codron, as were *The Real Inspector Hound*, *Night and Day*, *The Real Thing*, and *Indian Ink*. Clearly Stoppard could have prospered in a land where all theatre was commercial; subsidised theatre merely extended the range of what might be feasible.

Experimentation is most frequent, however, in small workshops; and Stoppard went also in that direction for a while, in his collaboration with the expatriate American Ed Berman, for whose lunch-time theatre he wrote brilliant plays which are even odder than usual: *After Magritte*, *Dogg's Our Pet* (later developed into *Dogg's Hamlet, Cahoot's Macbeth*), and *Dirty Linen / New-Found-Land*. Meanwhile he was in practice developing his own close team, the professionals with whom he would work again and again: in radio John Tydeman, and in theatre first the actor John Wood, then Peter Wood, Michael Codron, the designer Carl Toms, and later Felicity Kendal.

A different practical question is the social or cultural exclusiveness of Stoppard's plays. In radio this is less marked: you didn't have to live in a big city, or buy an expensive seat, to listen to *In the Native State*. Yet that play went out on Radio 3, a station to which the great majority of the British public tune in only by accident. An American critic, Enoch Brater, writes of a Stoppard audience as 'an intelligentsia'; his theatre 'will not work for slackers'[17]. Brater seems rather pleased about this, but I see it as a genuine limitation. As Trevor Nunn put it to me, 'Tom sets the bar very high.' One of the many decent things about Tom Stoppard is that he doesn't try to be what he isn't; and his plays are written for an audience that is not only intelligent but also well educated. Beckett's *Waiting for Godot* is said to work well in prisons; but a production of *Rosencrantz* there would be lucky not to sink under its weight of allusion. Nobody watching *Travesties* or *Arcadia* picks up every allusion or textual intricacy, but if you don't have the background (not

17 Kelly (ed.) Cambridge Companion, p. 212.

just the intelligence) to pick up a good many of them, you're missing out. Stoppard's plays were socially exclusive when first performed and with time will only become more so.

This means they've often been underestimated. Cohorts of drama students – of tomorrow's actors and directors – used to resist Stoppard's plays out of a kind of politico-social prejudice. But the plays are too good to be so missed. The actor Stephen Dillane (p. 246) admits to the prejudice, before taking on his first professional Stoppard role in *The Real Thing*: 'I imagined his audience to be conservative and self-satisfied, congratulating themselves for understanding the jokes. [In the event, however] I found the reasoning flawless, and surrendered to a greater mind than my own [embracing the play's] poetic reflection on time, vanity, futility, hope and passion (and love).'

As for the ultimate practicality, income, Stoppard, like other British playwrights, has written many screenplays. This is work he welcomes, not only because the money is big but because he enjoys sheer craftsmanship, putting his skills at the service of other people's work; and also because as an imaginative writer he is far too often 'blocked' to be doing his own things all the time. (His theatre translations, not discussed here, stand midway between being 'other people's work' and his own.) Most of Stoppard's screenplays are unpublished and self-effacing; in the next chapter I mention two which have been published and are more distinctively his: *Galileo* and *Shakespeare in Love*.

3

Stoppard's Development

Galileo, the screenplay for a film never made, was first published in 2003 in the literary journal *Areté*. With generous descriptive explanation in italics, it reads very well, though more like a novel than a film. What is most surprising is its sustained calm seriousness. Speeches here anticipate the poised rhetoric of *Arcadia* or *The Coast of Utopia*.

> I do not understand why perfection should be a state of rest rather than a state of change. I am very fond of this Earth; it is not, of course, perfect, but that which I find noble and admirable in it is all to do with change: the change of a bud to a flower, of a deer feeding to a deer running, the change of grape to wine, child to man, wood to flame; and the ash is thrown on the soil to help the buds change to flowers again. Alteration, novelty, decay, regeneration – these are not the blemishes of an imperfect world.

The surprise is that *Galileo* was written as early as 1970. The standard account of Stoppard sees his work developing from a heartless frivolity to a deeper humanity and gravity; but that's a misleading oversimplification. His 'squibs' and cartoon plays are certainly youthful (the last of them, the 1982 radio play *The Dog It Was That Died*, does feel like self-pastiche); yet even early on he chooses to write about people who – even when caricatures rather than characters – are incapacitated by anxiety and mental pain. Vast generalised insecurities obsess them, and clearly at least *interest* their creator. And although the later plays are indeed deeper and darker, their basic mode is that of comedy. Even at the start, a brooding Tom Stoppard is not far away; while as late as *The Coast of Utopia* he remains amused at human pretension.

His apprentice piece was written in 1960, under the title *A Walk on the Water*. Televised in 1963, it was later revised and staged as **Enter a Free Man**. Like many first works this is derivative, an uncertain mixture of working-class realism and broadcast sit-com. Riley is an unsuccessful inventor with delusions of grandeur ('First Watt and the steam engine – now Riley and the Sponge Principle!'); he is humoured by his wife and daughter. The names of Riley's pub cronies – 'Able the seaman' and 'Carmen the barman' – are characteristic of the rather laboured comedy. Though the play remains in print, Stoppard has described its successor, *The Gamblers* (never published), as 'the first play I really regard as *mine*'.

The best of his early writing is for radio. In 1964 the BBC broadcast two plays lasting only fifteen minutes each, **The Dissolution of Dominic Boot** and **'M' is for Moon among Other Things**. (Two years earlier Stoppard had used 'Boot' – the name of the journalist in Evelyn Waugh's *Scoop* – as a pseudonym in his own journalism, and in 1964 he also drafted a TV script about a character called Samuel Boot; 'Moon' became even more of a mock-obsession, both the name and the heavenly object.) Stoppard is always alert to what different genres can offer, and his notion for *Dominic Boot* is ideally suited to radio and the time limit. Dominic drops off his fiancée from his taxi and then, realising he has too little money to pay the fare, travels about London trying to raise it, all the time incurring higher debt on the meter. Radio makes possible the repeated desperate changes of scene and characters, locked together by the running of the taxi engine. *'M' is for Moon* is a conceit upon the letter 'M' – Constance, reading the M–N instalment of her mail-order encyclopedia, reveals that she used to be known as Millie; she 'doesn't want the moon' but yearns for the simple world of her childhood ABC: 'M was for Moon. It was ages before I knew that M was for anything else.' Her husband turns on the TV in time to catch the final credits of *Dial M for Murder* and hear the news of Marilyn Monroe's suicide.

A more substantial piece is **If You're Glad I'll be Frank** (1966): Gladys is the voice of the telephone speaking clock – not a tape, but a trapped person. She unwisely volunteered after being turned down by a nunnery because of her religious doubts – 'it was the serenity I was after, that and the clean linen'. She 'thought it would be peace', within the narrow logic of clock minutes and seconds; but instead she is on the verge of cracking. She grasps that the minutes and seconds are arbitrary human impositions on the shapelessness of infinity; humans have 'no sense of their scurrying insignificance'. Contemplating time is like looking down from a great height (as Stoppard's Albert will later from his bridge), 'reducing the life-size to nothing'. Gladys's voice has been recognised on the speaking clock by her husband, Frank, who attempts to speak back: 'I'll get you out of there, Gladys!' Ironically he is a bus driver, precise in his time-keeping. The First Lord of the Post Office, who fields phone calls from all sides (including at one point from God), manages to defeat Frank's efforts and stave off Gladys's breakdown. Finally she has gained some independence, her last words commenting contemptuously on the First Lord: 'He thinks he's God.'

In *Glad/Frank*'s second scene various people arrive for work, entering '*on the first, third, fifth, seventh and ninth strokes of Big Ben respectively (the second, fourth, sixth and eighth strokes being heard through the closed door)*'. Each greets the Porter according to their station in life (that is, the British class system) as 'Tommy', 'Tom', 'Mr Thompson', or 'Thompson'. The First Lord is similarly greeted, in each case 'correctly' for the greeter's status, as 'my Lord', 'your Lordship', 'Lord Coot' or 'Cooty'. It's a brilliant sequence, a cartoon in *sound* about *language*.

Albert's Bridge (1967) occupies a full hour and uses radio even more imaginatively. Film might have shown four men, spaced vertically, painting a big railway bridge, and their view of the city ('quite ordered . . . From a vantage point like this, the idea of society is just about tenable'). Film might also have shown Albert on holiday in Paris (happiest on the Eiffel Tower), cutting back to the local councillors, debating the economics of bridge-painting. What film couldn't do is to also take us inside Albert's thoughts. He has a degree in philosophy but chooses to work forever painting his bridge, which is 'utterly fixed by the rules that make it stay up'; for Albert this is 'sublime', because 'My life is set out for me . . . to climb and clamber in a giant frame.'

Stoppard's early characters yearn for ultimate control, over the threatening mess and flux of life. They often resemble Antoine Rocquentin, in Jean-Paul Sartre's influential novel *Nausea* (1938), who finds refuge from the horrors of contingency in a jazz record, 'an unchanging order'. John Brown, in the TV play **A Separate Peace** (1966) tried for a monastery for the same reasons as Gladys – serenity and clean linen – and was similarly rejected; instead he hires a room at a private hospital. He wants to contract out of the 'wide-open' scene of the world: 'Fire, flood, and misery of all kinds, across the world or over the hill.' Hospitals have their own generators, 'in case of power cuts . . . a hospital can carry on, set loose from the world'. In the novel **Lord Malquist and Mr Moon** (1966), Moon sees a power station as 'at the mercy of a million variables any of which might fail in some way – strikes, silicosis, storms at sea, a broken gauge, an Arabian coup d'état, a drop in supply, a rise in demand, a derailment at Slough, a faux pas at a British Council cocktail party, a toothache in the wrong man at the wrong time . . .'

He intends to write 'a history of the world'; he knows it's 'all mixed up . . . but I'm *organising* it . . . into sequences, and categories . . . the grand design'.

This is Stoppard's only novel. It acknowledges its genre by literary pastiche ('From behind a scrub of thorn the lion watched her. He was not sure yet and the wind was wrong' . . . 'Jane was sitting at her toilette . . . dreaming of might-have-beens.') In other respects, however, it's more like theatre, and also 'camp': this black farce is frantically allusive, not only to canonical culture but also to itself. From the start horses are 'pigeon-coloured' and pigeons are 'dun-coloured'; Lord Malquist's 'cosmic accuracy' is instantly miscopied by Mr Moon as 'comic inaccuracy', the error thus describing itself (Stoppard's days as journalist may be recalled). Moon's name is a further self-allusion, and much of the second page deals with boots; later the butler is called Bird*boot* . . .

The setting is London on the day of a huge state funeral. Mr Moon is a young free-lance historian offering himself as a Boswell-like recorder of Malquist's sayings. He also carries about a bomb inherited from an eccentric uncle, and has every intention of exploding it somewhere soon. His malaise has 'something to do with no one being *good* any more, but that's part of the other things, of things all getting out of control, too big'.

The reader may suspect, however, that Moon might feel better if his wife Jane would allow their marriage to be consummated. As for Lord Malquist, he's an anachronistic aristocrat whose cheques bounce but who continues to live in style, scattering behind his coach gold 'coins' which turn out to be chocolates – a visual pun described in words. A mixture of Lord Chesterfield and Oscar Wilde, Malquist now appears more as a draft for Sir Archibald Jumper, callous to the most obvious suffering. The Risen Christ is a donkey-riding Irishman who appears to have superficially healed stigmata; there are also a black Catholic Irish Jewish Cockney coachman called O'Hara, two cowboys, a murdered French maid, a lion, and *another* bomber, who eventually blows Moon up, mistaking him for Malquist.

The novel flirts with Absurdism, but not persuasively; more often its voice seems that of a young writer trying frantically to be sophisticated. The outrageously tasteless lays tacit claim to some opposite, decent reaction:

> [Moon] stood in front of the mirror with the towel round his body and over his head. He looked at himself.

'I am veryfine saint, mygoodness yes. I will not break my fasting I tell you till the British give me back my country, esteemed sir.'

That was a mistake. He shook for forty million potbellied starvlings, and pulled the towel over his face, gagged on laundered freshness, and revived.

'That was a mistake' attempts to reassure, and 'shook' to suggest Moon's regret; but he, or the narrator, still settles for the words 'potbellied starvlings' . . .

Where the novel is most off-putting is in its imaging of women. Jane's 'toilette' turns out to be the toilet: 'her knickers were round her ankles'; her next appearance is 'all but naked', with a cowboy 'rubbing cream into her left buttock'. A French maid appears, to whom Moon instantly finds himself stammering, 'Your breasts are so little'; and within lines Jane returns 'quite naked except for a sapphire ring slotted into her navel' and, a moment later, 'with a lascivious ellipse of her pelvis . . . buttock aglint with cold cream: "Are you sitting on my knickers?"

'So unlike the home life of our own dear Queen.'

Like the Gandhi travesty just quoted, this is offered knowingly: it purports to satirise male prurience, as well as the royalty gossip columns. Yet the narration never withdraws to a plausible distance; rather, it continues to indulge that prurience, and the effect is dehumanising – most obviously when a third female character, Lady Malquist, having conveniently provided Moon's sexual initiation, then equally conveniently 'lay limp under him, the amazing deflatable woman of the funfair'. And it gets nastier: when Jane fears she has breast cancer,

'"One off, both off," said the ninth earl. "An asymmetrical body is vulgar both as body and as art."

'Jane laughed merrily – "Oh Falcon, you are awful!"'

It's as if the writer is straining to appear as heartless as Malquist, in some prolonged misjudgement. Stoppard may have soon regarded his novel as dead, since it had tiny early sales and he re-used elements of it (for example, articulate cynic intimately examines decent man's wife) for *Jumpers*.

A few days either side of the novel's publication, a documentary about chess and the play *A Separate Peace* were televised – and **Rosencrantz and Guildenstern Are Dead** opened in Edinburgh. This is still the play for which Stoppard is best known, and plenty has been written on it. W. S. Gilbert had created a farrago about the two attendant lords, and Stoppard's own first toying with such an idea ('Rosencrantz and Guildenstern Meet King Lear', suggested by his agent, Kenneth Ewing) may well have been equally frivolous; but suddenly now he achieves what he would later describe as the 'marriage between the play of ideas and farce or perhaps even high comedy'. Though John Wood, the first Guildenstern in America, rightly describes it to me as one great theatre joke, it does walk on the backs of two serious, though also funny, classics: *Hamlet* and *Waiting for Godot*. As a 'play of ideas' it can offer mock-mathematical 'laws', mock-philosophical syllogisms, the artifice of theatre, human identity, and the certain destination of death. Yet its comedy is insistent and wide-ranging, from repeated Stoppardian slippages of word (and, in this play, name) to wry comment on Shakespeare's story, familiar to most theatre audiences.

The comedy, however, is not primarily of language but of situation – the human condition – and also what we're doing in the theatre. Pirandello's Six Characters carry within them a powerful story, but can't find the play they're in; just the opposite is true for Ros and Guil. They know what they have to do on stage, as does the audience; what they don't know about is their deaths – whereas the audience knows the play's title. The parallels with our general human situation are evident: we know the day-to-day expectations of us, but not what (if any) ultimate scheme we're part of, or how and when we will die.

Parallels with theatre permit many self-referential in-jokes: actors forgetting who's playing whom, or catching cold on stage ('There isn't any wind. *Draught*, yes'), or desperate for some 'action'. In Shakespeare, the First Player's ability to feign emotion shocks Hamlet. Stoppard's players have drifted down-market, almost into Beckett country: although they now dignify themselves with the name of Tragedians, they are actually reduced to playing anything, certainly including obscenity, for anyone who will pay. Their skilled feigning is now largely sensationalist; they're particularly good at 'dying', as they eventually and lengthily show. This drift/shift is masterly, helping to make the play a gloss not just on Shakespeare but on a distinctly 1960s, seedy version, since Ros and Guil too have entirely modern sensibilities – they may not talk about motorbikes or movies, but they think and feel like members of their twentieth-century audience.

For years afterwards Stoppard was in the habit of saying that he wasn't interested in characterisation. But by this he meant psychological realism; in practice the characterisation in *Rosencrantz* is quite sufficient. The fragments of Shakespeare should seem conventional – what we expect from a routine performance of *Hamlet*: Stoppard's play is subverted if they are played in 'interesting' ways or (as has occasionally happened) as puppets. The supporting Tragedians have to do little more than mime athletically. *Rosencrantz* thus has just three 'characters', all attractive parts.

Whereas Shakespeare's pair are indistinguishable, Ros and Guil are gently differentiated. As in *Waiting for Godot*, there is some slight overlap with traditional comic double acts: the smart talker and the dullard; but here neither is a simple fool and they always share the same predicament. Stoppard described them to Giles Gordon as carrying out 'a dialogue which I carry out with myself. One of them is fairly intellectual, fairly incisive; the other one is thicker, nicer in a curious way, more sympathetic.'[18]

Their reactions to the letter ordering the death of Hamlet anticipate later Stoppard work in which natural innocence

18 Delaney p. 19.

shows up clever talk: Guil's sweetly reasonable speech excusing them from doing anything about it anticipates Archie in *Jumpers*. But mostly Guil is decent, and gentle towards Ros. He is the one always trying to *interpret* their situation.

The Player is, of course, the only one who *understands* it. He is wearily at ease onstage, an old theatre queen who has been here, done this, far too often already and is disgusted by the decline in his art, himself and his audiences (Stoppard finely takes up Shakespeare's own topical reference to companies forced to tour because they've lost their audiences in the city). The Player is equally at home either side of the looking glass, in the Elizabethan play and the modern theatre; he realises that they exist only when an audience sees them, and that their fate is predestined by a script: 'It is *written*.'

He already *knows*; and throughout Stoppard's work knowers are bad news. *Travesties* is full of them, a babble of fanatics. Elsewhere the knowers are Malquist, Archie, and in *The Coast of Utopia* Bakunin (his certainties changing like a schoolboy's) and Marx. These later characters do *harm*, a charge that can't be levelled against the Player; but his 'knowing' is about death, and therefore includes the audience, within that other Stoppardian anathema: determinism.

Women are absent here, except for momentary appearances of Shakespeare's Gertrude and Ophelia. Any hint of sex is merely adolescent: Ros's grubby curiosity and Guil's alarmed recoiling. But here's a delicate touch: 'GUIL: Has it ever happened to you that all of a sudden and for no reason at all you haven't the faintest idea how to spell the word "wife"– or "house" . . .?'

Guil's random choice of words is, we might say, 'Freudian': if he and Ros are amnesiacs (that would be the good news) then 'wife' and 'house' may well be important aspects of their offstage lives. Their growing terror is that in fact they have no life offstage, and therefore of course no wives or homes. With further subtlety this blankness is intimated in terms of a hiatus of language, immediately after a panicky sequence when neither can get a stock phrase right ('home and high – dry and home', and so on for a dozen lines).

The weakness of *Rosencrantz* is that it's too long: stretches of the comic double act are dispensable, and for his own film in 1990 Stoppard cut the text by up to half. The third act was written at the request of the RSC, and is somewhat cruder than the previous two: it allows itself comic anachronisms (the beach umbrella and deckchair and possible smoking), has Ros considering vomiting into the audience and Hamlet actually spitting at them (but the 'fourth wall' seems to be glass, since he gets it back in his face, a somewhat basic metatheatrical joke). It also transgresses (though why should we care?) two previously implied conventions: that Ros and Guil can't leave this particular stage space, and that they are always immediately adjacent to (if not present at) the action of Shakespeare's play. What does now seem essential is the ending of Act Three – the Player's feigned death, the Tragedians' 'real' deaths, and the sudden but separate disappearances of Ros and Guil.

After *Rosencrantz* Stoppard returned to television. The 'squib' *Teeth* gave John Wood his first Stoppard role, *Another Moon Called Earth* was later developed into *Jumpers*, and *Neutral Ground* is a neat transference of the classical myth of Philoctetes to the double-agent thriller. These scripts remain in print, but deservedly better known are the stage plays **The Real Inspector Hound** (1968) and **After Magritte** (1970). Each takes up half an evening, so they can be paired.

At the start of *Hound* a looking-glass audience seems to rise into the back wall; we are not sure whether we are on the outside looking in or on the inside looking out. This Chinese-boxes feeling is multiplied for Stoppard followers when the two main characters turn out to be called Moon and Birdboot. They are critics, prejudging the play within the play and then identifying its clichés and stereotypes – and here the allusions are popular, since the framed play is a parody of a country-house whodunnit, perhaps by Agatha Christie. The more jaded features of realist theatre are mocked – the informatively answered phone call, the tedious offering and handing round of coffee. And the metatheatrical potential is richly realised: when the phone rings and rings on an empty stage, Moon impatiently gets up and answers it. The American critic Robert Benchley is said to have done just this, declared 'That's for me', and promptly left the theatre; here the twist is that the call turns out to be for the *other* critic, Birdboot. The barrier between watchers and watched has been breached, and from here on, as also happens in Pirandello's *Six Characters* and in *Rosencrantz*, the frame play and the framed bloodily merge.

After Magritte has been mentioned before for its characteristic pattern of grotesque juxtapositions rationally explained. One trigger in this case was a friend's account of finding himself – in real life and for quite logical reasons – a figure of absurdity: waiting to cross a busy road in pyjamas which were slipping down and with shaving cream on his face and a peacock under each arm. This play is the kind of theatrical *tour de force* where the audience are so busy laughing they probably don't notice the technique. Like *Hound*, it's a potential display piece for drama school. *After Magritte* requires some physical and technical virtuosity, on or offstage, for the gradual dismantling of the first ludicrous tableau and the gradual building of the final one: it's a highly visual play, very specifically for theatre. It was first performed at the lunch-time theatre in Soho of Ed Berman, who called himself Professor R. L. Dogg so that in references he would appear as 'Dogg, R. L.' ('doggerel': this spectacularly awful pun clearly won Stoppard's heart). Berman thus called his company Dogg's Troupe, of which *Dogg's Our Pet*, the mini-play written for him in 1971, is an anagram. This toyed with a thought-experiment of Wittgenstein about the arbitrary, non-referential nature of language, and was developed later within the larger framework of *Dogg's Hamlet, Cahoot's Macbeth*.

In late 1970 came the (initially Schools) radio play **Where Are They Now?**, written for just £75 but entirely Stoppardian in its deft, funny and poignant use of the genre. An Old Boys' reunion is intercut with the voices of the young boys they once were. Beyond the usual but well-made points about boarding schools and nostalgia, the audience is neatly 'ambushed' (a word Stoppard often used at that time): Gale, Brindley and Marks are the grown-up selves of schoolboys Chico, Groucho and Harpo, but not until late in the play do we learn which is (was) which. As in the Marx Brothers, Chico and Groucho are ebullient, while Harpo speaks only two words. Of the Old Boys, Brindley and Marks are talkative, while Gale is silent for a long time, and when he does speak is largely morose about his schooldays. But Gale turns out to have been not Harpo but Groucho, and was a good deal happier at school than he now cares to believe – a typically Stoppardian reversal.

Jumpers (1972) has been mentioned above (pp. 29–30). Stoppard's first full-length play for six years, long awaited by the National, it turned out to be bigger and bolder and odder than could have been foreseen. Stoppard here moves to a new level of seriousness, even though the play is riotously funny; and for perhaps the first time, apart from some passages in *Rosencrantz*, seems to convey something of his own thinking. He appears to endorse George's intuitionist faith in absolutes of good and perhaps, by logical extension, God. George, an academic moral philosopher, speaks the best sense in the play – but only intermittently, within many confused digressions, and he will never be able to out-talk his fluent Vice-Chancellor, Sir Archibald Jumper. Archie and his fellow professors have learnt to prosper in a modern relativist amorality, finely imaged as the ability to 'jump' into any intellectual position; they form an actual acrobatic troupe which Archie directs (a terrific stage idea, which seems, if anything, under-used).

Not only the university but the whole country has adopted amoral relativism, the Radical Liberals having won a general-election victory which Archie describes as a *coup d'état*, saluted with processions and fly-pasts. Meanwhile the first British astronauts are on the moon – their images televised on stage – but damage on impact means that only one can return. The

Captain, Scott, briskly strikes the other astronaut, called Oates, to the ground and boards the spaceship alone, with the words: 'I may be gone for some time.' The black-comic reference is to the real Captain Scott's expedition to the Antarctic (1910–12), where the words were spoken not by a selfish Scott but by an altruistic Oates, walking out to die in the snow rather than burden his colleagues. The new Rad-Lib universe stands on its head a legendary image of unselfishness.

Dotty, George's wife, once studied philosophy under him, then became a musical comedy star; now she is in a mental breakdown, partly triggered by the fact that men have stood on the moon. Lunacy gets its name, of course, from its supposed links to changes of the moon; and material here is expanded from the TV play *Another Moon Called Earth* (1967 – two years before the first actual moon landing). There the astronaut 'has stood outside and seen us all whole, all in one go, little'; has seen us relatively, in other words. In *Jumpers*, Dotty notes that 'to somebody on it, the moon is always full, so the local idea of a sane action may well differ from ours'; again, relativism rules.

This interweaving of Stoppard's joke-obsession with moons is typical of the play's ebullient clutter. Its sensational opening sequence – cabaret singer, striptease on a swinging chandelier, farce of near-misses and eventual breaking glass, further music, Jumpers, domestic row, murderous gunshot, slow bloody death of one Jumper, and images of the surface of the moon – constitute a riddle like the initial tableau of *After Magritte*, to be gradually explained. *Jumpers* 'breaks its neck to be entertaining', as admitted to *Theatre Quarterly* (p. 129): 'My preoccupation as a writer, which possibly betokens a degree of insecurity, takes the form of contriving to inject some sort of interest and colour into every line, rather than counting on the general situation having a general interest which will hold an audience.'

Stoppard has repeatedly dreamed of writing 'a quiet play', but in practice he's always inclined to 'add lots of people, and, you know, naked women on chandeliers' (p. 173). In the later plays there are more quiet moments, and more sympathetic characterisation, but in *Jumpers* everything is more or less manic, and our laughter is harsh – as of course is intended: the writer's sympathies may be with George, but the play's mood, tone and action are set against him, the last word being given to Archie.

The notional plot is a zany murder mystery (who shot the Jumper?) complete with statutory cod cop: a fan of Dotty's singing, his name is Bones and his brother is an osteopath . . . A subsidiary mystery is what is wrong with Dotty; it 'looks as if' she may be having an affair with her doctor, who is none other than Archie the ubiquitous Vice-Chancellor. The murdered Jumper is Professor McFee, George's current philosophical opponent; and it also 'looks as if' Dotty may have fired the shot, not least because the corpse now hangs in her bedroom. But entirely opposite explanations may equally well 'look as if' they are true: it looks just as likely that the earth goes round the sun as vice versa (Stoppard gave this to Galileo two years earlier, but here to Wittgenstein); and there's an ingenious late plot twist about McFee and his girl-friend which, as they say, it would be a pity to reveal here.

George, though the comic butt of the play, caricatured in his demonstrations with bow and arrow, hare and tortoise, is nevertheless the character for whom most sympathy is invited. Bones is a stock cartoon figure, from the same stable as Inspector Hound, Foot of the Yard (*After Magritte*) and the Inspector in *Cahoot's Macbeth*. The caretaker Crouch starts as just another stereotype ('I've seen a rabbit around the place of a morning, and it's as much as my job's worth') until his hobby, in equally cartoon style, turns out to be philosophy ('I grant you he's answered Russell's first point . . . but –'). Where *Jumpers* is most opaque is in its two female characters.

Women are still seen here through what feminists call 'the male gaze' – the Secretary in a striptease in the opening minutes, Dotty nude on her bed fifteen minutes later; the Secretary, though onstage virtually throughout, never given either a name or a single word to speak, Dotty a stereotype of feminine irrationality, lovable yet also exasperating. The deliberate bad taste of the joke about Scott and Oates is one thing, but of a different order is the appropriation of the names not just of the real philosopher George Moore but also of his wife, Dorothy, and in particular its contraction to Dotty (slang for 'daft', 'deranged'). Rather than an intended nastiness, I suspect this simply wasn't sufficiently thought through.

Casting can ensure that Dotty is convincing as a former musical comedy star; but her years as a student of philosophy are harder to credit. Apart from the conceit about the moon, her story is never told; the comments of Essie Davis, who played the role in 2003, are interesting (p. 243). Years later Stoppard described George as 'culpable . . . shutting out his wife' (to Shusha Guppy, p. 143). That point is never made explicit, but the original Coda did highlight George failing a fellow man: appealed to by the unfortunate Clegthorpe, he hesitated, then retreated into his own cocoon: 'Well, this seems to be a political quarrel . . . Surely only a proper respect for absolute values . . . universal truths – philosophy –'

Unfortunately this is lost in the 1984 revision: Clegthorpe now appeals to George too late, when already shot, and George's only reaction (in the script) is to cry 'Dotty!' – as if after all she is to blame for both gunshots. No longer is he shown to be a moral coward; instead there's a renewed hint of the murderous female.

Far more delicately treated is Sophie, the young woman at the heart of the radio play **Artist Descending a Staircase** (also 1972). It has been staged, though its framing joke, a misunderstood tape-recording of a death, is pure radio. Once again we are in the Stoppardian territory of explanation and unravelling – not only of that death but of a nexus of relationships and misunderstandings over sixty years. The play is constructed in an elegant palindrome, the scenes occurring in the sequence: now / a couple of hours ago / last week / 1922 / 1920 / 1914 / 1920

/ 1922 / last week / a couple of hours ago / now. The chronological story starts in 1914 with three brash young men,
Beauchamp, Donner and Martello, on a walking tour in
France. The tricks of Modernist art are pitted against traditional skills: Beauchamp anticipates Dadaism in a sustained
radio joke about his 'horse', as he walks along knocking
coconut shells together. After the war all three become artists,
and their joint exhibition in 1919 is visited by the young
Sophie, whose sight is failing. When she meets them again in
1920 she has become fully blind, but does remember being
attracted to the one who had painted a border fence in the
snow. This suggests Beauchamp, who duly starts a liaison with
her, though Donner is her true adorer. In 1922 she is abandoned by Beauchamp, and though Donner intends to stay on
with her, she declares: 'I can't love you back,' and with startling
promptness kills herself by jumping through an upstairs window. Fifty years later the three aged artists still live together;
and Martello discloses that it may really have been Donner that
Sophie was attracted to, since his painting was of a thick white
fence with black gaps between it . . . Two weeks later, Donner
has died in what the listener learns was an innocent accident,
but Martello and Beauchamp are each convinced that the other
is his murderer.

More than anything previous of Stoppard, *Artist Descending*
suggests intensities of pain: Sophie abandoned in her blindness,
and Donner grasping, fifty years too late, the truth of their
mutual love. As in *Jumpers*, callous cynicism is pitted against
moral decency:

MARTELLO: It's an odd word to exist, defenestration, isn't it? I
  mean when you consider the comparatively few people who
  have jumped or been thrown from windows to account for
  it . . . here we are, having seen much pain and many deaths
  . . . all much of a muchness after a brief delay between the
  fall of one body and another –
DONNER: No, no, each one is vital and every moment counts

60

– what other reason is there for trying to work well and
love well and choose well?

But these are still figures in a sort of cartoon – three heterosexual males who have chosen to live together for fifty years. The story doesn't stand up well to questioning. Even if Sophie's remembered image is of Donner not of Beauchamp, it is with Beauchamp that she lives physically for two years – and evidently with some success, or why would she kill herself when he leaves? The idea that another man who merely looked different is her truly destined love is romantic – and ironically appropriate to radio, where we can't see any of them; but it's also sentimental, and ultimately unconvincing. Overall the play remains essentially at the level of a finely etched diagram.

Artist leads on to **Travesties**, Stoppard's major play of 1974, in its glances at the First World War and at Modernist art. Exiled from their various homelands during the war, Lenin, James Joyce, and the young Romanian poet who founded Dada, Tristan Tzara, all spent time in Zurich, though not in any way together. There Joyce directed an amateur performance of Oscar Wilde's *The Importance of Being Earnest*, over which he quarrelled with a young Englishman, Henry Carr, who worked in the consulate after being invalided from the trenches. These ingredients are whisked together in a wild unhistorical mix, excused partly by its title and partly because it all notionally occurs within Carr's senile reminiscences. At the time Stoppard described *Jumpers* and *Travesties* as being 'the same kind of pig's breakfast', though seeing the later play as in some ways 'a great advance'. Personally I prefer *Travesties*; but its major limitation is that it requires an audience familiar with at least some of its cultural hinterland.

For a start, they need to know Wilde's play (not a problem for most Western audiences). Whereas *Rosencrantz* takes place at the periphery of *Hamlet*, here the actual action of *Earnest* is travestied; the irascible famous Modernists are thrown into Wildean situations. The dialogue contrives to be a pastiche of

Wilde, though hardly ever using his exact words. Yet part of the edginess of *Travesties* is that whereas Wilde's characters behave with elegant decorum, and would think it bad form to display any violent emotion, Stoppard's frequently rant and rave. And whereas Wilde's sophisticates imply a certain underlying cynicism, the main personages of *Travesties* are fanatics.

Neither play can find room for the distressed innocents of Stoppard's other early work. Here almost all the principals utter harangues of ideological certainty. Even the manservant Bennett turns out to be a secret doctrinaire socialist who on his final appearance looks at his employer 'implacably'. All these personages know they are right.

Since there is no possibility of their yielding or changing in any way, the play can make no real progress. This is no problem until well into the second act, because the succession of monologues, exchanges and set pieces is exhilarating, as are the intermittent glimpses of the framework of *Earnest*. That framework continues to be visible in Act Two, where the Gwendolen/ Cecily duel over afternoon tea becomes a duel in song, and the baby returned becomes an exchange of manuscripts. But it seems that Stoppard was always determined to make the second act different. Both acts are, of course, Carr's, overall; but within that, the first is Joyce's and the second is Lenin's, each largely excluded from the other's. Joyce is, more or less, Stoppard's hero; Lenin a sort of Antichrist.

Part of the strangeness of *Travesties* rises first from the fact that Lenin is included onstage alongside, yet not part of, a glittering burlesque; and second from the fact that he is not fictionalised. We are told: 'Nearly everything spoken by Lenin and Nadezhda Krupskaya herein comes from his *Collected Writings* and from her *Memories of Lenin*.' In other words, the playwright wears protective gloves, lifting the Lenins' historical words and dumping them with a kind of shudder into his farcical flow, which midway through Act Two dwindles to a trickle, then dries, as Nadya recounts the events of 1917 and Lenin harangues the audience. Critics in 1974 complained about this, yet it was clearly the intended effect; the Cold War was at its height, and Lenin was meant to kill the laughs. The *Theatre Quarterly* interview, given when rehearsals for *Travesties* were beginning, shows the intensity of Stoppard's views at the time (p. 122). By the time of his 1993 revision, however, the Cold War was over and it was now safe to laugh at Lenin. Fortunately, the gravest and best moment, late in the play, remains: the running theme in the evening's altercations and tirades has been the function of art, and even Lenin now admits being deeply moved by Beethoven's Appassionata Sonata – before hastily catching himself and reverting to talk of hitting heads. He leaves; a poignant memory from Nadya ends 'Something went wrong. I forget what'; the stage darkens and the music swells.

In spite of a new stage direction referring to her as Prism, Nadya's role is essentially unchanged in the revised text. She is a dully serious, anxious wife; and as such, although a minor role, Stoppard's first consistently realistic woman. Gwendolen (rather marginalised) and Cecily (whom Tzara describes as 'a librarianess') belong with his earlier imaginings: women admitted only in subservience, or as decoration, to what are essentially inter-male discourses about art and political power. Both are cast as personal assistants to male maestros; Gwendolen is made to read aloud to Tzara a suggestive cut-up of a Shakespeare sonnet ('see, this lovely hot possession grows / so long'), and although Cecily has a tirade of her own, it comes from Marx and Lenin. She soon recognises that 'all the time . . . you're trying to imagine how I'd look stripped off to my knickers', whereupon she climbs on to her desk and delivers the rest as a striptease to a big-band sound. Woman speaking politics is thus hastily transmuted to female in male fantasy, where – as it were – she belongs. It may be significant that Wilde's really intimidating woman, Lady Bracknell, is here relocated in a male character, Joyce.

The striptease and knickers predilections are suitably worked out of Stoppard's writing in **Dirty Linen** (1976). A West End entertainment patently beamed at the businessmen's evening out (though a distinctly short one) this is ironically aware of its unreconstructed attitudes: the apparent dumb blonde, Maddie Gotobed, turns out to have far more sense than anyone else. She is the secretary to the Parliamentary Select Committee on Promiscuity in High Places, and has had sex with almost all of its members. The committee is interrupted by **New-Found-Land**, which shows two civil servants discussing Ed Berman's application for British citizenship (the play was first performed on the day he got it). The title neatly links it to the framing farce, since John Donne, undressing his 'Mistress Going to Bed', calls her 'my America, my new-found-land'; the obvious extra twist is that in Berman's case an American saw Britain as new-found. The crafting throughout is brilliant, rather as if bawdy seaside postcards were drawn by a master; and there are characteristic flicks about language. Most memorable is a virtuoso dance in sound round the phallic maypole of 'cock', as each character tries to deny having visited a restaurant called the Coq d'Or:

I was at various times at Crockford's, Claridge's and the
   Golden Cock, Clock, the Old Clock in Golden Square, not
   the Coq d'Or . . .
I was at the Crock of Gold, Selfridge's and the Green
   Cockatoo . . .
I was at the Cockatoo, too, and the Charing Cross, the Open
   Door, the Golden Ox and the Cuckoo Clock . . .

The play's last words, like its first, are in a foreign language: 'Finita La Commedia'; and they seem most appropriate with hindsight, since *Dirty Linen* is pretty much the end of the road, in this playwright, for uncomplicated fooling-about and the humour of the male locker-room. As it was first performed, he was already contemplating a TV play about Russian dissidents; and two years later, in *Night and Day*, he wrote a largely realist play in which a woman is the central character. The year 1976, then, if one wants to periodise Stoppard, is where a very rough line might be drawn.

The pattern of his work had become established: commissions of various kinds, now including screenplays and adaptations of European plays from literal translations, other one-off ventures (in 1973 he directed a West End play himself) – and relatively few full-length plays of his own. Since the first performance of *Rosencrantz*, he has averaged a full-length play roughly every four years: he says he would prefer to be doing his own thing all the time but that the right ideas come rarely. Possibly they might have come more frequently if he had been less ready to take on commissioned work, but Stoppard would not be Stoppard without his enthusiasm for show business in general and his pride in the craft of writing, perhaps most enjoyed – because least anxious – when at someone else's service.

In his introduction to **Every Good Boy Deserves Favour**, Stoppard writes: 'As the principal conductor of the London Symphony Orchestra, Mr Previn invited me in 1974 to write something which had the need of a live full-size orchestra on stage. Invitations don't come much rarer than that, and I jumped at the chance.'

'Jumped' because he was already the man who had devised a play about the voice behind the speaking clock, who had unknotted the opening tableau of *After Magritte* and knotted up the concluding one, and who had gleefully dragged together the Zurich expatriates. Absurd juxtapositions, cleverly rationalised, were his stock-in-trade; and another glittering ingenuity seemed likely. What resulted, as Stoppard tells it, was for a long time nothing – and then something unexpected, even from a writer who specialised in surprise: a work of political protest.

The change wasn't actually so remarkable. In *Jumpers* and *Travesties* he had attempted to foreground fundamentally serious questions within theatrical frivolity. He knew and admired Vaclav Havel's political satires of the mid-1960s; and by this time – 1977 – he himself had become active on behalf of Soviet and Czech dissidents. 'He was now a militant,' remembers Trevor Nunn, who directed the play; 'now he wanted theatre directly to bring about change.'

Names are always crucial in Stoppard; here only three characters are granted a name at all, and they have just the one between them: Alexander Ivanov. This barely emerges for a Western audience, who may not spot that the boy Sacha's name is the diminutive of his father's, Alexander. But it exemplifies how the totalitarian state depersonalises, and also how the play generalises: this is offered not as a *particular* story but as what may be an all too common situation. The identical names also furnish the play's denouement – a deliberate fudge by the Colonel/Doctor who runs the prison/psychiatric hospital.

Alexander is detained there because he has expressed opinions that this or that action of the State was 'an odd thing to do' or 'really wasn't fair'. The devastating understatement, here and throughout his monologue, is coupled with the identification of the dissidents only by letters of the alphabet – getting as far as the letter 'T', and of course including 'I'. The minimalism of all this (unforgettable in Ian McKellen's clipped, dry delivery) conveys through language a bleak darkness.

'You see all the trouble writers cause . . . They spoil things for ordinary people.'

The character who does get Stoppardian verbal pyrotechnics is the genuine lunatic, Ivanov, with whom Alexander is forced to share a cell. His delusion is that he conducts a symphony orchestra. Meanwhile the boy Sacha plays the triangle, exasperating his teacher by subverting the orchestra. There's an insoluble problem here with the play's underlying concept: André Previn's music offers a lyrical, sympathetic commentary, yet the orchestra playing it represents the totalitarian state, no one out of line. It's almost as if the play is an unconscious *attack* – by a devotee of improvisation, perhaps – on the classical tradition that the LSO represents.

Every Good Boy was performed at the Royal Festival Hall in July 1977. In the previous month Stoppard had revisited Czechoslovakia for the first time, to meet Havel; and in September BBC TV broadcast **Professional Foul**, which was dedicated to him. Anderson is the J. S. Mill Professor of Ethics at Cambridge, visiting Prague to lecture at a conference, though he really wants to watch England play Czechoslovakia at football (a private glance at A. J. Ayer's enthusiasm for the game). In Prague he is approached by a former student, Hollar, now reduced to being a lavatory cleaner and under police surveillance. Hollar has written a paper concluding that 'there is an obligation, a human responsibility, to fight against the State correctness'. He expects Anderson to smuggle the paper back to Britain, where it can be published. To his dismay, Anderson refuses: 'It's just not ethical.'

A professional foul goes flagrantly against the *spirit* of a game (for example, hacking down a footballer about to score) though it accepts the *letter* of the laws (the hacker expects to be penalised). Anderson's refusal, excusing himself from hazardous involvement, pleads the letter of ethical law – smuggling the paper would be deceiving the State – and ignores a deeper moral priority. Immediately after refusing, however, he witnesses Hollar being falsely arrested; his mind is changed, and he still holds Hollar's manuscript. In his public lecture the next day he departs from the script previously vetted to reassert fundamental moral priorities – 'a sense of right and wrong', even when this means conflict with 'a collective or State ethic'. He then smuggles Hollar's paper back to Britain by a different kind of foul: since he himself is now likely to be searched at the airport, he secretes the paper in a colleague's briefcase without telling him. Both make it through to the plane without being stopped, but a third, younger colleague, who has always defended 'classical' beliefs in moral absolutes, is detained, white-faced.

Further twists and ironic humour are provided by the boorish relativist McKendrick, the fact that philosophers share a hotel with England footballers (who lose, after a professional foul), debates about language, pastiche of different styles of sports reporting, and ingenious verbal misunderstandings and overlaps, all of them natural and believable.

Professional Foul works faultlessly; the critic Laurence Lerner once described it to me as 'the best television play ever written'. As usual, Stoppard is alert to the chosen medium; this play is entirely realist in method, and accessible to the wide audience of mainstream TV (three showings in the 1970s were seen by nearly six million people in the United Kingdom alone). There are no literary allusions, and Anderson's lecture is a model of how some basic ideas from moral philosophy may be expressed lucidly to non-specialists. The developing climax, during the lecture, uses frequent intercutting, including the simultaneity of one scene on visual and another on sound. Film allows the play to begin and end on board aircraft, and the opening is brilliantly televisual, before any dialogue: a girlie magazine being shuffled with the brochure for the Colloquium Philosophicum. This attracts amused interest, gives information, and introduces the themes of double standards and of concealed documents. Later there's a crisp point *about* television: McKendrick, having greeted a footballer as if he were a familiar philosopher, remains puzzled: 'I knew his face.' Anderson explains: '*Match of the Day*.'

In **Night and Day** (1978), his first full-length play for four years, Stoppard surprised some by not seeming surprising enough. With a cast of just eight, it was written for Michael Codron and the commercial theatre; and in several respects it resembles an old-fashioned realist 'well-made play' with ideas, on the lines of Shaw or Galsworthy. In it Stoppard pays his dues, as it were, to his years in journalism, and also expresses his own mixture of conservative and liberal attitudes: 'People do awful things to each other. But it's worse in places where everybody is kept in the dark. It really is. Information is light. Information, in itself, about anything, is light.'

Press freedom is therefore one of the themes, but so is the awfulness of much journalism. ('I'm with you on the free press; it's the newspapers I can't stand.') Nevertheless, according to the young, not yet cynical reporter Milne: 'Junk journalism is the evidence of a society that has got at least one thing right, that there should be nobody with the power to dictate where responsible journalism begins.'

Such power Stoppard had recently witnessed, in Soviet Russia and Czechoslovakia. But the power Milne has clashed with is that of trade unions; he lost his previous reporting job for objecting to a closed shop – rather as Stoppard himself was once suspended.

The play's setting and post-colonial characters, in a supposed modern African republic, are inevitably pastiche. Keen young Milne and his rival, world-weary Dick Wagner (accustomed to jokes about his name) together with a photographer, Guthrie, are in Kambawe to report an uprising; they meet at the house of a wealthy businessman, Geoffrey Carson. (A businessman of this name attended the school in *Where Are They Now?*; Stoppard continues to repeat, or allude to, himself, and from *Professional Foul* onwards many characters have the surname Chamberlain – that of his secretary.) Wagner has been scooped to his own paper by Milne; now he telexes his union leader in London to protest that 'the Grimsby scab' (Milne) is still being employed. He also gets his own scoop interview with the country's president, only to find that this can no longer be printed: the whole paper has gone on strike as a result of his own telex about Milne – who has meanwhile been killed while attempting to reach the rebel leader.

Ruth, Carson's wife, is Stoppard's response to previous criticisms: the central figure, and a woman convincingly drawn. She is taken aback when Wagner turns up at her house, since she recently slept with him at a hotel in London; what's more, she now finds herself fiercely attracted to the boyish Milne. To tell Ruth's story the play departs from its predominantly realist manner: some of her lines are not speeches but overheard thoughts, without the direct address to the audience of the classical 'aside'. This is easily grasped; what is potentially confusing is an extended sequence which later turns out to have taken place only within Ruth's fantasy. At the end of Act One Milne is seen departing at dawn in search of the rebel leader; at the opening of Act Two he seems to have returned, late at night, and Ruth is there to meet him with quiet but highly charged amorous conversation. Yet late in the play we learn that, far from having come back, Milne was killed. A further complication is that even within her fantasy Ruth retains both 'speeches' and 'thoughts overheard': thus we hear her *think*: 'Why don't you shut up and kiss me?' and then again: 'So kiss me,' but the third time – as if by accident – she says aloud: 'I would prefer you to kiss me.' Stoppard teases the notion yet further by having Ruth persuade the fantasy Milne to disclose his own sexual fantasy about *her*.

'It was in a parallel world. No day or night, no responsibilities, no friction, almost no gravity.'

Later, within a few moments, Ruth disappears momentarily from view and returns played by a double. Milne leaves, Ruth Two steps out of her dress and follows him into the dark, now watched 'thoughtfully' by her husband; then Ruth One's voice is heard from behind him and she is seen lying, dressed, on the sofa. 'There's no need for you to stay up,' says Carson; 'he may not come for hours.' Only then do we grasp the extended metatheatrical trick played on us: we have been watching the 'parallel world' of one character's imagination within what is, like any play, itself an equally parallel world. The device reverses the theatre tradition of twins played by one actor who goes off and instantly returns by another door; here, two represent one. There is some continuity here from *Rosencrantz*, together with anticipations of *Hapgood* (the parallel possibilities of light, twinning and false twinning), *Arcadia* (modern Gus dressed in Regency clothes is indistinguishable from Lord Augustus), and the dialogue between old and young Housman in *The Invention of Love* (the whole play a dying man's dream).

Night and Day begins with a more routine departure from realism, a sequence of violence – the noise of a helicopter, an onstage jeep (on which Stoppard adamantly insisted), machine-gun fire, spotlight, death – which then turns out to have been a dream. The bewildering opening sequence, later explained, is typical of Stoppard; in this case it sketches the background of violent warfare for a play which thereafter stays within a domestic setting, and is never again so exciting.

Featuring Diana Rigg as Ruth, the play was a commercial success. Critical reception was more mixed; by this time Stoppard's name raised very high expectations. There are jokes, and sharp ironic perceptions, but the plot and outcome are uncharacteristically bleak, which may be partly because – again uncharacteristically – the play deals with the modern material and political world, about which Stoppard is not ebullient and is sometimes downright angry. The dedication to Paul Johnson probably reflects more than the mere fact that Johnson had also been a journalist.

In **Dogg's Hamlet, Cahoot's Macbeth** (1979) bewilderingly different ingredients are again brought together – starting with *Dogg's Our Pet*, a piece previously written for Ed Berman, which toyed with a notion from Wittgenstein. A word has no essential connection to what it signifies; and in theory, as Stoppard explains in his printed Introduction, a satisfactory understanding might be reached between two workmen even though their words had different meanings for them. A theatre audience can rapidly learn new meanings for familiar words. This sounds heavy stuff but doesn't turn out to be; schoolboy humour (for 'sir', say 'git') is located amongst schoolboys, and never before was a Speech Day address so geared to its audience:

LADY (*nicely*): Scabs, slobs, yobs, yids, spicks, wops . . . (*as one might say Your Grace, ladies and gentlemen, boys and girls . . .*) Sad fact, brats pule puke crap-pot stink, spit; grow up dunces crooks; rank socks dank snotrags, conkers, ticks; crib books, cock snooks, block bogs, jack off, catch pox pick spots, scabs, padlocks, seek kicks, kinks, slack; nick swag, swig coke, bank kickbacks . . . frankly can't stick kids.

Stoppard then stirs in his fifteen-minute *Hamlet* (with 'encore') also written earlier for Berman, and adds *Cahoot's Macbeth*, a tribute to the Czech playwright Pavel Kohout, who had shortened Shakespeare's play for private performance in Prague flats by banned actors. There are repeated interruptions by a police inspector:

> If I can make just one tiny criticism . . . Shakespeare – or the Old Bill, as we call him in the force – is not a popular choice with my chief, owing to his popularity with the public, or, as we call it in the force, the filth . . . The chief says he'd rather you stood up and said, 'There is no freedom in this country,' then there's nothing underhand and we all know where we stand. You get your lads together and we get our lads together and when it's all over, one of us is in power and you're in gaol. That's freedom in action. But what we don't like is a lot of people being cheeky and saying they are only Julius Caesar or Coriolanus or Macbeth. Otherwise we are going to start treating them the same as the ones who say they are Napoleon.

The last sentence glances back to *Every Good Boy*. Further interruptions come from a lorry driver looking to rejoin the action of *Dogg's Hamlet*; he enters where we expect Shakespeare's Third Murderer ('But who did bid thee join with us?') and again where we expect Banquo's Ghost. Finally Shakespeare's text becomes hopelessly corrupted with the virus of Dogg-speak ('Rafter Birnam cakehops hobble Dunsinane').

Stoppard had shown in *Every Good Boy* that political protest in cartoon form can be as powerful onstage as in newsprint. This time the balance is different, however; the courageous enterprise of the Czech playwright and actors can seem trivialised, and the Inspector, representing the sinister police state, is not only funny but disconcertingly likeable. On the other hand, the play has already outlasted that particular oppressive regime, and is well worth further revivals; it's no bad thing that what has survived is the laughter.

Between *Night and Day* in 1978 and *Hapgood* ten years later Stoppard produced only one new full-length play of his own but adaptations of four European classics: *Undiscovered Country* starred John Wood and was based on a play by Arthur Schnitzler; *On the Razzle* was yet another adaptation of a farce by Johann Nestroy which had already formed the basis of the musical *Hello, Dolly!*; *Rough Crossing* came from a Hungarian dramatist, Ferenc Molnar; and *Dalliance* again from Schnitzler. Carl Toms designed three of the four and all were directed by Peter Wood, who knew the originals from his frequent work in Vienna. The one of these most likely to survive in the British repertory, and the most Stoppardian, is *On the Razzle*, a joy both on the page and in performance.

Playing the boy apprentice there was Felicity Kendal. Four years later she starred in **The Real Thing**, the just-finished type-script of which Stoppard sent me in the spring of 1982. 'It's pretty straightforward,' he wrote disingenuously, 'as these things go.' Ho hum: the title alone invites mistrust, and the writer of the opening scene is a character in the second . . . and so on. What 'straightforward' might conceivably mean is that this is his first theatre play to be fully realist both in its staging (no overheard thoughts or fantasy sequences this time) and in its characterisation (no cartoons). Far from being therefore dull, *The Real Thing* is untroubled by either limitation. Shaped for the commercial theatre, it shakes hands with the main-stream while remaining intensely Stoppardian.

The opening scene, which an audience could well trust as 'the real thing' if unaware of the playwright's string of previous offences, is funny from the outset, but also tense and com-pelling. Wife gets back from overnight business trip to Switzerland; husband has meanwhile found her passport, so assumes the overnight to have been in England and adulterous. It's a gripping opening and the dry repartee is funny, fierce, yet packed with pain. Scene two shows us Henry, who wrote it. His wife Charlotte was playing the scene-one wife, and Max, who was playing her husband, comes round to their house for a drink, joined later by his partner Annie, another actor. (Three actors and a playwright: one of the *frissons* of *The Real Thing* is that Stoppard, a very private writer, here unlocks at least his garden gate.) Annie is having an affair with Henry, and soon they have set up house together. In the second act it's Henry's turn to be jealous, as Annie is involved first with a radical protester called Brodie, whose bad play she wants to perform, and second with Billy, her co-star in John Ford's Jacobean drama *'Tis Pity She's a Whore*. There's also a strong scene in which Henry and Charlotte discuss sex and love with their seventeen-year-old daughter Debbie and, ruefully, with each other.

Without departing from the letter of realism, Stoppard contrives highly characteristic 'structural cross-references' (he discusses this play on p. 157) – scenes, stage directions and lines which echo either the opening scene or each other. The play is persistently metatheatrical, and self-referential not only to the nature of acting but also to the craft of writing, not excluding Stoppard's own:

CHARLOTTE: Oh yes, without you I'd be like one of your women. 'Fancy a drink?' [one of his lines for her in the opening scene] 'Let me get you a drink.' 'Care for a drink?' That's Henry's idea of women's parts . . .

HENRY: . . . (*Blithely, knowing what he is doing,* HENRY *holds his empty glass towards* CHARLOTTE.) Is there any more of that?

Travelling by train to demonstrate against nuclear missile bases, Annie met Brodie, a soldier, who tagged along with her, then set fire to a wreath for the Unknown Soldier. Imprisoned for this act of protest, he has written a play, which Annie wants to perform. Henry howls at the ineptness of the writing, reading out Brodie's version of the meeting on the train. He insists on the importance of his craft. In at least some things, value is not equivocal or relative: his cricket bat 'isn't better because someone says it's better, or because there's a conspiracy by the MCC to keep cudgels out of Lords. It's better because it's better.'

The scene is strengthened by Annie's shrewd opposition: 'You're jealous of the idea of the writer. You want to keep it

74

sacred, special, not something anybody can do . . . Even when you write *about* something, you have to think up something to write about just so you can keep on writing . . . You teach a lot of people what to expect from good writing, and you end up with a lot of people saying you write well.'

Earlier, in Act One, Henry was seen helping Annie go through her lines as Strindberg's Miss Julie. It depressed him because, he says, 'I can't do mine. I don't know how to write love. I try to write it properly, and it just comes out embarrassing. It's either childish or it's rude . . . Perhaps I should write it completely artificial. Blank verse. Poetic imagery . . . more of the "By my troth, thy beauty makest the moon hide her radiance."'

'I don't know how to write love' provokes a shiver in the theatre. Though the dialogue in earlier scenes has been generally brash and bitchy, it's increasingly apparent that this play may endeavour to write about love 'properly', whereas in the past Stoppard has always resorted to the 'artificial' – pastiche, parody, cartoon. The opening of Act Two of *Night and Day* was a sort of love scene, but proved to be (as if it still somehow *had* to be) a character's fantasy. Henry's admission occurs after Stoppard has once again turned for support to the 'artificial' – Strindberg's words. As for 'By my troth', we are shortly to see Annie and Billie rehearsing the classic blank verse of John Ford – first jokily, later with passion. So isn't this the mixture much as before?

Not in the later scenes. There Stoppard risks dispensing with all 'artificial' support. Henry's instinctive verbal fluency is acknowledged as a potential barrier, and when it seems his daughter has inherited it, he tells her sharply: 'Don't get too good at that . . . persuasive nonsense. Sophistry in a phrase so neat you can't see the loose end that would unravel it. It's flawless but wrong. A perfect dud. You can do that with words, bless 'em.'

It takes one to know one, indeed. A moment later Debbie is fully justified in reversing the attack: '*Fa*. You're going on . . . Don't write it, Fa. Just say it.'

Henry nevertheless follows with another big speech, though Debbie abruptly deflates it at the end. It's about love as 'knowledge . . . Knowing, being known . . . and when it's gone everything is pain . . . Pain. (*Pause.*)' – and Debbie asks: 'Has Annie got someone else then?'

The previous scene showed Annie – on another train – meeting and being attracted by her fellow actor, Billy. Much later they record Brodie's train scene for television, rewritten by Henry, against his professional instinct, as a love-gift for Annie – who promptly sleeps with Billy. This is all handled deftly, almost perfunctorily. When Annie is late for her next shooting session she takes a phone call from Billy, then turns to Henry with the words: 'I love you. Do you understand?' Yet she still wants to let Billy down lightly: 'I just want him to stop needing me so I can stop behaving well. This is me behaving well. I have to choose who I hurt and I choose you because I'm yours.'

Eventually this play transcends its clever metatheatricality, its self-consciousness about the difficulty of 'writing love', and simply gets on with it. The love-scenes are of our time, messy, agonised, and fractured with irony. This perception of the instability of love and marriage, the provisionality of partnership, does however sit strangely with its writer's earlier insistence on moral absolutes. 'The difference between moral rules and the rules of tennis is that the rules of tennis can be changed' is not only George's ringing line in *Jumpers* but Stoppard's own in interview; yet now he seems to attach a sort of wrecking amendment: *except of course in sex*. In *Night and Day*, jokily, 'hotel rooms shouldn't count as infidelity. They constitute a separate moral universe,' and in *The Real Thing* no traditional 'rules' are even discussed. As Henry and Annie prepare to leave their partners, the only hint of a qualm is her deliberately brazen: 'It's only a couple of marriages and a child.'

Nevertheless Charlotte can still later describe Henry as 'the last romantic'; and he can settle for the tag. 'No commitments. Only bargains. The trouble is I don't really believe it. I'd rather be an idiot. It's a kind of idiocy I like . . . Everything should be romantic.'

As in this case, the script frequently indulges Henry. To Annie he does eventually admit: 'I can't cope with more than one moral system at a time. Mine is that what you think is right is right.'

(Four years later, in *Hapgood*, Kerner remarks: 'There is something terrible about love. It uses up all one's moral judgement. Afterwards it is like returning to a system of values, or at least the attempt.')

Thus love overrules all else, yet the words 'at a time' suggest that this possibly 'real thing' remains vulnerable to further changes of preference. And indeed the earlier effect of a series of clever repetitions (Charlotte was also an actor, she also played the lead in Ford's play, and in parallel domestic scenes she and Annie are each seen wearing a garment of Henry's which is too large for them) has been to suggest that the women around Henry could be interchangeable. As Annie leaves to go to her shooting session:

ANNIE: Please don't let it wear away what you feel for me. It won't, will it?

HENRY: No, not like that. It will go on or it will flip into its opposite.

A shrewd perception, maybe; but the phrase 'the real thing' now hangs somewhat in tatters, and we've long lost sight of rules that can't be changed – though in interviews Stoppard has continued to affirm such beliefs (as on p. 143, here).

Where the play shows no shift of attitude is on politics; there it lapses into complacent caricature. The joke seems (or does it?) to be on Henry when there's talk of 'their bloody missiles' –

HENRY: *Theirs?* I thought they were ours.

MAX: No, they're American.

– but to the extent that Henry is a self-portrait, he is knowingly and unapologetically so. More than twenty years after *The*

Real Thing, the playwright Alan Bennett, approaching his seventieth birthday, noted bitterly in his *London Review of Books* diary for 2003: 'While I was trudging up Whitehall past the end of Downing Street on the second anti-war march, Tom Stoppard was in Downing Street having lunch with Mrs Bush.'

Henry derides Annie for joining the demonstration. People like her 'desire to be taken for properly motivated members of the caring society', and we've already heard that this last phrase makes Henry draw his knees up into his chest. As for Private Brodie, in the play's final scene he arrives newly released from prison and having just watched 'his' play. '*He is wearing a cheap suit*' [but of course] and '*holding a tumbler of neat Scotch*' – [doubly 'of course', since] '*he speaks with a Scottish accent*'. He also behaves oafishly. Thus stereotyped, he seems not to threaten the play's dominant and – to put it politically – bourgeois concerns.

Annie's recollection is that Brodie's supposedly heroic protest was nothing of the kind; it was merely an impulsive attempt to please her. A sincere radicalism is thus excised from the play's possibilities, where previously it seemed at least to lurk offstage; instead, in Henry's words, 'public postures have the configuration of private *derangement*' (my italics). Brodie didn't really 'march for a cause', he just got caught up in a middle-class woman's aberration, and it's her we should feel for. Though Brodie is there beside her, Annie speaks of him in the third person, essentially patronising and dismissing him. She shows no remorse for what happened to him because of her, but she does regret his having become so coarse; in her memory he was 'nervous as anything. A boy on the train. Chatting me up. Nice.' Meanwhile, Henry's new interest in why Brodie did what he did is professional: this, the true story, 'I would have known how to write'.

'Listen,' says Brodie, 'I'm still here.' Ah: the dramatist knows what he's doing. Yet four lines later, because Brodie seems to be getting above himself, Annie '*picks up the bowl of dip and smashes it into his face*'. He walks out with a minimal dignity, and the dramatist seems to bid him good riddance. There's a phone call from Max, Annie's former partner – who is excited by his new love affair; the play is determined to end in laughter as Henry patronises him and then ignores him, turning up the volume of an ancient pop song.

The Real Thing is an uneasy mix (as, of course, are many good plays). It's often very funny, and also eloquent. In its love scenes it sharpens and refines an audience's sensibilities; yet in its politics it tends to deaden them. It's strong and lucid on the familiar Stoppard ground of artistic ethics – the importance of writing well; but vapid and vague on ground also seen as his, that of moral conduct. In the development of his craft, he here seems at ease with realist characterisation, including that of women (it's the men other than Henry who are somewhat marginalised), and the play represents an increased nerve, a readiness to attempt to write 'properly' about emotions with fewer ironic defences and without the props of clever artifice.

Stoppard wrote a bruised introduction to the published screenplay **Squaring the Circle** (1984), his TV film about Solidarity, the illegal association of trade unions which from 1980 challenged Poland's Communist government. Already as a screenplay writer familiar with the film world with 'American strings', he was nevertheless upset when its vagaries affected his own original work, initially a British project and in his mind 'a kind of personal dramatised essay'. The eventual film was a multiple compromise, and the printed text often makes heavy reading – partly because it deals with a leaden political system, and in a realist mode which allows little room for fun.

A 'main worry' from the start was integrity to the truth. 'We don't *know* what happened,' yet a 'docudrama' insinuated into people's homes – as distinct from a theatre play which they travel and pay to see – may be swallowed as fact. Stoppard wanted 'a narrator with acknowledged fallibility', possibly played by himself; what instead transpired was 'an unexplained American in Poland' – though the frame of fallibility at least survives in the Narrator's first line to camera: 'Everything is true except the words and the pictures.'

Authentic Stoppard breaks through occasionally: 'I've got a Catholic Church which doesn't want me to provoke the Russians, and a Communist Party two-thirds of whom believe in God. And to top it all I've got a police force which can't break the habit, and a Public Prosecutor with the political nous of a bull in a china shop. As First Secretary of the Polish United Workers' Party, Al Capone wouldn't have lasted out the week.'

There's also typically alert sport with the television medium. In front of what proves to be a fake bookcase, First Secretary Gierek broadcasts his standard platitudes, while a watching electrician mutters: 'Typical bloody August . . . nothing but repeats.' Later (perhaps a vestige from an earlier more radical script) the screen tears itself in half, then the Narrator is seen scribbling an alternative narrative, which when performed meets the same fate.

Yet what Stoppard most wanted to say is already there in his title. A free trade union cannot co-exist with 'socialism as defined by the Eastern European Communist bloc' any more than a circle can be turned into a square with the same area. As he explained to the producer, 'A mathematician knows that certain things cannot happen, not because no one has found out how to do them but because they are internally contradictory.'

The playwright who never went to university but read so keenly in the humanities was now evidently also conversant with some mathematics; soon afterwards he was reading about quantum physics. If *The Real Thing* showed that moral rules are much harder to pin down than the rules of tennis, **Hapgood** (1988) plays with the 'shocking' idea that there *is* no real thing: 'there is no underlying reality to the world'. The quotations are from John Gribbin's layman's guide of 1984, *In Search of Schrödinger's Cat*, which Stoppard appears to have used; Gribbin does qualify the latter statement a moment later – 'no reality in the everyday sense of the word'. Early Stoppard plays delighted in providing rational explanations for the apparently irrational; now he found quantum physics declaring more or less the opposite: that things don't work according to our rationality. His character Kerner attempts to explain: 'An electron can be here or there at the same moment . . . Its movements cannot be anticipated because it has no reasons . . . there is *no such thing* as an electron with a definite position and a definite momentum.'

The discovery that underlies quantum physics is the dual nature of light, which can behave either as waves or as particles, depending on how it is observed. *Hapgood* attempts an analogy between this and the doubleness of Cold War spies – either when one person is a double agent, spying for both sides ('A double agent is more like a trick of the light') or, more theatrically, as actual twins. Theatre is a highly appropriate medium for this material, since everyone who appears on stage is claiming a double identity while under observation: dissembling is the nature of the game.

Spy thrillers are often relished precisely for their success in deceiving their audience as frequently and as long as possible. Stoppard wrote one – *Neutral Ground*, in 1968 – and he parodied the genre in the radio play *The Dog It Was That Died* (1982), which is something of a throwback to his earlier cartoon manner. But at the end of such yarns all is revealed and understood, which is not the case in quantum physics and therefore (he has argued) not in *Hapgood* either. Peter Wood kept pleading for the audience to be given more information, and eventually, for the successful 1994 production at the Lincoln Center in New York, as the playwright tells me (p. 174), 'I simplified it. It was a bit too complicated for its own good.' (It has to be said that the 1994 text remains quite complicated enough.)

Hapgood recalls Stoppard's earlier mode, in being a conspicuously *clever* play which operates like a succession of diagrams, both in its intricate spy plot and almost literally in the cubicle-and-briefcase swaps of the opening scene. It's characteristic of his later work, however, in placing a woman at its centre (unusual in spy fiction) and in proposing a convincing and tender adult relationship. Elizabeth Hapgood runs a unit of the British Secret Service, within a cliché Cold War set-up, Brits and CIA against the KGB. Her Russian double agent (or 'joe') Joseph Kerner, a physicist, is also the father of her eleven-year-old son, Joe. The information Kerner passes back to the KGB is usually of no value, but recently has contained real secrets, and the play turns on a series of attempts to trap the culprit, who turns out to be Hapgood's right-hand man, Ridley.

The many complications include two pairs of twins but also, more entertainingly, the reverse idea: Hapgood's pretence that she herself has a twin sister. Ridley is told that the boy Joe has been kidnapped and that to bargain for his release Hapgood must arrange a 'meet' with the KGB yet all the time appear to be at her office. He visits the supposed twin, a slatternly Mrs Newton, and persuades her to come to the office to imperson-ate her sister – even though she will not know what to do there and will have to change her clothing, manner and language. The audience by now knows that Joe remains safe at school after all, but is still inclined to believe in Mrs Newton, and to wonder how she will cope in the office. Of course Hapgood is a brilliant dissembler, convincing both as Mrs Newton and as Mrs Newton trying to be Hapgood. Only in the scene's final line, when Hapgood makes her latest move in a telephone chess game, do we grasp that she has been herself all the time, and that we, along with Ridley, have been thoroughly conned.

Stoppard's reading about quantum physics, with its doubling and contrary observations, may have pointed him towards the spy plot; but the analogies merely *decorate* his story and give no real insight into the science. A non-scientific audience may retain the idea of the dual nature of light, but anything more requires a lecture (one rewrite, for Los Angeles in 1989, includ-ed an explanatory monologue lasting for eighteen minutes). The spy story itself is exhaustingly over-ingenious, as well as synthetic, in a dated genre: by 1988 the Cold War was about to end. For all the talk of nuclear warheads, we don't care because we don't believe; and most of the characters are obvious cardboard – not excluding Ridley and Blair, who happen to have the names of real British politicians at the time. (That's probably coincidence; a likelier rumour is that all the surnames were those of a junior Stoppard's classmates. There is certainly a private joke for the play's producer, when Joe's rugby team takes on 'St Codron's'.)

The play's emotional capital, such as it is, is invested in Hapgood, Kerner and Joe, their son, who is realistic enough as an eleven-year-old at a private boarding school ('it's silly to buy new boots for Colts B'). The play's most poignant moment hints at another story, of greater human interest:

HAPGOOD: Once when he was really little, he got unhappy
    about something, he was crying, he couldn't tell me what it
    was, he didn't *know* what it was, and he said, 'The thing is,
    Mummy, I've been unhappy for *years*.' He was only as big
    as a gumboot.

(Boots, boots, again.) But this is instantly dropped; she knows all about the British stiff upper lip.

Hapgood is an attractive role for a female actor – or would be if the play were more likely to be revived. Caring mother, still sexually attractive, thoroughly in power but bouncy, funny and vulnerable, she also gets to play her imaginary sister. Arguably the most striking progression in Stoppard's work is in his writing about women. Here it is Kerner who is more of a fantasy figure, expressive about physics but at other times almost out of Lewis Carroll, as in this implausible line: 'Frankly, I can't remember which side I'm supposed to be working for, and it is not in fact necessary for me to know.'

Little went right for *Hapgood*. Even its title seems lame: neither of its hints – at chance and at goodness – illuminate the play, and the unmemorable name can't have helped at the box office. The lead role was written for Felicity Kendal as much as Carr in *Travesties* was for John Wood, but then she became pregnant and it was decided – a considerable tribute to her – that the play should wait. When she did start rehearsing, she found it 'very difficult' and the eventual opening felt 'bumpy' (p. 256), which seems to be the general recollection: Peter Wood described to me the gloomy playwright, in the rain outside the preview theatre having noticed Michael Codron and his partner inside, murmuring: 'I see the undertakers are in.'

Nevertheless, the affection between Kendal and Stoppard was growing into love. His next play – one of his finest – was written for her, dedicated to her, and set in India, where she had grown up ('I don't feel remotely English', p. 259). Stoppard himself did not revisit India until after **In the Native State** (1991) was written; the Indian scenes are set in 1930 and could be drawn from his reading and from his own memories of the 1940s. They alternate with scenes from modern England, in the bungalow of the elderly widow of Francis Swan, a former District Commissioner in India. Mrs Swan is visited by a young Indian painter, Anish, who has glimpsed in a bookshop a painting by his father, Nirad Das, reproduced on the *Selected Letters* of Mrs Swan's sister, Flora Crewe, an English poet who died young in India in 1930. We hear of the portrait being painted, the growing intimacy between painter and sitter, together with other events of Flora's months in Jummapur, a 'native state' still notionally ruled by its rajah. (An American academic in *The Cambridge Companion* declares earnestly: 'Stoppard spent several years of his childhood in Jummapur,' but in fact the place is entirely fictitious.)

When the play opens it is nearly April and the heat is becoming unbearable, particularly for a woman who is new to India and is seriously unwell. The first words heard are Flora's voicing her erotic poem ('I am in heat like a bride in a bath'); suddenly Das says, 'Do you want me to stop, Miss Crewe?' and the radio listener instantly wonders, stop what? Radio also allows effortless cross-cutting with her letters home and with the annotations of their modern editor, another but fictional American academic, whose name – Pike – is a tease for

Stoppard's own very English editor, Frank Pike. His clunky footnotes reveal Flora's previous life and loves in London and Paris, including very funny circumstantial detail about actual personalities (she is said to have 'poured a pint of beer over the head of J. C. Squire in the Fitzroy Tavern in January 1921', and her photograph with Maynard Keynes supposedly appears in a book called *Ottoline Morrell and Her Circle in Hell*). Mrs Swan feels 'so cross that she missed it all, the *Collected Poems*, and now the *Letters*, with her name all over the place and students and professors so *interested* and so sweet about her poetry. Nobody gave tuppence about her while she was alive except to get her knickers off.'

Flora is viewed askance by the British in Jummapur. A young arty woman travelling alone, she is following in the footsteps of a Communist friend (another Chamberlain to tease the playwright's secretary) who spoke 'on the subject of Empire' three years earlier. The play begins a few days after Gandhi's Salt March, and the 1930 scenes repeatedly suggest rumblings towards Indian independence, the trouble ahead, while the modern scenes review the trouble now behind, and the intricacies of colonial and post-colonial relationship. It's typical of Stoppard to sketch political confrontation somewhere at the margins of a play, rather as if writing always from Zurich during the First World War: momentous events, it seems, keep calling to be addressed, but then only obliquely. The tendency culminates in the trilogy *The Coast of Utopia*, which depicts the social environment and theoretical debates of men who had a huge influence on later political history. The last words of *In the Native State* are historically its earliest, from the (real) diary of Emily Eden in 1839: 'I sometimes wonder they do not cut all our heads off and say nothing more about it.'

In Jummapur, Chamberlain's lecture caused the Rajah to suspend the Theosophical Society for a year. More seriously for Flora, as a young white woman she has no business associating closely with Indian men, yet the Rajah presents her with an erotic watercolour and Das, in addition to his conventional portrait, also paints her nude (that is, in *the* native state).

Radio, which can show nothing visually, here plays most elegantly on the listener's imagination; and, paradoxically, paintings are a linking theme throughout. Pike explains that an earlier nude of Flora was painted by Modigliani and was shown in a notorious exhibition of 1919 (her then fiancé bought the painting and promptly burned it). When Anish shows Mrs Swan the Das nude, which has been kept wrapped up for sixty years, she exclaims, 'How like Flora,' referring not to the likeness but to her sister's having stripped so riskily.

Das explains to Flora that both paintings and poems need *rasa* ('juice . . . essence . . . emotion'). The poem she is writing while he paints is about heat, and its *rasa* – she declares briskly – is sex. Das 'unhesitatingly' begins a disquisition on the *rasa* of erotic love; and she is startled by his sudden eloquence: 'Mr Das, you sounded just like somebody else. Yourself, I expect' – the barrier of race and culture between them has collapsed. On the morning of her departure for the cooler hill country, Das is met leaving her house at dawn; and after taking her 'second shower of the day' she writes to her sister: 'Oh dear, guess what? You won't approve,' but later: 'something good happened here'. This play is unlike anything previous by Stoppard in being genuinely and intensely erotic. Das first sees Flora naked when her shower has failed and she asks him to bathe her, and the heat, her physical weakness, the splashing water and the towel as he rubs her dry are powerfully suggested. A line might technically be traced back to the stripteases in early Stoppard; but here, though the writer and the male listener are surely stirred by the bathing scene, it comes across primarily as from within Flora's sensuality, that of a particular person vividly known.

Meanwhile she has been courted in orthodox fashion by a young British official, David Durance, who is conventional but decent. He takes her riding ('Don't point your toes out') and abruptly proposes marriage. Given a brisk 'No', he apologises gruffly, and hastily reverts to equestrian advice: 'Knees together.' ''Fraid so,' replies the irrepressible Flora.

A moment later Pike tells us that Durance 'was killed in Malaya in 1942 during the Japanese advance on Singapore' – the fate (more or less) of Stoppard's father. This disturbing private reference not only recalls the bleak realities behind the fiction, but also tugs in the playwright himself, to a drama which for all its humour is intense, poignant and, as a work of and about love, personal. Durance eventually sees Flora off to the hill country, and there a year later another young British official escorts her sister to see her grave; his name is Francis Swan. Mrs Swan's memory is akin to a stunning film moment, but in radio it is 'filmed' by the listener's imagination: 'I have never seen such blossom, it blew everywhere, there were drifts of snow-white flowers piled up against the walls of the graveyard. I had to kneel on the ground and sweep the petals off her stone to read her name.'

Stoppard finds plots hard to devise and has frequently turned to other people's, or the given frame of history. But when he *does* invent plots they work well, and the story of Flora Crewe is most delicately worked out, not least in its simulated reference points in real people and real history. Thus, for example, the premature death of Modigliani, a historical fact, is tied in so cunningly that Flora's unpunctuality, when due to be painted by him for a second time, lies convincingly on her conscience, partly explaining why she later poses nude for Das.

Except *Professional Foul*, no previous Stoppard work is so movingly realistic, about credible characters in credible and gripping situations, or achieves so much without his usual supports of stylisation, caricature or self-allusive patterns. This is not to say that psychological realism should be the aim of all drama, or that the earlier writing was misdirected: this man's genius is originally comic, and no one has ever been better at verbal and intellectual frivolity. Yet as early as *Rosencrantz* there were signs of an artist who might aspire to something more, to a true comic *gravitas* such as that in, say, Chekhov or

Mozart. Later plays also hinted at some similar direction, but were restricted by – or rather, perhaps, took refuge in – their own dazzling cleverness and cartoon principles, while *Night and Day* ventured into realism but lacked exuberance and also tenderness. *The Real Thing* reached out much further, though uncertainly, towards some dreamed-of synthesis of the Stoppardian comic mode with psychological realism and intense feeling. That synthesis was eventually achieved in *Arcadia*, but within its smaller scope *In the Native State* can stand even that comparison.

All three plays of the 1990s – this one, *Arcadia* and *The Invention of Love* – speculate on an impossible dialogue, the might-have-been encounter that in fact could *never* have been, between a youthful ardour and a later sceptical world-weariness. It's natural material for a playwright in his fifties; and this one was at the peak of his craft. In 1995 he adapted *In the Native State* for the stage, calling it **Indian Ink**; and the old team of Michael Codron, Felicity Kendal, Peter Wood, and Carl Toms worked together for the last time. The drama was extended to fill an evening, with good new material about India, about Nirad Das – and also about America, since Eldon Pike is now seen in person pursuing his researches, both at Mrs Swan's bungalow and in Jummapur. Though Stoppard had not yet received the attentions of Professor Nadel, Pike is burlesqued in lines of his own such as: 'This is why God made writers, so the rest of us can publish,' and: 'It must exist – look how far I've come to find it'; and Mrs Swan warns him sharply that '*biography* is the worst possible excuse for getting people wrong'. Pike's presence, and the associated changes to the character of Mrs Swan, who is now more of a humorist ('Where is the bit?' / 'Between your teeth, Eldon'), shift the overall balance more towards comedy.

The translation from radio is imaginatively done. In a note, Stoppard pays special tribute to Peter Wood's direction, but he himself probably made the basic decision not to attempt two or more separate sets but to merge present and past, England and

India, fluidly onstage – so that, for example, Flora arrives in her bungalow as Mrs Swan speaks from hers. This instantly releases the play from the constraints of strict realism, and builds on the recent success of *Arcadia*, where present and past use the same set and props and finally take the stage together. The scene which suffers most in adaptation is that in which Das bathes the exhausted Flora: on radio so intensely *imaginable*, almost as from within, this onstage becomes literal, more voyeuristic even as more distanced; and when a little later Flora asks whether Das can see her through her mosquito net, his reply seems to come from the earlier Stoppard: 'Barely.' The wittiest change is that two gymnasium horses in the Jummapur Club, 'fitted out with stirrups and reins' and 'used for practising polo swings', turn into the horses on which Durance and Flora ride out early next morning

Arcadia (1993) is the play in which everything came right. Stoppard invented here a complex story-line, delivered with skilful use of suspense and false trails; its situations are believable and it has a cast of convincing characters, for some of whom an audience comes to care deeply. It achieves the highest kind of comedy, where laughter is never very far away but nor is the futility of human pretension, or the reality of death. An astonishing range of intellectual material is geared to the plot yet also reaches out to the lives of an audience today, all of whom experience *sexual attraction*, many of whom have *gardens*, some of whom are aware of the tension within them between *classical* and *romantic* inclinations, and all of whom live in *a world that is doomed*; and that's not to mention the mathematics. Additionally and beyond all this it's a masterpiece of stagecraft. This is unmistakably a great play.

The title is perfect. The Arcadia of the Latin poet Virgil was a literary fantasy of rural life, in which idealised shepherds and shepherdesses, never smelling remotely of sheep, conducted their affairs well away from the nasty corrupting city. The single set of Stoppard's play is a large room in a grand country house among vast gardens, an Arcadia constructed to provide similar escape for eighteenth-century aristocrats. Yet a famous painting (1638–9) of Nicolas Poussin shows Virgil's shepherds puzzling over the inscription on a tomb, '*Et in Arcadia ego*', which is ambiguous but most probably represents the voice of Death: 'Even in Arcadia I am present.' In Stoppard, the characters we first meet, who are young and attractive and clever and funny, turn out in the second scene to be long dead; the first scene was in the Regency period, 1809, the second is 1993 – then we return to 1809, and get involved there again; and so on in alternation.

Though the country house, Sidley Park, is still occupied today by the same aristocratic family, its members tend to be living in or off their past: the modern Lady Croom retraces the former gardens, her batty husband resists Japanese cars and anything typewritten, the tongue-tied boy Gus spends hours in the library, going through old family books and papers, and his older brother Valentine, though thoroughly up to date in maths and computer technology, has chosen to base his postgraduate research on the family game books, which record the creatures shot in sport over the centuries. These are joined by Hannah, a popular writer researching Lord Byron's stay in the house in 1809, and by her rival Bernard, a brash academic similarly on the trail of Byron though pretending that his quarry is a minor poet also resident in 1809. The Regency scenes tantalisingly suggest that at any moment Byron may saunter on to the stage; he is at Sidley Park because his school friend Septimus is resident tutor to the house's two children, Lady Thomasina and Lord Augustus. As fits a story involving Byron, a good deal of sleeping-around is going on.

Generically, then, the plot is not unusual: modern characters 'detecting' the past. But whereas such fictions usually work from present-day to flashback, Stoppard reverses this (as he also did in *In the Native State*). The year 1809 is not 'other' or mysterious, but seems to be home ground for the evening. Delightful and eloquent characters appear in a beautiful costume drama, an Arcadian escape for a modern urban audience;

there's also a promisingly tangled plot, on the lines of post-Restoration comedy. When the stage empties and then modern characters intrude on the same set, the initial effect is deflation and disappointment: boring modern dress and impoverished language. (It will improve, but at first it's 'Oh! Well, she *was* here. / Ah . . . the French window . . . / Hang on. / Sod. / The best thing is, you wait here, save you tramping around.') It emerges that the room resembles its 1809 self because it has been temporarily cleared of later acquisitions; it will function as a passageway during a dance. Glumly we acknowledge that this is our *true* home ground, which for some reason the dramatist isn't, after all, going to let us forget.

The *single set* is Stoppard's best theatrical notion since that of *Rosencrantz*; as he says (to me, p. 171) a film of *Arcadia* would tend to miss the point. At a time when theatre is habitually fluid, the opposite and harder minimalist choice is made: to alter nothing as the periods switch forwards and back. The problem of anachronism in the props is defiantly turned into a feature: '*By the end of the play the table has collected an inventory of objects.*' Books and papers are literally the same; a tortoise, an apple, its leaf (and offstage gunshots) are made to double, as the boy playing Gus/Augustus doubles, for both periods. Each is realistic in either era and yet forms an ironic comment on theatrical realism itself, which Stoppard finally subverts with a deliberately comic anachronism: a dance band playing modern music while people in 1812 attempt to waltz.

By this time, in the long and amazing last scene, present and past are occupying the set simultaneously, neither period aware of the other. For the dance, all the modern characters save Hannah wear Regency fancy dress, which makes the boy Gus look identical to his ancestor Lord Augustus, whose actual clothes he may indeed be wearing. The scene sustains an extraordinary and ever-increasing theatrical tension: Septimus and Valentine study the same diagram, Hannah pours herself Septimus's wine in his glass, and the play ends with the independent dance of two couples, one from each era.

The symbolism of the single large room shared by all characters emerges as Valentine expounds the inevitability of *entropy*: 'we're all going to end up at room temperature'. What's happening when tea cools down 'is happening to everything everywhere. The sun and the stars.' All is part of the same vast stage set, which will ultimately be darkened. Hannah recalls a poem by Byron, 'Darkness':

> The bright sun was extinguished, and the stars
> Did wander darkling in the eternal space
> Rayless, and pathless, and the icy earth
> Swung blind and blackening in the moonless air . . .

The science here is not something pasted in as metaphor, as it was in *Hapgood*; it's what the play is ultimately about. Death is present even in Arcadia – not just human death but the death of everything. More specifically, the perception that 'you can't unstir the jam in your rice pudding' is made in 1809 – more than fifty years in advance of the formulation of the second law of thermodynamics – by Septimus's thirteen-year-old pupil, Thomasina. Three years later, in 1812, Septimus passes to her a scientific paper dealing with *heat exchange*, and she understands its alarming implications; by then she is teaching her tutor, who doesn't.

Earlier, Septimus told her of Fermat's last theorem, the most famous marginal note ever written: a claim to have proved something for which no proof survived. (With what Stoppard described in another context as 'like little signs from God that you're on the right track' the theorem was eventually proved a few months after *Arcadia* opened.) She proceeded to fantasise about a 'truly wonderful method' by which even such irregular forms as a leaf 'must draw themselves through number alone'. She even began to do the algebra, but that would have taken her 'a few million' calculations, possible only on a modern computer. Valentine, coming across her notes 180 years later, understands that her dream of fractal geometry anticipated the iterated algorithms which he applies to his game books. *Chaos theory* shows how the shape of a leaf happens, and the computer can simulate the occurrence of imaginary leaves. What seems 'chaotic' is the product of deterministic processes, but they resist prediction. In James Gleick's popular guide *Chaos*, which Stoppard had been reading, the scientist Doyne Farmer is quoted saying: 'It struck me as . . . a way that allowed you to reconcile free will with determinism. The system is deterministic, but you can't say what it's going to do next.'[19]

The play pursues this hint. Its science recognises *determinism*; Stoppard's humanism clings to the opposite notion of *free will*. Whatever is interesting in life is unpredictable – so we think we might have influence over it; yet everything, whether interesting or not, will eventually 'run down'. This tension is not something devised by the dramatist: it's intrinsic to our current knowledge. Stoppard's achievement is to clarify it intellectually within a play which nevertheless tingles with more pressing realities of human emotions.

Brilliantly, in persistent comedy, the irrationality of *sexual attraction* further complicates the tale: almost every character experiences some such perplexity, as of course has every member of the audience. The one who seems determined not to be caught is Hannah (first played by Felicity Kendal); she insists to the sex-driven teenager Chloe that 'it gets less important', and later refuses to fancy-dress for the final dance or to appear in a photograph – yet this reserve may only intensify the 'romantic', idealised love of fifteen-year-old Gus, whose last-minute love-offering confirms the final unravelling. Valentine, who is also in love with Hannah, tells her sharply: 'Your classical reserve is only a mannerism; and neurotic.' She may be simply opting out of human involvement; Chloe asks: 'What do you know about anything?' and she replies (twice) 'Nothing.' The play offers no resolution for Hannah; it ends with her dancing with a teenage boy, but only after 'hesitation' and at 'a decorous distance' – nothing long-term there.

19 Gleick, p. 251.

Thomasina, however, in 1812 is in love with her tutor, Septimus, and invites him to her bedroom. He is much tempted, but tells her he 'cannot'. Possibly he recalls with some embarrassment that he has already slept with her mother . . . but on the whole his refusal seems guided by deeper moral principles: she is very young and he is her tutor. In an agonising duel of auxiliary verbs – Stoppard's linguistic virtuosity distilled into a few monosyllables – Thomasina attempts to insist: 'You must'; to her, aged sixteen, their sexual destiny seems inevitable, predetermined. But Septimus's final line is: 'I will not'; he has free will, moral choice. Appallingly, however, we already know that if he had consented he might have saved her life, because she dies later that night in a fire, a disaster of heat exchange.

A further intellectual and emotional tension, between *classical* and *romantic* attitudes, is finely linked to the subsidiary theme of *garden design* – which in turn is tied into the main plot, because the Gothicised garden being installed at Sidley Park in 1812 requires the embellishment of a resident hermit, for whom an appropriate hovel is being constructed. The modern researchers know that there was indeed a hermit, who wasted away, obsessed by compulsive mathematical scribbling. The final twist confirms what the audience has for some time feared: that this hermit was the former tutor Septimus, frantically attempting after her death to honour Thomasina's intuition of entropy, and yet to prove her wrong. The bad news, for him and for all of us, is that she was right.

One excellence of Stoppard's sustained achievement – and one reason it has been sustained – is his refusal to repeat a successful formula: '*Jumpers* and *Travesties* are . . . so similar that were I to do it a third time it would be a bore' (Hayman, p. 12). There are recurrent Stoppardian tricks, characteristics and preoccupations; but each play has its own ingenious concept and its own fresh subject matter, often first encountered in the playwright's voracious reading and then, once a play seems a possibility, followed up by a great deal more. Finding the right material, and then the notion for a play, is clearly the hard part, and he can be choosy because meanwhile there is always well-paid craftwork to be done on screenplays and adaptations. He resembles in this the composer who is so much in demand as a performer (Mahler, Rachmaninov, Boulez, Bernstein) that his composing suffers, or at least is less frequent.

Occasionally an idea is glimpsed in one play and developed in another, as Guil's sardonic conception of 'a short, blunt human pyramid' materialises in *Jumpers*. *In the Native State* includes an exchange at the Jummapur Club between Flora Crewe and a British official who was tutored by A. E. Housman at Cambridge:

RESIDENT: When it comes to love, he said, you're either an
  Ovid man or a Virgil man. *Omnia vincit amor* – that's
  Virgil – 'Love wins every time, and we give way to love' – *et
  nos cedamus amori*. Housman was an Ovid man – *et mihi
  cedet amor* – 'Love gives way to me.'
FLORA: I'm a Virgil man.
RESIDENT: Are you? Well, you meet more people that way.

which, as the play shows, is certainly true for Flora. This is clearly relevant to her story, and also to *Arcadia*; what no one can have expected is that it would lead, a few years later, to a play about Housman himself, **The Invention of Love** (1997).

The surprise in this case was the uncharacteristic choice of subject: the homosexual yearning of a thwarted, blocked character. Initially Stoppard knew nothing of Housman's sexuality: what attracted him, he said to Alistair Macaulay (*Financial Times*, 31 October 1998), was 'the Romantic/classicist contrast, isn't it? It's *Arcadia* again. I just realised there was something basically dramatic in the man who was two men . . . I could write an awfully good book about The Plays of Tom Stoppard – to me, it's so obvious: many of my plays are about unidentical twins, about double acts. Twins, in *Hapgood*; the two Housmans here.'

In the opening scene the boatman Charon, who ferries souls across the Styx after death, is expecting two passengers: 'a poet and a scholar . . . It sounded like two different people.' 'I know,' sadly replies AEH, the supposedly dead man, who was both.

Travesties notionally takes place within Henry Carr's suspect memory; *The Invention of Love* – which also starred John Wood – is dreamed by AEH in his nursing home, waiting to die (there's a minor strand about longing to urinate in his bed). To some extent he is himself a dream character, granted occasional exuberant moments which sound more like Carr than Housman (*'quietus interruptus* by monologue incontinent in the hind leg of a donkey class'). He dreams he has already died, and as a classicist he naturally expects to meet Charon first. Only in the play's last words does he indeed die – 'now I really do have to go' – and his sphincter relaxes – 'with the indifferent waters at my feet'. (John Wood himself clarified this for me.)

Stoppard's writing for some time had been inclining towards realism, but in this dream-play anything can happen – even, towards the end, the meeting of AEH with Oscar Wilde. Wilde's dandyism and epigrammatic skill hover behind much of Stoppard, for example in Lord Malquist, the framework of *Travesties*, or the speeches of Lady Croom in *Arcadia*. On Housman there seems no such influence; yet the publicity given to Wilde's trial and imprisonment for homosexual acts in 1895 probably triggered the homoerotic but melancholy lyrics of Housman's *A Shropshire Lad*, written in the following months. The two men never actually met, but were at Oxford at the same time, and for one ludicrous moment in Stoppard's play the repressed student Housman is mistaken for the flagrant Wilde. The joke there, and the more sombre point of their encounter later, is that they were so different. AEH pities Wilde: 'Your life is a terrible thing. A chronological error. The choice was not always between renunciation and folly. You should have lived in Megara . . .'

But in Wilde's view, and Stoppard's, the life to be pitied is Housman's: 'The betrayal of oneself is lifelong regret . . . Better a fallen rocket than never a burst of light. Dante reserved a place in his Inferno for those who wilfully live in sadness – sullen in the sweet air, he says. Your "honour" is all shame and timidity and compliance.'

Housman was right to be a scholar, Wilde tells him: 'all scruple'. The implication is that he failed as an artist, who 'is the agent of progress against authority' and 'must lie, cheat, deceive'. Even love – 'the ice that burns who clasps it' – depends on 'our invention', which to Wilde doesn't make it false but true, since 'Truth is the work of the imagination.'

The main literary hook for the play is Housman's classical scholarship, his scornful emendations of previous editions of Latin poets – rather than his *Shropshire Lad* lyrics, which are treated only briefly and with some irreverence. A more deviously ironic hook is Jerome K. Jerome's comic classic *Three Men in a Boat (Not to Mention the Dog)* (1889), which Stoppard had previously adapted for both television and radio. The dying Housman's dream keeps returning to an outing on the river with two fellow students – with one of whom, Moses Jackson, he will be for ever in love – and 'a small yapping dog'. Later Jerome himself is one of three men in another boat as it approaches Reading – where Wilde has been imprisoned, partly as a result of Jerome's aggressively homophobic journalism. In a further knot of ironies the other two men in the boat are a closet homosexual (yet another Chamberlain) who works with Housman, and the journalist Frank Harris. One of the 'three' in Jerome's comic novel is called Harris; but *this* Harris has been seen earlier in the play discussing Wilde's fate with the men who had helped to ensure it, two other newspapermen, Henry Labouchère and W. T. Stead. Labouchère was a Liberal MP, and in 1885 his parliamentary amendment criminalised, possibly unintentionally, 'a bit of what-you-fancy between two chaps safe at home with the door shut'.

As this quotation suggests, the play's notional mode is comic. In Act One travesty versions of Oxford scholars play 'Dream Croquet', which includes calls such as 'First-class return' and 'Mind the gap' (there is a minor strand about railways, and

British audiences may remember the radio nonsense game 'Mornington Crescent'). Even an uninformed audience is likely to pick up from their dialogue that these were sexually inhibited men, who nevertheless taught classical and sometimes homoerotic love poetry to male undergraduates. Their hypocrisy and double-think are briskly caricatured:

JOWETT: Nowhere was the ideal of morality, art and social order realised more harmoniously than in Greece in the age of the great philosophers.
RUSKIN: Buggery apart.
JOWETT: Buggery apart.
PATER: The ideal of morality, art and social order was realised more harmoniously in Italy in the fifteenth century, morality and social order apart.

This resembles Stoppard's early cartoon manner; but in *The Invention of Love* it becomes movingly conjoined with the mature, elegiac mood of the Flora Crewe plays and *Arcadia*, and is most memorable for its melancholy – about a life lived 'sullen in the sweet air'. Like that life, the play is claustrophobic: significantly, it returns on itself at times, rather as Carr's mental toy train jumps the rails, and there is only one female character, Housman's sister, who appears in just one scene; these are men ideologically and emotionally cut off from women.

The finest scene is an extended duet in which the dying AEH talks with his undergraduate self, who is idealist, already in love, but as yet still cheerful. Here too there are laughs, but the notion of such an encounter would be poignant for any of us, let alone for a man as repressed as Housman. In the early radio plays *Where Are They Now?* and *Artist Descending*, and in the Flora Crewe plays of the 1990s, present and past interact in an ironic montage. In *Arcadia* they occupy the same stage space simultaneously, but cannot communicate. Here, present and past selves actually converse together. Of necessity the irony remains one-way, the dry commentary of hindsight, but at least once the young man is allowed to answer back and win (as it were) applause:

AEH: Catullus 99 – *vester* for *tuus* is the point of interest there.
HOUSMAN: No, it isn't!
AEH: I'm sorry.
HOUSMAN: The point of interest is – what is virtue? what is the good and the beautiful really and truly?

This encounter was always going to be theatrically risky – it lasts a long time, with relatively few laughs, and according to Trevor Nunn (p. 204) it might even have been lost in authorial revision; but it is the play's boldest and best achievement.

Any anxiety that Stoppard had retreated into elegiac mode was removed by his next public success, the movie **Shakespeare in Love** (1999). As early as 1991 he had been called in to anglicise and make Elizabethan the originally American screenplay by Marc Norman. The initial nonsense notion is that Shakespeare, actually one of the most productive of artists, might have suffered from writer's block. He is stuck on his proposed play 'Romeo and Ethel the Pirate's Daughter' – and is similarly 'humbled in the act of love', as he admits to his analyst. Additionally the script takes up, without acknowledgement, the idea of *No Bed for Bacon*, by Caryl Brahms and S. J. Simon, in which an aristocratic lady called Viola disguises herself as a boy player in order to work in Shakespeare's company. In *Shakespeare in Love* Viola ends up playing Juliet to Shakespeare as Romeo; one of the film's achievements is that the poetry of *Romeo and Juliet* is allowed to ring through and eventually, for some minutes, grips the audience. The screenplay is, of course, allusive, lifting lines from many places in Shakespeare, entangling the plot with the death of Marlowe, and identifying a sadistic young urchin as John Webster (this met by a silence of non-recognition in the cinema where I first saw it); yet no advance knowledge is essential to its enjoyment and it works for an international mass audience as most Stoppard plays cannot.

The screenplay ends with Viola emerging alone on 'a vast and empty beach . . . a stranger shore', as in *Twelfth Night*, the play Queen Elizabeth has requested. Septimus in *Arcadia* speaks of being 'alone, on a stranger shore' and *The Invention of Love* ends: 'on this empty shore, with the indifferent waters at my feet'. However unconsciously, the playwright is moving towards the imagery underlying his most ambitious work, **The Coast of Utopia** (2002), a trilogy of plays individually entitled *Voyage*, *Shipwreck* and *Salvage*.

I know of no previous trilogy prepared all at once in this way; usually such plays would appear separately over a period of years. The total playing time was more than nine hours. Following individual previews of each play, audiences could choose between experiencing all three over a twelve-hour day, or seeing each on a different evening.

Once again, now nearly sixty-five, Stoppard was seeking to extend his range. *Utopia* is relatively realist, in spite of the odd time-slip or dream sequence, and fundamentally serious beneath an intermittently comic surface. The plays present a large cast of historical characters, who frequently declaim their philosophical or political opinions. To that extent the work is driven by ideas: it broadcasts ideologies. Yet it is also partly about families, and often there is a child or an adolescent onstage. The playwright's most expansive, grandly sweeping work turns out also to be his most domestic. A decent humanism is held up against murderous dogma, and Stephen Dillane, who played Alexander Herzen, the central character, felt himself to be 'the mouthpiece for Tom's most passionately held beliefs about how a good life is lived'.

Stoppard pays tribute to *Russian Thinkers* (1978), a collection of essays by the historian of ideas, Isaiah Berlin. During 'a remarkable decade', 1838 to 1848, a group of young radicals, 'the original founders of the Russian intelligentsia . . . set the moral tone for the kind of talk and action which continued throughout the nineteenth and early twentieth centuries, until the final climax in 1917'.[20]

20 Berlin, p. 115.

That climax, the October Revolution, inflicted Communism on Russia for more than seventy years. It proleptically haunts *Utopia*, as indeed it haunts much of Stoppard's earlier work: on p. 113 we find him, at the age of thirty, imagining a play about aristocratic refugees from the Revolution; *Travesties* builds up to Lenin's train journey back to Russia; *Every Good Boy* and *Professional Foul* show totalitarian Communism in action. The playwright's intense anger at how 'Lenin perverted Marxism, and Stalin carried on from there' is eloquently expressed in the *Theatre Quarterly* interview (p. 123); but Marx himself had already 'got it wrong'. *Utopia* shows Western Europeans, not merely Russians, expounding their idealist and socialist visions – mostly with sympathy, as if Stoppard is determined to prove to those on the left that he has always understood where they are coming from. But there is no sympathy for Marx, the one name sure to be recognised by all audiences.

Behind Marx lies the philosopher Hegel, whose writings excite Nicholas Stankevitch and Vissarion Belinsky with a vision of 'the dialectical logic of history' through a 'zigzag' of superseding ideas. Herzen, however, tells Belinsky: 'You've got Hegel's Dialectical Spirit of History upside down and so has he. People don't storm the Bastille because history proceeds by zigzags. History zigzags because when people have had enough, they storm the Bastille. When you turn him right way up, Hegel is the algebra of revolution.'

Marx turned Hegel upside down in another way, seeing the zigzags of history as inevitably provoked by material forces rather than ideas. But Herzen resists the determinist thinking which underlies them both. History is not 'necessity'; it is created by individual human beings – and most of all by chance. Tuberculosis kills off key characters, Herzen's second son and his own mother are drowned; two later children die of diphtheria. In *Voyage*, the most theatrically imaginative of the three plays, the arbitrariness of historical event is represented by a six-foot Ginger Cat, silently smoking and ironically raising its glass at fancy-dress parties. Herzen acknowledges it, yet still asserts free will: '[T]he Cat has no plan, no favourites or resentments, no memory, no mind, no rhyme or reason. It kills without purpose, and spares without purpose, too. So, when it catches your eye, what happens next is not up to the Cat, it's up to you.'

His sharp realism makes Herzen also, politically, the gradualist, and wins Stoppard's vote as well as Berlin's: in their view, Herzen is how (if at all) to be a socialist.

The young Karl Marx appears briefly on stage, almost like a character from *Travesties*, in the second play, *Shipwreck*, found in Paris at the time of the 1848 revolution. Satirical reference is made to him in other scenes, and he reappears, further caricatured, in two sequences dreamed by Herzen in *Salvage*. The trilogy's last two big speeches – still within the dream – distil the implied argument of the previous nine hours, and of some earlier Stoppard work.

MARX: Now at last the unity and rationality of history's purpose will be clear to everyone . . . a higher reality, a superior morality, against which resistance is irrational . . . the culmination of history. I see the Neva lit by flames and running red, the coconut palms hung with corpses all along the shining strand from Kronstadt to the Nevsky Prospect . . .

HERZEN: But history has no culmination! There is always as much in front as behind. There is no libretto. History knocks at a thousand gates at every moment, and the gatekeeper is chance. We shout into the mist for this one or that one to be opened for us, but through every gate there are a thousand more. We need wit and courage to make our way while our way is making us. But that is our dignity as human beings, and we rob ourselves if we pardon us by the absolution of historical necessity. What kind of beast is it, this Ginger Cat with its insatiable appetite for human sacrifice? This Moloch who promises that everything will be beautiful after we're dead? A distant end is not an end but a trap. The end we work for must be closer, the labourer's wage, the pleasure in the work done, the summer lightning of personal happiness . . .

Utopia grants its characters many sustained speeches such as this, crafted with Stoppard's usual skill. They are mostly framed ironically, however, in some domestic context (at the end of this final dream, '*Herzen half-falls out of his chair*'). The character most obviously de-bunked is Michael Bakunin, the central figure in *Voyage*, a naïve young aristocrat with too much money to make him take a job but not enough to finance his self-indulgent intellectual lifestyle. He provides two long-running jokes: the way he latches on to and then discards one idealist philosophy after another, and his chronic borrowing of money. He is depicted as incorrigibly selfish and yet somehow unaware of it; early on his resolve is to be able to say: 'Whatever I want, that's what God wants.' That may seem like Stoppard in cartoon mode, yet Bakunin's family is drawn more delicately, and gradually it becomes clear that he selfishly sabotages the marriage prospects of three of his four sisters. He recurs in the second and third parts of the trilogy, slightly indulged but essentially a whipping boy, a foil for Herzen's sharper and dryer thinking.

Two other key figures traverse the trilogy with Herzen from the outset in 1833 till its close in 1868. One is his boyhood friend Nicholas Ogarev, with whose wife they form a *ménage à trois* in the third play; the other is the writer Ivan Turgenev, a somewhat detached fellow-traveller and dandy with whom Stoppard identifies: 'I'm being called a traitor by both the left and the right, on the one hand for my malicious travesty of radical youth, and on the other for sucking up to it.'

PEROTKIN: And what was your attitude really? . . . your purpose?
TURGENEV: My purpose? My purpose was to write a novel.
PEROTKIN: So you don't take sides between the fathers and the children?

TURGENEV: On the contrary, I take every possible side.

Others, the Ginger Cat being what it is, are dead before the start of the third play: Herzen's mother, his wife, and his son Kolya, and also the most dynamic of the Russian radicals, Belinsky. Another twenty or thirty historical figures come and go, their names and significance hard for an audience to retain. Much of *Shipwreck*, the second play, is set outside Russia: Herzen and many other radicals are in Paris for the 1848 revolution, and Herzen's exile continues in Nice, where his family tragedy occurs. He never returns to Russia, most of *Salvage* being set in England among Russian, French, German, Polish, Hungarian and Italian exiles.

Years, characters and debates roll through the three plays, usually in domestic settings with more dramatic events taking place offstage. Much is briefly sketched; some scenes have only a line or two, like battle scenes in Shakespeare – or a screen-play. Modern theatre is habitually fluid, but *The Coast of Utopia* often seems more filmic than theatrical and might work well as a television series of, say, six or eight episodes: many moments seem to cry out for close-up. Instead the plays were staged in the vast Olivier auditorium at the National Theatre in London, and that did give audiences a contrary advantage: the sense of the sweep of history, crowds and clusters and individuals coming and going, in front of a huge and brilliantly changing panoramic screen. The direction was indeed partly filmic, though not at the intimate level of television: William Dudley, the designer, used video projections to create superb images of a summer garden with birch forest, cityscapes, seascapes, storms, as well as many interiors.

Dudley's designs were for some the most memorable element. Though seats sold well for the marathon drama – the biggest ever venture of an important and popular playwright – many spectators were ultimately disappointed. Reviews showed deep respect for Stoppard and the company, but generally found the enterprise misjudged: too long, too uneven, and too unrewardingly earnest, from a dramatist who until then had been reliably entertaining. Stoppard audiences accept and relish intellectual challenge, not grasping everything at first hearing; they cope with that. In *Utopia*, on the other hand, they found themselves expected to listen to lengthy expositions of arguments which were not new and perhaps not so difficult; one reviewer commented that whereas previous Stoppard plays made an audience feel cleverer than they actually were (because that was implied), here they might feel more stupid (because they were being lectured at). Others felt that the playwright had settled uncritically for the rather vague liberalism of Isaiah Berlin, or that more than a decade after the fall of Communism in Europe the case against Marx's dogma was unnecessary: this was not Stoppard moving on, after all, but returning to an obsession.

Twenty-four years earlier, as he recalls to me (p. 172), '*Night and Day* disappointed people who would have loved another *Travesties* type of evening'; and in *The Real Thing* Henry remarks that 'all us artists' suffer from 'people saying they preferred the early stuff'. As I have argued, Stoppard's readiness to move on is generally a strength; and for better or worse *Utopia* is not the place to seek former pleasures. The eloquence remains, and some of the humour, but whereas in many past successes, to use his own image, two trains arrive on the same line, *Utopia* tends to lack that structural and conceptual complexity.

In this respect the first play, *Voyage*, is the most Stoppardian. The events of its second act, in Moscow, follow roughly the same time sequence as, and gradually clarify, the events of the first act in the country estate of Premukhino: that's an invigorating idea. The play begins well, under the benign influence of Chekhov, with the four Bakunin sisters and their ineffectual brother: 'Tata, Tata, don't you know? Dawn has broken! In Germany the sun is already high in the sky! . . . The outer world of material existence is mere illusion. I'll explain it all to Father.'

These last words become a catchphrase, as Bakunin changes philosophies like shirts; and the wars of words and ideas continue to be somewhat leavened by Chekhovian comedy in this first play, where the trilogy has not yet narrowed around Herzen.

At the start of the second, *Shipwreck*, the undertones are not so much of Chekhov as of Ibsen: 'Not too close to the river, darling!' heavily anticipates the later drownings. Here the only departures from conventional chronology are the 'reprises' which end both acts; otherwise the play follows Herzen and his associates steadily through Paris in 1848 and 1849. The political rhetoric dominates; yet it sometimes takes place in the presence of Herzen's small son Kolya – who is not only far too young to follow the arguments but cannot even hear them, since he is deaf. Delicately, not yet noticed by most audiences, a human and domestic reality distances itself from the utopian verbiage. In Act Two Kolya, after being taught to lip-read, triumphantly speaks a few words, including: 'I speak Russian,' but alas he speaks them in *German*, and in Nice, which was then an *Italian* town.

This child is a displaced person, forever in exile from his homeland, as his father will remain. Nor is Kolya seen again. The news of his drowning, a notional climax, is rendered minimally, lamely – perhaps intentionally; the play's rhetoric appears suddenly in tatters. Nine months later, however, Herzen does find the words, for the trilogy's finest speech:

> His life was what it was. Because children grow up, we think a child's purpose is to grow up. But a child's purpose is to be a child. Nature doesn't disdain what lives only for a *day*. It pours the whole of itself into the each moment. We don't value the lily less for not being made of flint and built to last . . . It's only we humans who want to own the future too . . . Was the child happy while he lived? That is a proper question, the only question. [And instantly, seamlessly, Herzen then returns to the political agenda.] If we can't

arrange our own happiness, it's a conceit beyond vulgarity to arrange the happiness of those who come after us.

At the start of the third play, *Salvage*, a whirling, *Travesties*-like dream sequence does call to mind the earlier Stoppard – or even Beckett, as the catcalls at Marx run 'Abortionist! / Parasite! Sponger! / Onanist! / Economist!' When realism is restored, however, there is less theatrical interest; the trilogy proceeds towards a conclusion through Herzen's years in London, a swirl of other European exiles and a family badly missing his wife, who is now dead. Children again figure onstage, along with a presumptuous governess, to alleviate the otherwise unstoppable political exchanges; on the other hand the second-act complication of Herzen's new relationship with Ogarev's wife is strangely under-dramatised. Turgenev and Bakunin revisit, and a representative of the younger generation arrives from Russia to tell Herzen, as was promised thirty-four years earlier by Polevoy in *Voyage*, that he is now 'behind the times'. Eventually another Herzen dream (quoted above: 'But history has no culmination!') allows an ending.

Utopia presented a huge challenge, most of all to its large and gifted company of actors. The playwright also found it 'completely draining', and the director, Trevor Nunn, though famously responsible for the six-hour *Nicholas Nickleby*, looks back on it as his biggest project. The leading actor, Stephen Dillane, feels that 'lack of time' prevented the full realisation of a 'masterpiece', although 'as the fog began to clear . . . the great shapes of the plays began to emerge like a new landscape'. (These quotations are from interviews which appear later in this book.) Everyone hoped that the trilogy would prove to be Stoppard's towering achievement, the triumphant fruition of his earlier themes and talents. Instead what is remembered (as I write) is more the sheer heroic scale of the enterprise. In the words of Browning's Andrea del Sarto, 'A man's reach should exceed his grasp': Andrea recognises the greatness of a Raphael not in detail – which he himself might actually improve – but in conception. Stoppard's trilogy reached for an imagined artistic coast to which even the voyage was a concept of greatness; it may not have managed a landing, but nor was it a shipwreck.

4

Stoppard on Stoppard

Throughout his career Stoppard has given interviews generously, perhaps partly because he once worked as a journalist himself. He speaks superbly off the cuff, but his epigrammatic brilliance is often self-shielding, as he admits ('I now have a repertoire of plausible answers which evade the whole truth'[21]). His commonest reason for agreeing to be interviewed is to publicise a new production, in loyalty to those putting it on.

The selection here appears in chronological order. The first piece is a newspaper article, though possibly based on an interviewer's questions. Included later is most of a lecture which Stoppard gave in various forms at North American universities, where he emerges as something of a teacher. The final interview is new for this book, my own 'update'.

'Something to Declare', 25 February 1968

This essay appeared in the Sunday Times, *when Stoppard was thirty. The piece is briefly discussed on p. 19.*

One thing which has begun to interest me more than anything else about writing, not necessarily plays, is the relationship between one's conscious and unconscious level of creation. When I'm talking about my own work to somebody, my relationship with them is rather like that of a duped smuggler confronted with a customs officer. I truthfully declare that I am indeed responsible for this piece about two specific individuals in a particular situation. Then he starts ransacking my luggage

21 To Jon Bradshaw, quoted Delaney, p. 92.

and comes up with all manner of exotic contraband like truth and illusion, the nature of identity, what I feel about life and death – and I have to admit the stuff is there but I can't for the life of me remember packing it.

One is therefore the beneficiary and victim of one's subconscious: that is, of one's personal history, experience and environment. It took me quite a long time to reconcile myself to this, because I liked to feel that I was in total control of my material.

A concrete example. My mother married again and my name was changed to my stepfather's when I was about eight years old. This I didn't care one way or the other about; but then it occurred to me that in practically everything I had written there was something about people getting each other's names wrong, usually in a completely gratuitous way, nothing to do with character or plot.

I think of myself as a reactionary in many ways. When I'm struck by something I want to write about it; very often it doesn't appear to have much to do with my main existence. It doesn't reflect what I've been reading in the newspapers or any of my own preoccupations. I have very few social preoccupations. I am preoccupied rather more with things I find difficult to express.

One element of this preoccupation is simply an enormous love of language itself. For a lot of writers the language they use is merely a fairly efficient tool. For me the particular use of a particular word in the right place, or a group of words in the right order, to create a particular effect is important; it gives me more pleasure than to make a point which I might consider to be profound. On the other hand, when one does concentrate mainly on the language itself, with luck this appears to have some meaning, often in a general sense and, when one is very lucky, in a universal sense.

There is quite a strong undercurrent in the theatre now of not so much written plays as theatrical experiences created by a group of intelligent people – who might without disadvantage include a writer among them. I am not really being snide about it, because I have never achieved through words a moment in a theatre which would even approach the extraordinary feeling created by Peter Brook's *US* when a few white butterflies started to flap around the auditorium and one, the last one taken out of a tin, was set aflame. I shall never forget that; it's a useful corrective whenever I start feeling a certain indulgence towards the idea of language as an end in itself.

And I do think in visual terms – not in terms of colours, or an actual stage, but certainly in terms of movement. I do not expect a theatre to adapt itself to my play very much, I don't set out in fact to write a play that will demand a new kind of theatre or a new kind of audience. But my feeling still is that the theatre ought to start from writing, come what may, even though in my view it is delusion that a play is the end product of an idea; in my experience the idea is the end product of the play.

After *Look Back in Anger* young writers tended to be young playwrights, not because what they had to say I think was particularly suited to dramatic form but because the theatre was clearly the most interesting and dynamic medium. (As for the other media, television in theory is one thing and television in practice is another. As a medium it is flexible, but in practice the television set-up is such that in most cases a space is looking for a particular thing to fill it. Television likes things to have an air of continuity; therefore there has turned out to be a sort of code suggesting a certain atmosphere, that the audience will be able to identify with at least one and possibly all the characters in a television play. This isn't always necessary or desirable with stage plays.)

It seemed clear to us, that is to say the people who began writing about the same time that I did, about 1960, that you could do a lot more in the theatre than had been previously demonstrated. *Waiting for Godot* – there's just no telling what sort of effect it had on our society, who wrote because of it, or wrote in a different way because of it. But it really redefined the minima of theatrical experience. Up to then you had to have X; suddenly you had X minus one.

Of course it would be absurd to deny my enormous debt to it, and love for it. To me the representative attitude is 'I am a human nothing'. Beckett qualifies as he goes along. He picks up a proposition and then dismantles and qualifies each part of its structure as he goes along, until he nullifies what he started out with. Beckett gives me more pleasure than I can express because he always ends up with a man surrounded by the wreckage of a proposition he had made in confidence only ten minutes before.

I feel some guilt about being a writer. Probably all artists feel guilty. The reason is – at least this is how I analyse it for myself – that we are still lumbered with an enormous heritage of art, which has become something which folks place on the edge of society. Artists are made to feel decorators, embroiderers, who operate not precisely at the hub of society, who don't in fact contribute in the way that one can contribute a bicycle or a pound of butter, who somehow are in a business that can barely justify itself until we have enough butter and all that butter stands for.

It took me quite a while to justify my own credentials; yet artists do not in fact need to justify themselves – they are producing something which crystallises and makes concrete something in the air.

We all, on a much smaller scale, do this whenever we write anything. Yet as for real social stuff which makes headlines, I haven't got the slightest desire to write about it on its own terms. One thing that had an enormous effect on me was the evidence at the trial of the people who killed three Civil Rights workers at Meridian, Mississippi. I couldn't get out of my head the awful fact of those murders; but I couldn't begin to write about that kind of subject in real terms. I think what I would write about if I ever got to the subject at all would be the fact that I was so personally revolted and disturbed by the cold-blooded killing of those three people that I'd like to get the people who did it and cold-bloodedly kill them.

My intention still is to write a play to commemorate, probably rather sceptically, the fiftieth anniversary of the Russian Revolution. I started it about the beginning of 1966; but confronted with the enormous importance and reality of that revolution, I absolutely boggle, I don't know what to do about it. I think I want to write about that lovely group of octogenarians who I believe inhabit a house in Bayswater, who had to flee in 1917 and who are hanging about waiting for the whole thing to blow over so that they can go back.

When I'm asked why I write I tend to put up a sort of front answer, because the real answer is enormously complicated, and one I haven't worked out successfully. Some writers write because they burn with a cause which they further by writing about it. I burn with no causes. I cannot say that I write with any social objective. One writes because one loves writing, really.

'Ambushes for the Audience: Towards a High Comedy of Ideas', 1974

This interview is a sort of classic for Stoppard-watchers; if just one such encounter had to be selected, it is still probably the most instructive. The engagement on both sides is simply more serious here than in most interviews for publication. The editors of the magazine Theatre Quarterly *(Roger Hudson, Catherine Itzin and Simon Trussler) allow the playwright plenty of time but clearly want to challenge his reluctance to be political according to their own orthodoxy, and Stoppard responds vigorously. The interview took place early in 1974 (when* Travesties *was in rehearsal) and appeared as the lead feature in the magazine's May–July 1974 issue. The extract here begins, after autobiographical ground has been gone over, on the topic of* Rosencrantz.

TS: What was actually calculated was to entertain a roomful of people with the situation of Rosencrantz and Guildenstern at Elsinore. The chief thing that added one line to another line was that the combination of the two should retain an audience's interest in some way. I tend to write through a series of small, large and microscopic ambushes – which might consist of a body falling out of a cupboard, or simply an unexpected word in a sentence. But my preoccupation as a writer, which possibly betokens a degree of insecurity, takes the form of contriving to inject some sort of interest and colour into every line, rather than counting on the general situation having a general interest which will hold an audience.

Process of Solving Problems

TQ: *So really* Rosencrantz and Guildenstern *doesn't embody any particular philosophy but is a process of solving craft problems?*
That's absolutely the case *on a conscious level*, but one is a victim and beneficiary of one's subconscious all the time and, obviously, one is making choices all the time. And the kind of things which I personally enjoy, which I personally judge to be . . . quirky, and therefore interesting enough or funny enough or resonant enough to do the job of retaining an audience's interest, involve rather more than a simple matter of craft. *Why* do these things appeal to me? What is it about them that I find satisfying? There one starts to get into an area where a more interpretive attitude to the material is not irrelevant. It's difficult for me to endorse or discourage particular theories – I mean, I get lots of letters from students, and people who are doing the play, asking me questions about it, which seem to expect a yes-or-no answer. It is a mistake to assume that such questions have that kind of answer. I personally think *that anybody's* set of ideas which grows out of the play has its own validity.

With hindsight, do you think Rosencrantz *was more a play about, well, existential problems posed by bit-part characters in* Shakespeare, *or was it, maybe subconsciously, asking questions*

about more general, more 'real' philosophical problems?
First I must say that I didn't know what the word 'existential'
meant until it was applied to *Rosencrantz*. And even now exis-
tentialism is not a philosophy I find either attractive or plausible. But it's certainly true that the play can be interpreted in
existential terms, as well as in other terms. But I must make
clear that, insofar as it's possible for me to look at my own
work objectively at all, the element which I find most valuable
is the one that other people are put off by – that is, that there is
very often *no* single, clear statement in my plays. What there is,
is a series of conflicting statements made by conflicting characters, and they tend to play a sort of infinite leap-frog. You
know, an argument, a refutation, then a rebuttal of the refutation, then a counter-rebuttal, so that there is never any point in
this intellectual leap-frog at which I feel *that* is the speech to
stop it on, *that* is the last word.

*That's curious, because I would have thought it could be said of
quite a few of your plays, the more recent ones particularly,
that they are solutions to problems – in a quite precise though
often a very comic sense – After Magritte, for example, Real
Inspector Hound or Artist Descending a Staircase . . .*
If you're thinking of a situation as being a metaphor for a more
general confusion then of course that's true of *After Magritte*;
but that's not an intellectual play, it's a nuts-and-bolts comedy.

*But isn't it true to say that most of your plays have a fascina-
tion with the eccentric in human behaviour, at least as a starting point? Aren't you more interested in that than in trying to
explore the nuances of ordinary social activity?*
What I try to do, is to end up by contriving the perfect marriage
between the play of ideas and farce or perhaps even high comedy. Now, whether this is a desirable objective, or why it should
be, is a matter which I'm not in the least interested in going into.
But it *is* the objective, and to that end I have been writing plays
which are farcical and without an idea in their funny heads, and

I have also written plays which are all mouth, like *The Gamblers*, and don't bring off the comedy. And occasionally, I think *Jumpers* would be an example, I've got fairly close to a play which works as a funny play and which makes coherent, in terms of theatre, a fairly complicated intellectual argument.

How conscious are you before you start that this play is going to be a nuts-and-bolts comedy, and this other play's going to have philosophical complications?
Wholly. You see, I've only written four full-length plays, one being *Walk on the Water* which doesn't really count in this respect. Now the other three – that includes the new one, *Travesties* – are in this area of trying to marry the play of ideas to comedy or farce. At the same time, I don't think of myself, I don't think of any writer, as ploughing that narrow a field. *After Magritte* and *The Real Inspector Hound* are short plays and they really are an attempt to bring off a sort of comic coup in pure mechanistic terms. They were *conceived* as short plays. The one thing that *The Real Inspector Hound* isn't about, as far as I'm concerned, is theatre critics. I originally conceived a play, exactly the same play, with simply two members of an audience getting involved in the play-within-the-play. But when it comes actually to writing something down which has integral entertainment value, if you like, it very quickly occurred to me that it would be a lot easier to do it with critics, because you've got something known and defined to parody. So it was never a play *about* drama critics. If one wishes to say that it is a play about something more than that, then it's about the dangers of wish-fulfilment. But as soon as the word's out of my mouth I think, shit, it's a play about these two guys, and they're going along to this play, and the whole thing is tragic and hilarious and very, very carefully constructed. I'm very fond of the play because I didn't know how to do it. I just got into it, and I knew that I wanted it somehow to resolve itself in a breathtakingly neat, complex but utterly comprehensible way.

I find it very interesting, this combination of your not knowing what's going to happen and of knowing exactly what's going to happen – or exactly what you want it to come out like, anyway.
Well, for anyone who is actually familiar with *Hound*, I didn't know that the body was Higgs, and I didn't know that Magnus was going to be Puckeridge. I mean, as soon as I realised the body had to be Higgs and, later, Magnus had to be Puckeridge, as solutions to the problems in writing that play, it made sense of all the things I'd been trying to keep going. But it's a sort of risk operation, that particular play. *After Magritte* was worked out very carefully.

There's something equally careful about how many of your plays operate, yet one does wonder very much how particularly the more eccentric situations germinate.
Before *The Real Inspector Hound*, I wrote a sort of goon-show version of it, which had no kind of structure – it was just a situation of two people watching a whodunnit and getting involved in it. I wrote that in Bristol after *The Gamblers*, and then didn't finish it and kept it about, and brought it out again in 1967. But I have enormous difficulty in working out plots, so actually to use *Hamlet*, or a classical whodunnit, or another play (which I'm afraid I've just done again) for a basic structure takes a lot of the pressure off me.

I suppose even plays like Albert's Bridge *or* If You're Glad I'll Be Frank *also rely on . . . not so much familiar situations as familiar metaphors – painting the Forth Bridge, and the faintly ridiculous concept of a 'speaking clock', in those cases.*
Yes – in fact *If You're Glad . . .* actually had its origins in a series the BBC were contemplating, which I don't think ever happened, about people in absurd jobs which didn't really exist, and the idea of doing one about the speaking-clock girl occurred to me then. For me, it is such a relief to get an idea! I know there are writers who are not going to live long enough to do justice to all the ideas they have, but to me it's like being

struck by lightning – and I feel just as powerless to *make* it happen – even, as it were, by hanging about under trees in thunder storms.

Visions and Revisions

Is your working method different when you know you're writing for radio rather than the stage?
Not at all. I mean the structure is obviously geared to radio, but I write the same way – in fact, overwrite, just as much for radio as for anything else. Once I've got an idea and I've got it worked out, I do this incredible ground plan for a play, and I always end up having to create a new first-act curtain, because my intended first-act curtain is an hour further on. Stepping on the tortoise in *Jumpers* was always, as far as I was concerned, going to be the first-act curtain. By the time my people had shut up, an hour and ten minutes had gone, and we were only halfway there. And that tends to happen with my plays.

But the ground plan gives you confidence or something . . .?
Yes, but it turns out to be almost irrelevant, because I am in this terrible self-imposed trap, where I feel I can't begin without knowing exactly what I'm going to do, and then the only way you know what you're going to do is by beginning. The play I've just finished, I started working on it and thinking about it round about March, and I vaguely said to the RSC I'd try and do it by the end of July, because I knew what the nucleus was. As it turned out, I couldn't get going before May, and between March and May I was just plodding about trying to make sense of the material, because I didn't quite know what to do with it. And I think it was June when I actually started writing this play which I'd said I could do by the end of July. But by simply *writing something*, in the space of half a second as you reach a certain point, you create the whole next two scenes, which you simply couldn't have reached after weeks of walking around just thinking – it's a ludicrous procedure and I never seem to

learn from it. Yet it still seems to be necessary in a way, because one always feels one is writing oneself into a tunnel, and one might be going completely on the wrong track.

When it suddenly gels you then find yourself writing quite quickly?
Yes, it's always been smashing except this last time, as it happens, when I was still looking for answers all the way through . . .

You write consecutively once you get started?
Yes, absolutely.

Do you find then that the first version goes through many revisions?
No, it goes through revisions when I'm doing it, in the sense that I tend to rewrite each page half a dozen times, four times or twenty times, so by the time I've done the first draft it's *been* revised so often on the way that the only thing to do is either to tidy it or to change it totally, if you see what I mean.

Do you talk to people whose opinions you trust while you're writing?
No.

Do you discuss what's probably going to be the final draft with the director or company you're going to work with?
No, I just do it and deliver it, like a parcel.

How disciplined and organised are you when you're writing a play?
When there's no pressure on me I'm not disciplined at all, but when I'm writing seriously I get up and write and eat my lunch in four minutes and write, stop when my wife gets home, and see the children for about two hours, 'be daddy' for two hours, and eat, and then I work from about nine until one or two in the morning, and go to bed and then do it again. The thing is

that, through character-flaw, I always end up being late anyway, that's why I do it. It's not because I'm disciplined, it's
because I'm panicked when I'm in the shit again. I bring the
whole thing on myself by walking about the garden for two
months thinking that I'm actually getting somewhere, and then
abruptly I realise that I'm going to be incredibly late and incon-
venience a great number of people. From that moment on, it's
absolutely impossible for me to, say, put a plug on the hoover
– *there's no time for that for God's sake, I'm late!*

A Writer for Hire

You talked earlier about Rosencrantz and Guildenstern *being
very much a play for the middle sixties – do you feel yourself
aware of a 'contemporary mood' while you're writing?*
No, I don't know that I could define such a thing. It was just
that in that play the resonances happened to be in tune with the
resonances associated with all sorts of other writers at the time.

*You clearly don't feel yourself part of a 'movement' either, and
your plays could hardly be called social or political. Does this
mean you have no strong political feelings, or simply that
they're not what you want to write plays about?*
Look, can we clear a few decks to avoid confusion? I'm a professional writer – I'm for hire, if you like – as well as being
someone who pursues his own path in his writing. Latterly I
have been able to stick to accepting the kind of jobs which happen to lie on my own path, but in the past I've written all kinds
of stuff, everything from seventy episodes of a serial translated
into Arabic for Bush House, to a one-off spy thing for
Granada. Furthermore, the plays which I do from pure choice
are not all of a kind either. I find it confusing to talk about 'my
plays' as though *Hound* and *Jumpers* were the same sort of
thing. Obviously, the two have things in common – for example, *Jumpers* is a serious play dealt with in the farcical terms
which in *Hound* actually *constitute* the play. Much the same is

true of the play I have just finished, *Travesties*, which (and this is pertinent to your question) asks whether the words 'revolutionary' and 'artist' are capable of being synonymous, or whether they are mutually exclusive, or something in between. Okay. So forget the Arabs and *Hound* and whatever, and here I am as the author of *Jumpers*, *Travesties*, and of my next unwritten unthought-of play which we will, optimistically, assume represents perfectly the kind of theatre I am interested in. That's 'my plays'. Next – 'political plays'. Well, here are some plays which I have seen or read in the last year or so and which I assume all go into your political bag: Hampton's *Savages*, Griffiths's *The Party*, Fugard's *Sizwe Bansi is Dead*, and his *Hello and Goodbye*, and for that matter the old one, *The Blood Knot* (I haven't seen the latest one yet), Hare's *The Great Exhibition* – and *Slag* if you like – and Brenton, again I haven't seen *Magnificence*, only the earlier ones, and there was another very good Griffiths – *Occupations* – and then the combined work, *Lay By*. Well anyway, regardless of how political or social any or all of these plays are as far as you are concerned, I'll proceed on the assumption that you wouldn't ask any of these playwrights why they didn't write political plays.

I'd have quibbles with one or two, but go ahead.
Well, there are political plays which are about specific situations, and there are political plays which are about a general political situation, and there are plays which are *political acts* in themselves, insofar as it can be said that attacking or insulting or shocking an audience is a political act (and it *is* said). There are even plays *about* politics which are about as *political* as *Charley's Aunt*. The term 'political play' is a loose one if one is thinking of *Roots* as well as *Lear* – I mean Bond's – as well as *Lay By*. So much so that I don't think it is meaningful or useful to make that distinction between them and *Jumpers* – still less so in the case of *Travesties*, and down to zero in the case of my next play but three which I'll call *XYZ*.

Well, I don't know yet about XYZ *or* Travesties, *but in terms of* Jumpers . . .

Jumpers obviously isn't a political act, nor is it a play about politics, nor is it a play about ideology. There is an element in it which satirises a joke-fascist outfit but you can safely ignore that too. On the other hand the play reflects my belief that all political acts have a moral basis to them and are meaningless without it.

Is that disputable?

Absolutely. For a start it goes against Marxist-Leninism in particular, and against all materialistic philosophy. I believe all political acts must be judged in moral terms, in terms of their consequences. Otherwise they are simply attempts to put the boot on some other foot. There is a sense in which contradictory political arguments are restatements of each other. For example, Leninism and Fascism are restatements of totalitarianism.

Two Faces of Totalitarianism

I disagree profoundly. Doesn't this reduce politics entirely to theory, whether it's for better or worse, whereas one has got to take into account the actual effects on human beings of what it's done and is doing?

Exactly. The repression which for better or worse turned out to be Leninism in action after 1917 was very much worse than anything which had gone on in Tsarist Russia. I mean, in purely mundane boring statistical terms, which sometimes can contain the essence of a situation, it is simply true that in the ten years after 1917 fifty times more people were done to death than in the *fifty years* before 1917. The boot, in other words, was on the other foot, and how, but the point is not to compare one ruthless regime against another – it is to set each one up against a moral standard, a consistent idea of what constitutes good and bad in the way human beings treat each other regardless of class, colour or ideology, and at least my poor professor in *Jumpers* got *that* right. Even before I read Lenin it always seemed to me – well, curious, that while he was in a Tsarist prison, and in Tsarist exile, he managed to research and write his book on the development of capitalism in Russia, and receive books and magazines, and write to friends, all that, whereas – well, compare Solzhenitsyn.

People tend to think of Stalinism as being something else, a perversion of Leninism. That is an absurd and foolish untruth, and it is one on which much of the Left bases itself. Lenin perverted Marxism, and Stalin carried on from there. When one reads pre-revolutionary Lenin, notably *What Is to Be Done?* but also all the letters and articles in which he railed against the early Marxists who had the temerity to disagree with him, one can see with awful clarity that ideological differences are often temperamental differences in ideological disguise – and also that the terror to come was implicit in the Lenin of 1900. (Incidentally, artistic differences are also liable to be temperamental differences in artistic disguise. Perhaps we can get back to that in a minute.) The great irony about Marx was that his impulses were deeply moral while his intellect insisted on a materialistic view of the world. His theory of capital, his theory of value, and his theory of revolution, have all been refuted by modern economics and by history. In short he got it wrong. But he was a giant whose shadow still reaches us precisely for the reason that, wrong as he was in detail, the force he represented sprung from a sense of universal moral justice. He realised which way things would *have* to go, and then he put together a materialistic theory which was quite irrelevant, like sticking scaffolding on a moving train. It was only a matter of time before somebody – it turned out to be Bernstein in 1900 – somebody with the benefit of an extra fifty years' hindsight, would actually point out that Marx had got it wrong, but that it didn't matter because social justice was going to come through other means. Bernstein reckoned that the class war wasn't the way, that human solidarity was a better bet than class solidarity. And this argument between 'hards' and 'softs' constitutes a great deal of radical argument today. It is not an argument about tactics – that's just surface dressing – it's an argument about philosophy, I mean Bernstein stuck his banner on the grave of Kant. So I'd like to write a play – say, XYZ – which would pertain to anything from a Latin American coup to the British Left, and probably when I've done it I'll still be asked why I don't write political plays.

If you are, perhaps it would be because your plays – to date, that is – are so philosophically opaque that they don't really make clear statements. I'm thinking particularly of the philosophical element in Jumpers.

Opacity would be a distinct failure in the play. I don't think of it as being opaque anyway, and I consider clarity is essential. On the other hand, if you mean that the mixing up of ideas in farce is a source of confusion, well, yes, God knows why I try to do it like that – presumably because I *am* like that. Plays are the people who write them. Seriousness compromised by frivolity. It gets up a few people's noses, but that's not important. At the same time I'm making all this sound much more self-confident than I feel. The thing is, if my plays were the end products of my ideas, they'd have it all more pat, but a lot of the time I've ended up trying to work out the ultimate implications of what I have written. My plays are a lot to do with the fact that *I just don't know*. This is something I tried to bring to the surface in a TV *One Pair of Eyes* programme, but to me it is even more evident in the thickets of dialogue. Few statements remain unrebutted. But I'm not going to rebut the things I have been saying just now. One thing I feel sure about is that a materialistic view of history is an insult to the human race.

Possibility of Political Art

Isn't there a danger that one just ends up with the conclusion that all political art is perhaps well-intentioned but impotent, so why bother?

The possibility of political art having a political effect in close-up, in specific terms, certainly exists, though I can't offhand think of an example of it happening, but it is in any case marginal compared to the possible and actual effects of, say, journalism. On that level, one *World in Action* is worth a thousand plays. Come to think of it, *Cathy Come Home* could be cited, though I don't know if it *changed* anything. Look, do you know who Adam Raphael is?

There are two, aren't there – one a BBC correspondent, one on the Guardian.
Right. The *Guardian* Adam Raphael is the one who broke the story on wages in South Africa. Within forty-eight hours the wages went up. Now Athol Fugard can't do that. God knows he can do things which Adam Raphael will never ever be able to do, but it is self-evident that the situation provokes a very important question, whether it is better to be Adam Raphael or Athol Fugard. But of course that sounds as though one is choosing between alternatives, whereas I am simply saying: one is doing a short-term job and one a long-term job. Both are important. I think I'd like to spell this out more because I usually cut corners and end up appearing to say that because art can't do what *World in Action* does, art is unimportant, plays are unimportant, and one might as well write *Pyjama Tops* as *Galileo*. The *Guardian* quoted me in 14 point bold quoting Auden saying that his poems hadn't saved a single Jew from the gas chambers, and ever since then I've wanted to pay homage to Auden, or his shade, with the rider that I was making a point about the short-term not the long-term. Briefly, art – Auden or Fugard or the entire cauldron – is important because it provides the moral matrix, the moral sensibility, from which we make our judgements about the world. Well, Auden and Fugard don't need to be told that, nor you, but that is ultimately the answer to your question –

What question?
The question about the impotence of political art –

Yes – and this is presumably why your plays tend to bear on life in an oblique, distant, generalised way –
Well, that's what art is best at. The objective is the universal perception, isn't it? By all means realise that perception in terms of a specific event, even a specific political event, but I'm not impressed by art *because* it's political, I believe in art being good art or bad art, not relevant art or irrelevant art. The plain truth is that if you are angered or disgusted by a particular injustice or immorality, and you want to do something about it, *now*, *at once*, then you can hardly do worse than write a play about it. That's what art is bad at. But the less plain truth is that *without* that play and plays like it, without artists, the injustice will *never* be eradicated. In other words, because of Athol Fugard, to stretch a point, the *Guardian* understood that the Raphael piece was worth leading the paper with, worth printing. That's why it's good and right that *Savages* has a long run in the West End. All kinds of people have said to me, how ridiculous to sit in the theatre and watch this, how pointless, how useless – what they were saying in effect was that Hampton's play wasn't going to save a single Indian, but that is to misunderstand what art means in the world. It's a terrible reason for *not* writing *Savages*.

At the same time, Hampton's plays, and Fugard's plays, are absolutely different from yours. You are neither Fugard nor World in Action.
Of course. Fugard writes out of his experience as a white South African living against the current in a white supremacist regime. I write out of my experience as a middle-class bourgeois who prefers to read a book almost to doing anything else. If you say, then Fugard is much more important, I'd say, yes, of course he is! He's very much more important than me, just as he's much more important than the gang of playwrights who

think that waving your cock at the audience is a revolutionary act and makes a play 'political'.

Brains as Well as Balls

Have you read or seen much of what's been happening in fringe theatre?
I've read much more than I've seen, and perhaps that isn't fair to some of the fringe playwrights. For example, I've got a lot of enjoyment out of reading Brenton – I've only seen *Gum and Goo* – and I think of him as a very good, very funny writer, and of course he's a scatological writer, but the easy equation between being *scatological* and being *political* is one I resist, it's intellectually shoddy.

Presumably you didn't see the Powellite Measure for Measure.
No – but I don't mean this point to revolve around Brenton particularly, it's not fair to him – I'm talking about the general and ubiquitous equation between the sexual and socialist revolutions. When *Lay By* is playing the Haymarket to a house packed with stockbrokers and property developers I hope the authors turn out to have brains as well as balls. And of course they do. *Occupations* and *The Party* are plays I respect. So is *The Great Exhibition* by David Hare, which I love, in fact Hare is the kind of writer-craftsman who appeals to me most. I said something earlier about artistic differences often being merely temperamental differences, and you can see what I'm getting at now. But in the published text of the Hare play there's an epigraph in the form of a statistical table showing that down the ages the top ten per cent of the population owned eighty per cent of the property – I'm going by memory, but it's something like that. Now he only took the table down to 1960, and it so happens, because it's one with which I'm familiar, that it goes on to show that by 1970 a huge change had taken place – a much less unequal distribution. Perhaps the later figures only became available after the play went to press.

Statistically they upset the argument, anyway, but the statistics are appended to a play which succeeds because it is a brilliant comedy which would fit comfortably in Shaftesbury Avenue (I can't think why it didn't transfer), and the West End is exactly the place where a political writer *should* put a play saying the Labour Party is a joke.

The point being –?
The point being that to me that play is 'important' because it is writing – comedy writing, as it happens – of a very high order, not because it is saying something 'important' about a statistical subtext. If Hare were a bad writer, the play would be totally unimportant. When I saw Bond's *Lear* I thought and still think that it contains a few things that are as good as anything in Shakespeare. Do you remember how the blind old man says how the holes in the ground 'cry out' before he puts his foot in them? And there's a line about somebody oversleeping on the morning after the battle 'because all the birds were dead'. Now that is probably the single image, the single line out of a whole year's playgoing, which I'll carry about with me till I'm dead, as I'll carry about, say, Auden's glacier knocking in the cupboard. Now I may be quite wrong about this, but I feel that that sort of response is the *least* important thing about the play as far as Bond is concerned. I imagine the thing which was supposed to make the experience rewarding was the overall statement about violence and power, which was simply a momentous restatement of something one walked *into* the theatre with.

You said that in Travesties *you asked the question whether the terms 'artist' and 'revolutionary' were capable of being synonymous – did you come to any sort of conclusion?*
The play puts the question in a more extreme form. It asks whether an artist has to justify himself in political terms *at all*. For example, if Joyce were alive today, he would say, juntas may come and juntas may go but Homer goes on for ever. And

when he was alive he *did* say that the history of Ireland, troubles and all, was justified because it produced *him* and *he* produced *Ulysses*. Okay. So clearly one now has to posit a political prisoner taking comfort from the thought that at least he is in the country of Joyce, or of Homer, and to ask oneself whether Joyce, in moral terms, was myopic or had better vision than lesser men. And my answer to that question is liable to depend on the moment at which you run out of tape. Of course one feels uneasy in trying to work out questions that involve *oneself*, in terms of authentic geniuses, but it helps to clarify the issue. How do you measure the legacy of a genius who believed in art for art's sake?

Moving towards 'Issues'

Your plays are evidently at least moving *in the direction of 'issues'.*
Jumpers still breaks its neck to be entertaining as well, which was the intention, and it's still the way I tend to write things, though I think it's gradually becoming less so. With *Rosencrantz*, whatever lessons could be drawn from it, they were all just implied and not necessarily by me at that. *Jumpers* was the first play in which I specifically set out to ask a question and try to answer it, or at any rate put the counter-question.

The way you've been talking, am I right in thinking that you feel that it's your full-length plays which constitute your more important work, and the shorter the play the more occasional it is?
Yes, in practice. But I've been asked to do a short play now, and though I've no idea what I'll do, if anything, there's absolutely no reason why it shouldn't be a serious play. I think actually that it probably isn't a matter of length, it just happens that at the time when I wrote the short plays my inclinations were slightly different.

Writer at Rehearsal

How far do you involve yourself in the first production of your plays?
Wholly.

And does the play itself undergo any change in the process?
Some, yes. One day when I was out for ten minutes, Peter Wood cut a scene in two and played it backwards, and it was better. So we kept it. That was in *Jumpers*.

Normally you're there all the time to make sure things like that don't happen?
No, I sit there to *do* things like that if they're necessary. I'm very free about that sort of thing as long as I'm there, and pretty rigid about it if I'm not. I think of rehearsal as being a very important part of getting the play right. Of the directors I've worked with, I had very good rapport with Robert Chetwyn, and with Peter Wood, and that is the main thing – it's not that somebody is born to direct your plays, or that they particularly understand them. I always feel it's like what Evelyn Waugh said about the Second World War, that the great thing was to spend it among friends. Getting a play on is so awful, the important thing is to spend it among friends.

'The Art of Theatre', interview with Shusha Guppy, *Paris Review*, 1988

Though it appeared in the magazine's Winter 1988 edition, the interview from which these extracts are taken took place early in that year, while Hapgood *was in rehearsal.*

SQ: *How are the rehearsals going?*
TS: So far they are conforming to pattern, alas! I mean I am suffering from the usual delusion that the play was ready before we went into production. It happens every time. I give my publish-

er the finished text of the play so that it can be published not too long after the opening in London, but by the time the galleys arrive they're hopelessly out of date because of all the changes I've made during rehearsals. This time I gave them *Hapgood* and told them that it was folly to pretend it would be unaltered, but I added, 'I think it won't be as bad as the others.' It turned out to be worse. Yesterday I realised that a chunk of information in the third scene ought to be in the second scene, and it's like pulling out entrails: as in any surgery there's blood. As I was doing it I watched a documentary about Crick and Watson's discovery of the structure of DNA – the double helix. There was only one way all the information they had could fit but they couldn't figure out what it was. I felt the same. So the answer to your question is that the rehearsals are going well and enjoyably, but that I'm very busy with my pencil.

What provokes the changes? Does the transfer from your imagination to the stage alter your perception? Or do the director and the actors make suggestions?

They make a few suggestions which I am often happy to act upon. In the theatre there is often a tension, almost a contradiction, between the way real people would think and behave, and a kind of imposed dramaticness. I like dialogue which is slightly more brittle than life. I have always admired and wished to write one of those 1940s film scripts where every line is written with a sharpness and economy which is frankly artificial. Peter Wood, the director with whom I've worked for sixteen years, sometimes feels obliged to find a humanity, perhaps a romantic ambiguity, in scenes which are not written like that but which, I hope, contain the possibility. I like surface gloss, but it's all too easy to get that right for the first night only to find that *that* was the best performance of the play; from then on the gloss starts cracking apart. The ideal is to make the groundwork so deep and solid that the actors are continually discovering new possibilities under the surface, so that the best performance turns out to be the last one. In my plays there are usually a few lines which Peter loathes, for their slickness or coldness, and we have a lot of fairly enjoyable squabbles which entail some messing about with the text as we rehearse. In the case of *Hapgood* there is a further problem which has to do with the narrative mechanics, because it's a plotty play, and I can't do plots and have no interest in plots.

Yet you have produced some complex and plausible plots. So why the aversion?
The subject matter of the play exists before the story and it is always something abstract. I get interested by a notion of some kind and see that it has dramatic possibilities. Gradually I see how a pure idea can be married with a dramatic event. But it is still not a play, until you invent a plausible narrative. Sometimes this is not too hard – *The Real Thing* was fairly straightforward. For *Hapgood*, the thing that I wanted to write about seemed to suit the form of an espionage thriller. It's not the sort of thing I read or write.

What was the original idea that made you think of an espionage thriller?
It had to do with mathematics. I am not a mathematician but I was aware that for centuries mathematics was considered the queen of the sciences because it claimed certainty. It was grounded on some fundamental certainties – axioms – which led to others. But then, in a sense, it all started going wrong, with concepts like non-Euclidean geometry – I mean, looking at it from Euclid's point of view. The mathematics of physics turned out to be grounded on *un*certainties, on probability and chance. And if you're me, you think – there's a play in that. Finding an idea for a play is like picking up a shell on a beach. I started reading about mathematics without finding what I was looking for. In the end I realised that what I was after was something which any first-year physics student is familiar with, namely quantum mechanics. So I started reading about that.

It is said that you research your plays thoroughly.
I don't think of it as research. I read for interest and enjoyment, and when I cease to enjoy it I stop. I didn't research quantum mechanics but I was fascinated by the mystery which lies in the foundation of the observable world, of which the most familiar example is the wave/particle duality of light. I thought it was a good metaphor for human personality. The language of espionage lends itself to this duality – think of the double agent.

You seem to think the success of the play has so much to do with its production. Do you, therefore, get involved with the lighting, costumes, etc.? Please give examples, anecdotes.
It is obvious that a given text (think of any classic) can give rise to a satisfying event or an unsatisfying one. These are the only relative values which end up mattering in the theatre. A great production of a *Black Comedy* is better than a mediocre production of a *Comedy of Errors*. When the writing is over, the event is the thing. I attend the first rehearsal of a new play and every rehearsal after that, as well as discussions with designers, lighting designers, costume designers . . . I like to be there, even though I'm doing more listening than talking. When *Hapgood* was being designed, I kept insisting that the shower in the first scene wouldn't work unless it was in the middle of the upper stage, so that Hapgood could approach us facing down the middle. Peter and Carl insisted that the scene wouldn't work unless the main entrance doors were facing the audience. They were quite right, but so was I. We opened out of town with the shower in the wings, and it didn't work at all, so we ended up having to find a way to have both the doors and the shower in view of the audience. The look of the thing is one thing. The sound of it is more important. David Lean was quoted as saying somewhere that the hardest part of making films is knowing how fast or slow to make the actors speak. I suddenly saw how *horribly* difficult that made it to make a film. Because you can't change your mind. When you write a play, it makes a certain kind of noise in your head, and for me rehearsals are

largely a process of trying to reproduce that noise. It is not always wise to reproduce it in every instance, but that's another question. The first time I met Laurence Olivier, we were casting *Rosencrantz and Guildenstern*. He asked me about the Player. I said the Player should be a sneaky, snake-like sort of person. Olivier looked dubious. The part was given, thank God, or Olivier, to Graham Crowden, who is about six-foot-four and roars like a lion. Olivier came to rehearsal one day. He watched for about fifteen minutes, and then, leaving, made one suggestion. I forget what it was. At the door he turned, twinkled at us all and said, 'Just the odd pearl,' and left.

Is it a very anxious moment for you, working up to the first night?
Yes. You are trying to imagine the effect on people who know nothing about what is going on and whom you are taking through the story. In a normal spy thriller you contrive to delude the reader until all is revealed in the denouement. This is the exact opposite of a scientific paper in which the denouement – the discovery – is announced at the beginning. *Hapgood* to some extent follows this latter procedure. It is not a whodunnit because we are told who has done it near the beginning of the first act, so the story becomes *how* he did it.

Did you draw on some famous spies, like Philby or Blunt, for your characters?
Not at all. I wasn't really interested in authenticity. John le Carré's *A Perfect Spy* uses the word 'joe' for an agent who is being run by somebody, and I picked it up. I have no idea whether it is authentic or invented by le Carré.

What happens on the first night? Do you sit among the audience or in a concealed place at the back? And what do you do afterwards?
The first *audience* is more interesting than the first night. We now have previews, which makes a difference. Actually, my

play *The Real Inspector Hound* was the first to have previews in London, in 1968. Previews are essential. The idea of going straight from a dress rehearsal to a first night is frightening. It happened with *Rosencrantz and Guildenstern* and we got away with it, but for *Jumpers* we had several previews by the end of which I had taken fifteen minutes out of the play. I hate first nights. I attend out of courtesy for the actors and afterwards we all have a drink and go home.

How does the London theatre world differ from New York?
Theatre in New York is nearer to the street. In London you have to go deep into the building, usually, to reach the place where theatre happens. On Broadway, only the fire doors separate you from the sidewalk and you're lucky if the sound of a police car doesn't rip the envelope twice a night. This difference means something, I'm not quite sure what. Well, as Peter Brook will tell you, the theatre has its roots in something holy, and perhaps we in London are still a little holier than thou. The potential rewards of theatre in New York are really too great for its own good. One bull's-eye and you're rich and famous. The rich get more famous and the famous get richer. You're the talk of the town. The taxi drivers have read about you and they remember you for a fortnight. You get to be photographed for *Vogue* with new clothes and Vuitton luggage, if that's your bag. If it's a new play, everyone owes the writer, they celebrate him – the theatre owners, the producers, the actors. Even the stage doorman is somehow touched by the wand. The sense of so much depending on success is very hard to ignore, perhaps impossible. It leads to disproportionate anxiety and disproportionate relief or disappointment. The British are more phlegmatic about these things. You know about British phlegm. The audiences, respectively, are included in this. In New York, expressions of appreciation have succumbed to galloping inflation – in London only the Americans stand up to applaud the actors, and only American audiences emit those high-pitched barks which signify the highest form of approval. But if you

mean the difference between what happens onstage in London and New York, there isn't much, and there's no difference between the best. Cross-fertilisation has evened out what I believe used to be quite a sharp difference between styles of American and British acting, although it is probably still a little harder to find American actors with an easy command of rhetoric, and British actors who can produce that controlled untidiness which, when we encountered it a generation ago, seemed to make acting lifelike for the first time.

I have heard that in New York people sit up and wait for the New York Times *review, which makes or breaks a show. It is not like that in London, but do you worry all night until the reviews come out the next day?*

Certainly I'm anxious. One is implicated in other people's fortunes – producers, directors, actors – and one wants the play to succeed for their sake as much as for one's own. If there is a favorable consensus among the reviewers, you accept it as a reasonable judgement. If you get mixed reviews, you are heartened by those who enjoyed it and depressed by the rejections. What one is anxious about is the judgement on the event rather than the play. None of us would have worked so hard if we didn't believe in the play, and so we don't need a critic to tell us whether we liked it, but whether we succeeded in putting it across. For the text is only one aspect of an evening at the theatre; often the most memorable moments have little to do with the words uttered. It is the totality – to use the jargon – which is being judged. A favourable judgement means that on that occasion the play has worked, which does not mean that it always will.

Do critics matter as much?

In the long term, not at all. In the short term they give an extra push, or conversely give you more to push against; but favourable reviews won't save a play for long if the audiences don't like it, and vice versa. The play has to *work*.

I would like to know what you mean by 'work'.
It has to be truthful. The audience must believe. But the play is also a physical mechanism. Getting that mechanism to work takes an awful lot of time and preoccupation. The way music comes in and out, lights vary, etc. When you've got all that right you can get back to the text. Otherwise, the fact that it seems right on paper won't help you.

Do you change things according to what the reviews say?
No. But I change things according to what happens to the play, and what I think of it. Sometimes one is involved in a revival and one wants to change things because one has changed oneself, and what used to seem intriguing or amusing might now strike one as banal. Any revival in which I am involved is liable to change.

It has been said that Kenneth Tynan was the last critic who had a definite point of view and was bold enough to express it, thereby influencing the direction of the theatre. So perhaps critics do make a difference.
Ken had enthusiasms. Some lasted longer than others and while he had them he pushed them. But you have to read critics critically and make the necessary adjustment according to what you know about them. When I was a critic – on my local paper in Bristol and later for a magazine in London – I floundered between pronouncing what I hoped were magisterial judgements and merely declaring my own taste. If I might quote myself from a previous interview – 'I was not a good critic because I never had the moral character to pan a friend. I'll rephrase that – I had the moral character never to pan a friend.'

But Tynan introduced into England what one associates with French intellectual life – a kind of intellectual terrorism, when suddenly one author or school is 'in' and another 'out', and woe betide he who disagrees! He destroyed people like Terence Rattigan and Christopher Fry and all those he called 'bour-

geois' playwrights, and you had to love Osborne and Brecht or
else! But I recently saw Rattigan's Separate Tables and thought
it very good indeed, infinitely better than some of the plays Ken
had praised and made fashionable.

Which shows that he didn't destroy them. However, I know
what you mean, and one or two of my close friends thoroughly disapproved of Ken. But I hope they know what I mean
when I stick up for him. The first time I met Ken was when I
was summoned to his tiny office when the National Theatre
offices consisted of a wooden hut on waste ground, and I was
so awed by being in a small room with him that I began to stut-
ter. Ken stuttered, as you know. So we sat stuttering at each
other, mainly about his shirt, which was pale lemon and came
from Turnbull and Asser in Jermyn Street. This was in the late
summer of 1966 when we wore roll-neck shirts.

*You have been praised for your eloquence, your use of language
– your aphorisms, puns, epigrams – as if you invented them,
wrote them down and put them into your characters' mouths.
Do you?*

No. They tend to show up when I need them. But perhaps it is
significant that very often a particular line is more or less arbi-
trarily attached to a particular character. I can take a line from
one character and give it to another. As I just told you, there
was something in the third scene of Hapgood which I had to
put in the second scene. But the dialogue was not between the
same two people – only one of them was the same. So the lines
of a female character became those of a male, and it made no
difference. In *Night and Day* I had to invent an African dictator, but there was no way I could do it unless he was the only
African dictator who had been to the London School of
Economics. You don't have to be African or a dictator to make
those observations about the British press. I rely heavily on an
actor's performance to help individualise a character.

Do you act out all the characters as you write?

Sometimes. I walk around the room speaking the dialogue.

Once you've got the idea and devised the narrative, do you take notes while you're reading up on the subject?
Not really. Sometimes, over the course of several months, I might cover a page with odds and ends, many of which might find their way into the play. But I don't write down in notebooks, nor jot down what I overhear – nothing like that.

In the course of writing the play, do you get surprises, because for example, you don't know what a character is going to do next, or how the story will end?
Absolutely.

What about the order of the play, the number of acts and scenes?
I don't work out the whole plot before I begin, just the general outline. The play alters as you write it. For example, in *Jumpers* the end of the first act in my scheme turned out to be the end of the second act, followed by only an epilogue. *Hapgood* was in three acts and is now in two. The reason for the change is partly intrinsic and partly circumstantial. Managements prefer two-act plays because they think that audiences like only one interval, and Peter thought it would be better for the play. It shows how pragmatic the theatre is, perhaps the most pragmatic art form, apart from advertising. For example, the male secretary, Maggs, used to be Madge, a woman. But when we came to choose the understudies we realised that if the secretary were male he could understudy so-and-so. It turned out to be better for the play also, because then Hapgood is the only woman surrounded by all these men. But at first it was a question of casting.

Having got your outline, do you proceed from the beginning to the end chronologically?
Yes I do. I write plays from beginning to end, without making

stabs at intermediate scenes, so the first thing I write is the first line of the play. By that time I have formed some idea of the set but I don't write that down. I don't write down anything which I can keep in my head – stage directions and so on. When I have got to the end of the play – which I write with a fountain pen; you can't scribble with a typewriter – there is almost nothing on the page except what people say. Then I dictate the play, ad-libbing all the stage directions into a tape machine from which my secretary transcribes the first script.

What are the pitfalls on the way? Things that might get you stuck?
It is not like playing the violin – not difficult in that way. The difficulties vary at different stages. The first is that you haven't got anything you wish to write a play about. Then you get an idea, but it might be several ideas that could belong to two or three plays. Finally, if you are lucky, they may fit into the same play. The next difficulty, as I said before, is to translate these abstract ideas into concrete situations. That is a very long and elaborate period. Another difficulty is knowing when to start; it's chicken-and-egg – you don't know what you're going to write until you start, and you can't start until you know. Finally, in some strange, quantum-mechanical way, the two trains arrive on the same line without colliding, and you can begin. The following stage is not exactly pleasant but exciting and absorbing – you live with the fear that 'it' may go away. There is a three–month period when I don't want to say good morning to anyone lest I miss the thought that would make all the difference.

Once the play begins to take shape, what do you feel?
Tremendous joy. Because whenever I finish a play I have no feeling that I would ever have another one to write.

Do you disappear from home to write?
I disappear into myself. Sometimes I go away for a short period,

say a week, to think and concentrate, then I come back home to carry on.

Where do you work and when?
I have a very nice long room, which used to be the stable. It has a desk and lots of paper, etc. But most of my plays are written on the kitchen table at night, when everybody has gone to bed and I feel completely at peace. During the day, somehow I don't get much done; although I have a secretary who answers the phone, I always want to know who it is, and I generally get distracted.

Do you have an ideal spectator in mind when you write?
Perhaps I do. Peter Wood has quite a different spectator in mind, one who is a cross between Rupert Bear and Winnie the Pooh. He assumes bafflement in order to force me to explain on a level of banality. If I had an ideal spectator it would be someone more sharp-witted and attentive than the average theatre-goer whom Peter thinks of. A lot of changes in rehearsals have to do with reconciling his spectator with mine.

You have said that all the characters talk like you. Does that mean that you have trouble creating female characters? You once said, 'There is an area of mystery about women which I find difficult to penetrate.' Yet the eponymous character of your new play, Hapgood, is a woman.
I wonder when I said that! It is not what I feel now. When I said I wasn't interested by plot or character I meant that they are not the point for me. Before writing Night and Day I thought, 'I'm sick of people saying there are no good parts for women in my plays, so I'll do one.' It turned out not to be just about a woman, and I thought, 'Well, one day I'll do a Joan of Arc.' But I never think, 'I'm writing for a woman so it had better be different.'

How important are curtain lines?

Very important, because they define the play's shape, like the spans of a bridge. It's like architecture – there is a structure and a conscious architect at work. Otherwise you could decide to have an interval at 8:30, and whatever was being said at that moment would be your curtain line. It wouldn't do.

You said that you have worked with Peter Wood for sixteen years, but are you always closely involved with your plays' productions?
In this country, yes. In America I was involved with the production of *The Real Thing*, which was directed by Mike Nichols. But who knows what's going on elsewhere? You are pleased the plays are being done and hope for the best.

You have been accused of superficiality; some people say that your plays are all linguistic pyrotechnics, dazzling wordplay, intelligent punning, but that they don't have much substance. How do you react to that charge?
I suppose there is a certain justice in it, insofar as if I were to write an essay instead of a play about any of these subjects it wouldn't be a profound essay.

Nowadays fame has become a thing in itself. In French the word is gloire, *which is nicer because it denotes achievement; it has connotations of glory. But fame doesn't: you can be famous just for being famous. Now that you are, do you still feel excited by it, or do you think it isn't that important?*
Oh, I like it. The benefits are psychological, social and material. The first because I don't have to worry about who I am – I am the man who has written these plays. The social advantages appeal to half of me because there are two of me: the recluse and the fan. And the fan in me is still thrilled to meet people I admire. As for the material side, I like having some money. The best way to gauge wealth is to consider the amount of money which you can spend *thoughtlessly* – a casual purchase which simply doesn't register. The really rich can do it in Cartier's; I'm

quite happy if I can do it in a good bookshop or a good restaurant.

What about the company of your peers, Harold Pinter?
The first time I met Harold Pinter was when I was a journalist in Bristol and he came down to see a student production of *The Birthday Party*. I realised he was sitting in the seat in front of me. I was tremendously intimidated and spent a good long time working out how to engage him in conversation. Finally, I tapped him on the shoulder and said, 'Are you Harold Pinter or do you just look like him?' He said, 'What?' So that was the end of that.

Going back to your work, Jumpers *was about moral philosophy, and in it you attacked logical positivism and its denial that metaphysical questions are valid . . .*
Ah, but remember that I was attacking a dodo – logical positivism was over by the time I wrote the play. I was amused to see Freddy [Sir Alfred] Ayer being interviewed on television. The interviewer asked him what were the defects of logical positivism, and Freddy answered, 'I suppose its main defect was that it wasn't true.' The play addressed itself to a set of attitudes which people didn't think of as philosophical but which in fact were. At the same time, it tried to be a moral play, because while George has the right ideas, he is also a culpable person; while he is defending his ideas and attacking the opposition, he is also neglecting everyone around him and shutting out his wife who is in need, not to mention shooting his hare and stepping on his tortoise.

In the play you say that the Ten Commandments, unlike tennis rules, can't be changed, implying that there are fundamental moral principles which are eternally valid because of their transcendental provenance – their foundation in religion. Do you believe that?
Yes, I do.

143

Are you religious?
Well, I keep looking over my shoulder. When I am asked whether I believe in God, my answer is that I don't know what the question means. I approve of belief in God and I try to behave as if there is one, but that hardly amounts to faith. I don't know what religious certainty would consist of, though many apparently have it. I am uneasy with religious ceremonials, because I think intellectually, and the case for God is not an intellectual one. However, militant humanism grates on me much more than evangelism.

'The Event and the Text', 1988

Stoppard lectured variously under this title in several North American universities during the 1980s; the extracts here are from the version given at McMaster University, Ontario. Talking to students rather than journalists, he emerges attractively as a teacher, encouraging their response more to theatre in general than to his own achievements. He makes two main points: the first (on which he has spoken frequently) is that theatre must be 'pragmatic'; the second, related point is that – though many see him as a highly literary dramatist – a play script should not be seen as 'literature'.

I'm going to begin with a description of part of a production which I never saw myself. When I started out trying to write plays there was a celebrated production of *The Tempest* at one of the Oxford colleges and later on I got to work with some people who had been to see this. Surprisingly often, over the years, the memory of this production would come up. The director I worked with, the designer I worked with – it was something which had stayed in their memory. This was now thirty years ago, and it's still a vignette which comes up in conversation occasionally among people I work with. This production of *The Tempest* took place in the open air in the early evening, and when it became time for Ariel to leave the action of the play he turned and he ran up the stage, away from the audience. Now the stage was a lawn, and the lawn backed on to a lake. He ran across the grass and got to the edge of the lake, and he just kept running, because the director had had the foresight to put a plank walkway just underneath the surface of the water. So you have to imagine: it's become dusk, and quite a lot of the artificial lighting has come on, and back there in the gloom is this lake. And Ariel says his last words and he turns and he runs and he gets to the water and he runs and he goes splish splash, splish splash, right across the lake and into the enfolding dark, until one can only just hear his footsteps making these little splashes, and then ultimately his little figure disappeared from view. And at that moment, from the further shore, a firework rocket was ignited and just went whoosh into the sky and burst into lots of sparks. All the sparks went out one by one and Ariel had gone. This is the thing: you can't write anything as good as that. If you look it up, it says, 'Exit Ariel.'

Now the thing you look it up in appears to be a book. It is a book. It appears to be the same kind of 'thing' that you hold in your hand when you're looking something up in *David Copperfield* or *The Golden Bowl* or whatever. It seems to be a piece of literature – this book thing. This is a coincidence. Really, the point of the distinction which this lecture is going to be making would be made much more quickly, indeed instantly, if there had been an alternative convention for the dissemination of plays. Suppose we just did scrolls, or it all came out on disk, and nobody ever thought of making it look like *David Copperfield* or *For Whom the Bell Tolls* or *Brighton Rock*, or whatever. But they keep looking as though they are the same sort of thing. If you work in the theatre, I think probably especially if you work in the theatre as a writer, you understand very early that they are not the same sort of thing.

I think that you are probably aware of the truism, that poems never get finished; they merely get abandoned. I think that plays never quite get finished either; they get interrupted by rehearsal. The production impedes a process which then very often continues after that first performance has evolved and gone its way and finished and so on. Not all playwrights would stand beside me here and say this. I think that there are a number of writers, perhaps for all I know the majority, who see what they do as nearer a piece of literature than I do: what gets handed in on the first day of rehearsal – I mean that is it – you don't mess about, you don't come back and rewrite it or ask the actors if they have a better idea.

I like a kind of rough theatre where everything goes into the melting pot. I'm extremely jealous of my frontiers, in the sense that I wish to be the only person who can move them, but I consider them to be moveable. When you write a play it makes a certain kind of noise in your head, and the rehearsal and staging is an attempt to persuade the actors to reproduce this noise. Sometimes the actors have a better noise to offer. You know what I'm saying, don't you, about this noise? 'She shouts', 'she whispers', 'she goes on her knees and pleads', 'she whines', or 'she laughs' . . . there's a cadence and a rhythm, and of course, it's expressed in language. But theatre is a curious equation in which language is merely one of the components. The point about this equation is that it has to come out nicely. In other words, you can't mess about with one side of the equals sign without doing some compensating act on the other side. It has to still work as a piece of algebra, if you like. But time and again one discovers that if one walks into the process of staging a play with an algebraic equation in mind, and everybody has to do exactly 4y and you do 3x and you do something cubed: what you get is a sort of very rigid structure which is never going to be as good again as it is on the night you open.

In the best possible world the best show you give is the last one because really you ought to come in with something which remains organic. This, of course, is sometimes a disadvantage as well because plays can go off, like fruit; and of course the soft part goes first, as in fruit. But nevertheless I think if you have the alternative idea that a play is something like this ashtray – here it is and you put it down and you come back in three weeks and there it is again; it hasn't moved, it hasn't changed: then I think what actually happens is that they break. The noise of a play breaking is something which keeps playwrights awake: once they hear it they never forget that noise.

The equation I'm talking about contains, among its elements, not merely the obvious things like the physical limitations: it contains the music of a play, it contains the lighting of a play. I don't know whether this sounds like a truism or something which is faintly surprising, but the length or even the necessary presence of a speech may be altered, one's sense of it, of its necessity, or one's sense of its being too long or not long enough – that can actually be altered by a light. This is why I'm trying to say that what we don't do is what people do when they write *David Copperfield*. We're doing something else. Of course this thing which contains the play, this book – I'm not saying that it doesn't contain bits of literature; very often it may well do; in the case of *The Tempest*, obviously it does. Let's be clear about that: of course there's literature in it. But the expression of it is slightly different. (All these things are my prejudices; don't buy everything!)

To me what is in this book is two things: the one turns into the other. The first thing is an attempt to describe an event which you wish to take place one day; you write this play and you're trying to describe what you want to happen here. The other thing is it's a record of some mythical production which has taken place. It becomes a description retroactively, not of a particular production but a description of an event which may take place again in one form or another – an event which has taken place. I make this distinction because there's a kind of pivot point; it's when the author dies. When you're dead you've had your chance and now it's somebody else's turn. The truism which I want to offer to you, and I think it is one, is that a given text, irrespective of its literary aspirations, or the degree to which it succeeds in realising these aspirations – a given text can give rise to an extraordinarily satisfying and a deeply satisfactory experience, or a lousy one. Otherwise there wouldn't be any bad productions of Shakespeare. Why would there be?

What in fact happens is that the manipulation of the elements tries to achieve some kind of balance with the utterance, the psychological relationships, and the movement of the narrative. I think I could actually now deliver this to you as a question, which you don't have to take as rhetorical, though you don't have to answer out loud either. The first time I ever lectured like this was eighteen years ago – I haven't done it much since – but eighteen years ago when I was a 'promising young playwright' I did this very thing at an American university, just like this, on a campus in the Midwest; I was very innocent in those days and without intending any kind of malice I remarked at one point that I'd never written anything for 'study'. A ripple of consternation went over the auditorium. That was what they did with plays: plays were what you 'studied'. It was a new idea to me that one studies plays. It was a new idea to my audience that one did anything else with plays. But when you look back, those of you who actually go to the theatre, when you look back on things that you've seen, when you remember things which happened to you in a theatre, very often, surprisingly often, what you remember is not actually to do with what anybody wrote – remember Ariel.

I find that that's true of me with my own plays. I'll probably refer to things I wrote myself now and again: this is not an incipient megalomania; it's because it's the only experience I have: I don't go to other people's rehearsals. I did an adaptation of a play by Schnitzler; it's called *Das weite Land* (we called it *Undiscovered Country*). It's a big play, and Schnitzler wanted it done in three acts, with two intermissions. This was at the National Theatre in London, and the director, Peter Wood, was insistent that he wanted to do it with one intermission. And this meant that we did the play right through Act One and halfway through Act Two; we had an intermission and then we did the second half of Act Two and Act Three. Now Act One of this play took place in the garden and conservatory of the house of a rich Viennese industrialist. Act Two took place in the lobby of a chic mountaineering hotel in the Dolomites – in this case it even had a working elevator. The idea was that without anybody going out and having a drink you would go from this garden and conservatory and then you'd be in this hotel lobby in the Dolomites, and you'd still be there, thinking this is great.

Come the technical rehearsal, we got to the end of Act One (because it was a translation/adaption I hadn't been quite as present during rehearsals as I normally am with my own plays) and they were about to embark on this transition. I sat at the back and what was on that stage was just too alarming and depressing for words. There were people wandering around trailing cables and there were greenhouses falling about and hotel lobbies falling in and everything had stopped and it just looked dreadful! The director (I'd known him for ten years by then, we'd done a lot of work together) was his usual insouciant self. I thought, 'This time he really has pushed it and blown it.' But that was a dry run, and I'll describe what happened ultimately when he got what he wanted. As we got to the end of Act One and time to do the scene change, a lot of dry ice began to be pumped from all around. After a very short time the stage was up to about shoulder height in this white fog. This gave a certain coherence to the chaos; it certainly improved matters. I was still reserving my judgement at that point. The next thing that happened was that in the middle of the stage – out of this fog – a fist holding an ice-axe went straight up and was followed by a shoulder with a coil of rope, and then a little woolly hat, and then a mountaineer was standing there; he started pulling on his rope, and pulled another mountaineer up out of this fog (there was no trapdoor; he crawled through the fog from the wings). Then these two guys started pulling on the rope, and a third person with woolly hat and ice-axe and whatever came through. It was very interesting. They all stood there and clapped each other on the back and congratulated each other, and looked around and all that and then by this time the fog was beginning to disperse because the dry ice just – whatever dry ice does – you chemistry people will tell me later. These three mountaineering guys were then just standing in this hotel lobby with the lift going up and down. For years afterwards, even occasionally now, somebody says, '*Undiscovered Country*, you . . . you did . . . you wrote that? That was wonderful, when that fog came in and the mountaineers . . .' I say, 'Yeah, I wrote that.'

The moment at which you give the audience 'the information' is something which can be under the control of the writer. This is the conventional view. As a matter of fact it was my view: you wrote a play and theatre was what happened to it. You gave it to them and they gratefully took it and then they did your play. The way this thing drip-fed from here to there was what you'd written and it drip-fed at the rate you wrote it and in the order in which you wrote it. This is nonsense. There was a production of *Comedy of Errors* Trevor Nunn did in London about fifteen years ago. It was a modern-dress thing. Now *Comedy of Errors* – I know you know but I'll bore you anyway: it begins in Ephesus. The situation is that Ephesus is at war with Syracuse. The play begins with this old guy who is this sort of chief fellow in Ephesus, and what he's saying is that we have this hostile situation with Syracuse and anybody from Syracuse caught here in Ephesus will be put to death. At which point one of the people who has been listening to this long speech turns around, and he's got this sort of wary, terrified smile on his face – he's wearing a Syracuse T-shirt. Now, Shakespeare didn't know that he would do this. And then there is some language which tells us what we've just been told. I'm not criticising, I'm just pointing this out. This production was absolutely wonderful; I say I absolutely adored it, to make the point that in fact it went just slightly soft at that point because the writer was dead and he wasn't there to take it out. They might have done it for him.

Shakespeare-theatre-going, Shakespeare-watching and so on, is actually in itself, as you can imagine, a rich enough field to explicate any point that I might make and more beyond. I hardly know where to stop. It does encourage what I suppose many people here might consider to be liberties, the taking of liberties, some of them quite notorious if that's the word. Some of you may know of a very famous production of *King Lear* by Peter Brook which Paul Scofield did I suppose twenty years ago. In *King Lear* there's a scene where Gloucester is blinded. They carried the play right through until Gloucester's blinding and then they had an intermission. So we had blind Gloucester staggering about, with blood pouring down from his eyes looking really horribly wounded; it was quite grisly. What made it worse was that the servants who were moving the furniture away and generally tidying up were jostling him and adding to his injury and being extremely callous towards him. As all this was going on, Brook brought up the house lights and – it was really extraordinarily effective – you were in the same world as it. In a strange kind of way you were implicated because the lights were just levelled off until it looked the same there as it was here. Gloucester was staggering about and then he'd gone. Then you had to kind of pull yourself together and look around and say, 'Well actually I didn't do anything,' and go and have a drink. It was very good theatre. The only thing is it wasn't what Shakespeare actually wrote: he didn't write these servants jostling him and ignoring him. They were actually running around offering him whites of egg and trying to make his eyes better and comforting him. Brook cut all that.

I do want you to ask yourselves where you stand on this point. And I'm not going to belabour it. It's just that we need to be reminded what happens in theatre, what the people who practise theatre feel they can do. I'm not in any sense standing here rebuking, 'j'accuse' stuff – not at all – it interests me too. It's going to interest me even more when I'm dead. Harold Pinter, you know, once flew to Rome with a lawyer because they were doing, I think, *Betrayal*, in a boxing ring. I don't mean that they decided oh well, we'll do the play right here. What I mean is that the set was a boxing ring and then they had two ladies making love in a bathtub. He never wrote that, and he moved in with his lawyer and stopped it. At the time I thought, 'Oh Harold, for God's sake. Somebody else will do it right later, don't worry.' But in the end my sympathies came round towards him. Principally because it was the first time the thing had been done in Italy; I feel – this is just pragmatic – I do feel different about the first time a play is done.

I saw a *Rosencrantz* in Italy where Rosencrantz was a woman. She didn't play it as a woman – she was the director's mistress, she always had a good role, and in this case she was wonderful, I loved the production. It also took place in a series of perspex boxes, which I also loved. The only thing which depresses a writer as a matter of fact, if he chances upon a play of his own years later, is to see a production which tries to mimic the original. That's not terribly interesting, and so I was quite pleased. If they'd done it in a boxing ring I might have felt slightly different.

All right, this equation. I'll tell you an anecdote about something which happened to a play of mine when it was done in France, and you'll see exactly what I mean by this algebraic equation. The second half of *Travesties* begins – well it began, with about twelve minutes of a young woman recounting a sort of potted history of how Lenin got from Zurich to the Finland Station in St Petersburg. In fact, the speech began with the publication of *Das Kapital* and it went on for about five pages. And I remember thinking I might be pushing my luck here. What I was counting on was that it was the first thing which happened after the interval, so people would come back and feel it's OK; secondly it was a relatively new character, an attractive young librarian lady called Cecily, and we hadn't seen much of her before in the play. I was tempted to try this thing partly because there was a slight sense of sadism I suppose towards the audience because the first act was jolly and full of jokes and people generally sat about laughing; I thought it would be quite nice if they all went out thinking, 'Oh this is fun isn't it,' came back, and just hit them with this boring thing, as though they'd come

back into the wrong theatre. So, she learned it, then we did previews and from the first moment it was clear that I'd over-
played my hand here, so I started cutting from the top and in
the end (I'm very pragmatic about these things) she did the last
paragraph. I mean the train was practically entering the station
by the time she . . .

The play was going to be done in Paris and the director gets
in touch with me and he says this and that, and any thoughts,
notes, and I said, 'No, that's fine – oh one thing, Cecily's
speech, top of Act Two, don't feel you have to do it all.' And he
said, '*Mais pourquoi pas? C'est magnifique.*' 'No, no, listen,
I've been there, I promise you, I thought it was a good idea but
I promise you – listen, in London we actually cut it down to
one paragraph.' And he said, 'But you know, you're crazy.' He
wanted to do it all. So I said, 'OK, I mean you do it,' and so on,
'*sur votre tête* be it'; back he went to Paris. I carried on with my
work and they did the play. I heard it went pretty well, and the
chap phoned up and he said everything was fine, and I said,
'How was Cecily's speech at the top of Act Two?' And he said,
'*Formidable, superbe!*' I was thinking, 'God, this is the sort of
audience I deserve.' So I go to Paris to see it, and it's fine, and
Act Two starts and he was right. She did every word and you
could have heard a pin drop. But she was stark naked! He'd
altered the equation.

It made me laugh too but you see what I'm saying, don't you,
that the thing which is going on up here is not literature walking about. That's not what it is. When I go back over my own
experience I just remember things all the time where the idea
was not a good idea, certainly with Shakespeare. And I don't
mean either let's all do it as though it's happening in 1930 or
something, let's all do it in jackboots to show what *The
Tempest* is really about or whatever. I don't mean that; in fact I
on the whole disapprove of that on purely practical grounds,
sort of artistic practical grounds. I don't think theatre works as
parable; it works as metaphor. This is an important difference.
Let's say that you see *Coriolanus* and you think to yourself,

'Mussolini.' Now many people I would think have done so, or something like that, thought of some twentieth-century dictator or nineteenth-century dictator; it depends on where the play is done. If it's done in Latin America it might be somebody I can't call on now, but there would be a sense of a reference and application. This is to me how the thing is supposed to work; but as soon as you make everybody Italian and give them a shining brown belt and big boots and walking around in 1930s Italian Fascist style then it's not metaphor, then it becomes a sort of parable. I think that seldom works because in a way you're denying the subtext's right to be sub, which is where its power is . . .

The empirical nature of the theatre as it happens is matched by a kind of brazen pragmatism on the part of writers like myself. I don't say that all writers are like myself, but I feel in a sense disappointingly pragmatic about these things. And very often a play takes its final form for reasons which are rather embarrassing to admit, and never more so than in this context and this milieu – where they are 'studied.' I'll give you a frivolous example from a play which I adapted and translated from one by Nestroy, the nineteenth-century Viennese comedian-actor who wrote innumerable plays and a handful of them are still in the Viennese repertoire. One of these we did at the National Theatre, we called it *On the Razzle*. There's a certain point in the play where they're in a restaurant, it was a curtain, it was a moment when an act finished and one wanted something, you know, which wasn't quite there.

I decided to have a waiter come on with what I called a flaming pudding, like a Christmas pudding, with lots of flaming spirit on it. It looked as though it would do the job. So we rehearsed and rehearsed, and of course you rehearse without props, the pudding or anything, you just do it, and finally we were there at the technical rehearsal: 'OK where is the flaming pudding?' It turned out that because of the fire regulations at the National Theatre we couldn't have a flaming pudding. So then there was a pause for consultation, and everyone turned to me as if it was my fault. Finally I said, 'Well, OK we'd better make it a cake with electric candles,' so the fire people wouldn't mind. They said, 'That's fine, we'll do that. Go and get me a cake and electric candles.' I said, 'Wait a minute, whose birthday is it?' Nobody in this play was having a birthday. So I then made it the birthday of one of the women in the hat shop. So I said, 'OK it's her birthday.'

When you do that – this isn't playwriting class, but I'll tell you anyway – you can't just suddenly say, 'Oops, it's my birthday, here comes my cake,' because the audience will not believe you. You have to get the birthday up front in Act One, and then have someone mention the birthday, and finally by the time it gets to the cake the birthday must have been in the play really and properly several times and then the cake will work. Now then, this play was translated from Nestroy, and without question somewhere there is an academic doing something about Nestroy or maybe even me and they say 'ah'. And then they write a paper or maybe set a question for some of you: 'In *Einen Jux will er sich machen* (in the original) Mrs Thing does not have a birthday. But in *On the Razzle* the plot has accommodated a whole new thread in which her birthday is really rather important. Why do you think that . . .?' If this ever comes up you just write down because the National Theatre fire officers said, 'Get that fucking pudding out of here!'

I want to say one more thing about this equation. Algebra doesn't actually offer the clearest image of this, perhaps a kind of three-dimensional geometry is involved because in fact the audience is implicated in this changing event. A lot of it is actually out of one's control, because what happens is the changes are entirely mysterious to the writer, the actors and everybody there. You can see the effect: you take these words on a Tuesday night and you get these people to say them and you get these light cues and you get these sound cues and you do everything, and on Tuesday night the whole thing takes off and it flies and everybody is happy and whatever and they understand it and they clap at the end and they go out and they say, 'My

God that was good, I'll tell all my friends to come and see it.' Wednesday night, you get the same piece of paper, the same people, the same actors, the same lights, and it just lies there absolutely, you sit at the back and think something terrible has happened to this play. But you don't know what it is. In fact it's you.

In some strange way there's some collective force which acts like a chemical agent on this, and we act on that. This fourth wall, here, which you can't see, is there, which is like those toffee windows they have for movies so you don't kill an actor when you throw him through it. It's there all the time and when something just goes like a needle through that wall the event is just destroyed. Sometimes you exploit this; there are often plays where one character conversés with the audience or at least addresses the audience and then turns back into the play. So in that sense the equation is extended deliberately. This is a very frail object, whoever the writer is, and maybe especially if it's Shakespeare – we always get back to Shakespeare but I think with good reason, because he's sort of there like a decanter, with that silver label around its neck saying 'World Champ'. Even with Shakespeare the extraordinary fragility of this event is something which I can hardly overstate for you. The paradisal dream of the playwright is to write a novel, because whatever you write – that's the way it stays. Everybody gets the same thing and it's the same tomorrow as well. It's a temptation all the time to get out of this appalling danger and write something which just stays the way you left it. The reason you don't is that it stays the way you left it.

The Real Thing: Donmar, 1999

The extracts here come from the programme for the Donmar Warehouse revival. Stoppard talks with the director, David Leveaux, and Lucy Davies, the Donmar's Literary Manager.

DL: *The interesting thing is what happens when this play is shared with a late nineties audience, when its last outing in London was in the early eighties.*

TS: Yes, if a play's locked into an event you cannot shift, like the sinking of the Titanic, for ever after everybody's in 1912 and that's that. But if the play is about love and friendship and marriage and fidelity, and has a general social background, then the emphases are very different.

DL: *I think that plays change their nature, as the years pass, in the sense that they have a built-in mechanism of prophecy if they are to persist or endure in the imagination and interest of an audience. You could say that if* The Real Thing *is about love, then of course one can think of other plays in other centuries that are about love that are bound, as it were, by certain discretions or certain considerations affecting the treatment of love in that particular time.*

Language, for example.

DL: *Somewhere in there it's almost as if you sent a memo to yourself about the limits of language . . . Henry's lucidity – his capacity for completing the analysis of an emotion in a phrase – eventually starts to fracture. I think it makes it rather an unusual play in and among your plays.*

I find it titillating to have structural cross-references, which are really quite separate from the real subject. There's a moment in *The Real Thing*, which is repeated at least twice. There's a man in a room and a woman's been away and she comes back and he believes that she's been unfaithful and she gives him a present and takes it out of a bag. And there is a scene which we see taking place in a real time and space in a railway carriage and then that scene is transmuted into a play within a play – a television play within the staged play. That kind of layering has always appealed to me.

LD: *Did people level the accusation that Henry was you?*

They did, but I can't blame them. I actually wanted to write about a novelist because I thought that if I wrote a play about a playwright I'd never get out from under. So I tried to make him a novelist, but of course I couldn't, it denied me all these tricks which I liked. Also, of course, he is me because it's intellectually autobiographical. In most of my plays, there's somebody who's nearer to being my spokesperson than anyone else. I used a lot of myself. I mean, for example, the pop music . . . that's completely me, I'm a musical dunce . . .

Everything I've written, I think, is supposed to work as comedy on one level or another. Periodically, from the very beginning of writing plays, I've thought, how does one write a tragedy – a real tragedy – in contemporary theatre? What would it be like? . . . I think irony is so hard to keep out because we're all so sophisticated. And we're no longer pure as an audience, so we're commenting.

LD: The Real Thing *is all about pain* . . .
DL: *Certainly when I reread the play a few months ago that was the thing that leapt out at me. Pain.*
Listening, it sounds as if one's launched in to deal with a grand theme. Pain, it's all fine, but I think that I was equally interested in the joy or at least in showing the mixture. The play often gets a bit self-referential. It's one of the titillations I was talking about. I mean, Henry is sitting on the stage saying, 'I don't know how to write love. It's either banality or rude.' So whatever else is going on, it's also a man writing the scene that he's in. So, I think that one way of looking at *The Real Thing* is that having a plot in a sense compromises the play (*laughter*). It would be quite nice to have no plot and just have this sort of messy, shapeless stuff going on that has to do with attraction and misunderstanding . . .

In comedy, laughter is often the sound of comprehension. Then you know you've communicated. This is why actors and directors are absolutely right to worry about a missing laugh at a first preview. One isn't there to score laughs in that simple sense, but if it's missing then you know you've just done something which has taken the mind away at the critical moment.

DL: *But what you just described is equally true of a play that does not invite a single laugh. If you are off rhythmically then comprehension is not with you. There is no recognition in an audience. The difference is, you don't necessarily get the direct evidence of that, until it's too late. What you're listening to is the silence of incomprehension, which is sometimes mistaken for the silence of fascination, and it's very important to be able to distinguish between the two. Everything, however profound or momentarily banal it is in the theatre, requires ferocious sense of rhythm. Even in a silence. Especially in a silence ... It's the coalescence of rhythm, intention, clarity, relationship. When those things come together you have recognition.*

My starting point is that all theatre is alienation. You go . . . You know you're there. You know why you're there . . . the whole trick is to make you forget that, for as long as it's possible to forget it . . . The form, the shape of where you are turns out to be much less important . . . because what's happening in the centre of that space is all that matters. The point is reached where the observer no longer knows or cares what kind of theatre he or she is sitting in – those are the moments which justify all of the work.

John Tusa, BBC Radio, 2002

John Tusa interviewed Stoppard shortly before the opening of The Coast of Utopia, *and began with the real possibility that his own birth had been overseen by Stoppard's father, Dr Straussler; both men's families then left Czechoslovakia in 1939. Some extracts from Tusa's interview have already appeared in the first chapter; here are other selections.*

JT: *I want to start with this question of openness. In your early years were you able to protect yourself, perhaps from self-revelation, by this sure ability with words?*

TS: I didn't think of it like that, but that's possibly how it operated. But on the whole I was following my inclination; it wasn't a principle or a plot. Then as now I wrote the way I wanted to write, the way that appealed to me at the time.

Were you deliberately concealing, or was it just that you didn't see why you should reveal more than you had to?
Well, I was shy; I'm still shy, and fairly timid. I've come to care less, or become braver or more fatalistic. But first of all I wasn't really interested in my own experience, biographically speaking. I wasn't really interested in myself as a source for my plays, though of course *all* plays have to originate with the author and – if you like – the plays expressed in part my temperament, in part my intellectual interest, and more than anything else I think they expressed the places where I found I could have fun.

And what were those places, where you found that you could have fun?
It was partly to do with language, linguistic fun. From as long – literally as far back as I remember – I've liked puns, word-jokes, I can literally recall looking at a comic at the age of about six or seven and I remember what I enjoyed and what it was precisely and how the joke worked. Certainly I was receptive to that, and it went in very deep, and is still, occasionally with unfortunate results, coming out.

But that didn't come from your parents or your stepfather, did it? By the sound of it your English stepfather, Kenneth Stoppard, was not the sort of man who did enjoy language or would necessarily have thought that it was the right thing to do? So have you any idea where it came from?
Well, to begin with, we mustn't make *that* sound like a moral judgement. I don't think that parentage and environment can have all that much to do with the kind of response I'm talking about, a completely instinctive like or dislike for certain kinds of language or literature. I mean, I wasn't a precocious intellectual literary child in any way, believe me: when I was in my

eight-to-thirteen period I wasn't reading Conrad, I was reading Biggles.

Quite right too. Now, the language; I know one can make too much of this, but do you feel that you're in the tradition that is sometimes identified of people who are called non-Britons, or at least non-Britons by birth, who appear to care for English more than the English do themselves – Naipaul, Vikram Seth, Conrad etc. etc. Do you feel that you're part of that tradition?
I do. Looking back at myself, I would say that I *am* part of it. I didn't *feel* I was part of something or anything; I was just being myself and liking what I liked, but I now am a little extreme about the English language. I mean just to take a point which I was going to say is trivial, but of course it's *not* . . . every time I see 'who' instead of 'whom' in a newspaper it's almost like a physical pain. It offends me deeply, it makes me angry.

Yes, but why is that reaction more than just a spasm of ageing pedantry, which a lot of us have?
But it's not pedantry, it's a question of something meaning what it means and not meaning something else; and while it's sometimes the case that it makes no difference to the sense of the sentence in which 'who' is used instead of 'whom', mostly, if you really understand the English language, the sentence is not saying what the writer thinks it's saying. The sad thing is that it means to the reader what the writer erroneously thinks it means, and then you've lost . . .

You've said how English you always have been, that you were brought up to be English, you felt it. When Kenneth Tynan said, 'You must never forget that Stoppard is an émigré,' was that an Englishman's total misunderstanding of your experience?
It was a judgement he made about my writing. I felt he was entitled to make it.

Meaning what? That you didn't write as he thought an English playwright at the time should write?

Perhaps so; perhaps he felt that my subject matter was not the subject matter of someone who had, as it were, grown out of this soil or the pavements here. He might have imagined that I discovered the English language as though it were a big toy box, rather than something that I merely grew into, grew up in. What people tend to underestimate is my capacity for not bothering, not caring, not minding, not being that interested. It's pretty awful actually, when I think about it myself I sometimes feel I really ought to do better than this!

But why? Doesn't that suggest that you know what you are, you know who you are, you know why you do it, and anybody else's opinions are just their opinions?

I think that's pretty much it. I've seldom minded other people's opinions; but the other side of that coin is that I've seldom been interested by them, their opinions of me, I mean.

You never stopped writing for radio; I wonder what it is particularly about the medium that you like?

It's fairer to say that I have continually stopped writing for radio, because the gaps have been long. To start with, I was jolly grateful to be asked to have a go at a short radio play at the time when this happened to me; because, you know, that was the public. When would this have been – sixty-three or four? – I did a couple of fifteen-minute radio plays.

But did you learn, subsequently, did you feel that your writing for radio had helped you to write more effectively for the stage, maybe even in the actual construction of the plays? Was there a direct carry-over of experience?

I think the carry-over comes from everything you write. I don't think the medium itself was that significant, but it was significant in my life because of simply learning how to write a play . . . all these things educated me. I say that sitting in the

National Theatre in a break from a rehearsal of another play; and I don't know how educated I've become. I'm still looking at the thing and feeling uncertain about its architecture. It's not as though there's a right answer for each play: there may be, but you certainly don't know what it is when you set out . . .

One of the things I like most about the theatre is not its literary side, although clearly that has an appeal to me; but what I love about the theatre is its pragmatism. It's a pragmatic art form. I love it for being adjustable at every point: there's no point where theatre gets frozen, unless you walk away from it.

You don't hand down your script as tablets of stone?
No. Before I'd written a play I thought of it rather like that: you know, that the playwright writes a text, and theatre is what happens to it, theatre is how it's served. That's true in the broadest possible way, but of course the reciprocal action between the writer and the director and the actors and the designer, and the audience ultimately, is continuous; and every single day I'm at rehearsal, including this morning, I'm adding or taking away words.

So you've never been upset if an actor says, 'I'm terribly sorry, Tom,' either 'I can't say that line' or 'That line seems absolutely wrong to this particular character'?
Oddly enough, that's not how actors feel about things. No, when I say that there's an empirical level to theatre, I mean that if two actors are having a conversation here while three are having a conversation there, and one of them has to walk four paces, you think, 'That's a silence I don't want, give him three more words.' When I got into movies the thing that I always loved was sitting in front of the steam deck, the editing machine, and being God, manipulating, changing reality. And rehearsals are a bit like that: you're still in control of the play, you're still creating it, it's not simply lying there like something that has to be pumped into life.

What might make you feel that you had lost control of the play
– if there was a director who was really so insensitive or a direc-
tor who was asking for changes which you knew were wrong
for the spirit of what you'd written?
Well, that's never happened. By the time you're in a rehearsal
room, you've got past that possibility. First of all, other than at
the very earliest stages of your career, you tend to be working
with people you already know, some of them. So you're not
going in with your fingers crossed thinking, Gosh I hope this
person isn't going to be rotten to me and so forth. Things are
much more collaborative and organic.

How long do ideas take to gestate? I mean, this trilogy: after
all, one new play's quite a thing, three new plays is heroic.
Looking back on it, when did some idea that Alexander Herzen
and his colleagues might form the basis of drama, how far back
did that go?
About five years. I'm always grateful to get to a point where
there's something I want to write a play about. And usually my
plays don't overlap, even in my mind. More recently, probably
because I'm aware that I've got less time than I used to have, I
try to hurry up the process; and the play before these plays,
which was a play about A. E. Housman the poet, I got that as
a thought very strongly and immediately almost before the previous play was on the stage. But somehow it still took about
four years for me to do it. Again with the play about Herzen
and these other Russians we're talking about, the mid nineteenth century Russian radical opposition, again this was
something that I wanted to write about five years ago when the
Housman play was barely on.

But you were able to park that at the back of your mind until
you could start thinking about it in detail?
No, not at all; I've been working solidly since that moment,
because it was a subject which expanded faster than I could
contain it, and master it. The material – there used to be one of

those toys where you took the lid off the box and foam covered the coffee table! – it was a bit like that. And I wasn't thinking that I'd be writing a trilogy at all, of course. But a year later, as I began to sort out the story of these people, I began to see that I'd have to abandon most of it and simply write a play; at that point I began to sort it out as three plays. But because these are plays about historical characters, involved in quite difficult philosophical and political, ideological matters, about which I knew very little – and certainly very little about *them* – it was a play which required a tremendous amount of reading. And I probably overloaded and went on reading too long.

Do you finish the reading before you start writing? And you let what you've absorbed from the reading digest itself and become fallow before you start writing, is that the process?
I take notes from what I read. I have to read everything two or three times for it to stick. And even then I'm always going back to something I've read a year earlier, two years earlier, to remind myself what I need. The notes for the trilogy occupy more paper than the trilogy occupies, of course; and I don't think I managed the process all that well. I felt I had to know everything in order to make the choice about which bits I wanted to use, and so forth.

That makes it sound far more like research than the creative process, which is clearly not the case. It's interesting that you feel you have to get such a secure hook on the facts of a particular situation before you can write about it.
Yes. 'Research' sounds rather joyless. All the time I'm reading, I'm as it were editing what I'm reading into things which I know I'll want.

And are you hearing the characters already?
Yes, one's hearing them, certainly. And I get a terrible early hang-up about being accurate – unnecessarily accurate, actually; and a lot of the time I'm trying to make things work the way

they happen simply because that's exactly how they happened. And now, looking back on the plays, I realise that from the plays' point of view there's no difference between those passages which I invented or compressed and the ones which are faithful representations of a particular moment. The audience doesn't know the difference, and there isn't any difference, in that sense.

When you create dialogue, are the characters yourself talking to yourself, or do you consciously say this is character A and this is character B and they must be different? Is it fundamentally an internal dialogue with yourself?
To some extent it is. One wouldn't altogether abandon character, and furthermore the way a person thinks and the way a person talks are sometimes inextricably confused and confusing. Character emerges out of content, too. But yes; it's a play, among other things, about people searching for the ideal society, to put it at its most high-flown. So there is a level where the terms of the argument are as important as the characterisation of the speaker, and all my writing life I've been guilty, if that's the word, of writing things which I wish to be said in the tone in which I wish them to be said. And occasionally I would be in the position where I would redistribute certain speeches among different characters – I'd change my mind about who said this or who said that, and clearly the demands of characterisation cannot in that instance prevail.

Do you believe in an ideal society?
Well, I believe in the desirability of an optimal society. I believe with Alexander Herzen, who ultimately is the focus of this trilogy – and with Isaiah Berlin, who is Herzen's cheerleader in modern times – that Utopia is an incoherent concept; that there is no overall right answer to all these questions which have puzzled people for several thousand years. What I do believe in is that it should be possible to have a fair society and a just society, without needing to feel that concepts such as justice

must have an absolute meaning and application for all people at all times and in all places. I think that the present is worth attention; one shouldn't sacrifice it to future conceptions of this future or that future. What he says in the play which I rather think I do feel in my own heart is, at one point he says that if we can't arrange our own happiness it's a conceit beyond vulgarity to arrange the happiness of those who come after us.

Looking at the whole of your career, the most common thing said about you is that there are two clear phases. The first is the period of the argumentative plays, the purely clever plays you might say, and then the second came after the watershed in 1982 of The Real Thing, *the play about love, pain, adultery, human relationships; and again the, perhaps glib, phrase is that there's the Stoppard of the mind and the Stoppard of the heart, and that there was a really big change. Do you recognise that as a way of looking at your work?*
Yes, yes I do. I'm aware that I kicked off as a language nerd, a language something. I've also come to understand that the humanity in theatre is and has to be provided by the people who perform the piece, to some extent. I think that I was saved in the past, more than I realised, by the humanity that the actors brought to a scene, to a play. And I recognise the picture because it's clear to me too that, as I remarked at the beginning, I've become much less shy about emotions. And now I think I'm writing in a way which is probably very different from a play like *Rosencrantz*.

Is there more of a sense of integration, that heart and mind now work together in a much more natural way, and that you don't argue with yourself about which one is in the ascendant?
I was probably too concerned when I set off to have a firework go off every few seconds, whether it was a sparkler or a Roman candle or a rocket or just a tiny flint, just sparking for an instant. I think I was always looking for the entertainer in myself, and I seemed to be able to entertain through manipu-

lating language . . . [Then] I came to be sitting in the theatre watching *The Cherry Orchard*, feeling the sense of instant diminution; I mean as one sort of diminishes in one's chair one thinks: 'Yes, I see, it's really about human beings, isn't it? It's not really about language at all.' I saw a Gorky play in this very building, Trevor Nunn's production of *Summer Folk*, and it was seeing that play which as much as anything made me determined, after many years of being determined, to try to write that kind of a play. I haven't done so, of course; but I think I've written some scenes which are not too far away. But yes, I thought I'd like to write a play for these people in this very set: I'd like to write a Russian play. And so the trilogy, you know, contains a few lines the like of which I would never have dreamed of including in any play associated with my name, like: 'Would you like a glass of milk?' or: 'How are you feeling today?' I mean, that small change –

– was a big change for you.
Well, yes, it is.

One of the things I've always found odd is the idea that you weren't some sort of political writer; and I suppose that's because of the narrow way in which 'political playwright' has been defined, or was defined in Britain for so long. That is that you had to be at the heart committed Left. But I mean way way back, certainly Professional Foul, *your television play about Czechoslovakia, that was* 1977, *you were deeply engaged in politics, though perhaps not the politics that the Left wanted you to be involved in. You were aware of the corruption of language in the Soviet Union, weren't you?*
I was always writing plays that I wanted to write, without worrying about what kind of plays I ought to be writing. *Professional Foul* is in a broad sense a very political play; but I didn't think of it as being a political play in its fundamental sense. I always said, and I still think, and it's certainly true of that play, that political questions resolve themselves into moral

questions. It was a play about conflicting moralities, and sometimes a play about conflicting moralities works itself out
through a political scenario, an ideological scenario . . .

*But it must have been easier – or was it? – that Havel was
analysing the corruption of the political system through the
corruption of its language, and therefore did that not have very
considerable impact on your own belief in language and its
connection with morality?*
I loved his plays because he was very good at what he did, you
know; I didn't love them because they were about the corruption of language. I mean, there are probably quite a lot of plays
around which are about the corruption of language, but they
may not be any good. Havel wrote wonderful plays; he had a
deft and sprightly intelligence, and a wit, which even in translation you couldn't miss; they were terrific plays. I also liked
him, I mean in his interviews and subsequently when I met him.
So there was a personal element in this, I really took to him and
wanted to help in some way.

*As far as the role of art, in politics, is concerned, do you still
sympathise with Auden's view that his poetry didn't save a single Jew from the gas chambers, so there's no point in trying to
justify art by saying it does something else?*
I think that if you imagine a culture, a society, and mentally
extract art from it, then one understands that art doesn't
require me or anybody else to defend it. It is an absolute essential: society without it becomes almost meaningless. I think to
focus in on what Auden wrote leads you into trying to make a
determination about a particular point; but the real point is
that art is a template, a matrix of some kind, for our morality;
it's always there, as politics' conscience . . .

*Is there anything else you want for yourself as an artist, apart
from the huge success of* The Coast of Utopia?
I think I'd like to – I won't be able to because it's a character

defect – but in theory I would like to alter my life completely, so that the next time I'm writing something nobody's waiting for it; I'd quite like to change the scale and the pace of the way I work.

But that's entirely in your hands, isn't it? And I think you've always said that the trouble with you is if somebody comes up with a bright idea you say, 'Yes I want to do it.'
I suppose it is in my hands, but it's also alas in my character. And while I would like now to spend a year saying, 'Well I think I might be writing a sonnet but I'm not sure,' and it doesn't matter if I do or I don't, I'll probably end up suddenly getting enthusiastic about a project or a play and I'll start assenting vaguely that yes, perhaps September 2003 might be a possibility; and suddenly there I am missing Wimbledon, missing going fishing, missing going to the theatre, missing dinner, because of this idiotic commitment that I've let myself in for.
It sounds like compulsive behaviour to me. Too late to change?
It sounds clinical behaviour. A clinical condition, yes.

For this book, May 2003

This interview was agreed as an update, not going over old ground. Stoppard and I met in the National Theatre, where he was attending early rehearsals of Jumpers. *Strolling between coffee bar and bookshop, stopping to talk to passers-by, he reminded me of an avuncular headmaster on his own patch (he had been on the Board of the National since 1989): a lofty but kindly presence.*

JH: *Coming back to* Jumpers *after thirty-odd years, how does it feel now to be watching the work of a young man?*
TS: A few things seem a bit clumsy – the odd phrase and so on. But so far actors think it's fine, director thinks it's fine. It's a difficult play to do: complicated in its staging. I tend to write with a rather naïve idea of stage design; I'm a bit over-literal. There

are two areas, the bedroom and the study, which can be tiresome . . . But now we're trying to do it without that sort of literal geography. With *Coast of Utopia*, one aspect of Trevor's whole take on it was that he wanted the entire stage for every scene, so there was no sense of slicing the cake with this bit for them and this bit for them. We would have the entire Olivier stage for every scene – which was rather wonderful, I thought, in the event. Though I suspect that you could do it with a table and a chair, if you really wanted.

There are so many scenes there that once you started to slice it up, you'd be in trouble. I wonder whether writing for screenplays had influenced you – this readiness to have a series of short scenes moving on very quickly?
It's not that it influences you directly, but one becomes aware, as the years go by, that you can have a freer form – and designers welcome it. I remember Bill Dudley saying to me: 'Don't worry about putting in more stuff; the more you have, the better it is for me.' So it's not so much films as the way that theatre form has evolved, I think.

On the other hand, Arcadia *is the opposite, isn't it? – very much fixed in one place and moving between the two periods? And that seems crucial to it?*
It is.

I read somewhere that you were thinking of doing a film of it. But in a way that would deny its nature?
I know. I've been asked to do it, and have thought about it for quite a while, but, I mean, you're quite right: what do you do? Film the play? Still, it's something I haven't completely abandoned, frankly. I've withheld *Arcadia* from various people who asked for it, because of a sense that, if I were to direct another film, that would be a good one for me to do. But I'm not really a film director, and I wouldn't do a film which I hadn't written.

When you filmed Rosencrantz, *you said that you could be freer than anyone else because you had written it.*
That's true; I was the only person who was willing to treat the whole thing with a certain amount of disrespect. I never mind the idea of people cutting things; but I hate the idea of them *adding* things . . . I've also been asked about doing a film of *The Real Thing*, but I always delay: I'm just baffled by the idea. I think that working within the physical limits of a theatre is part of its structure, of how it works.

And the opening of The Real Thing *would be much less significant in film terms.*
I know. People don't really appreciate how things unravel when you change one thing: they think that you can make the first scene into a film shoot instead of a play, that sort of thing. But the main impediment to doing a film of *Arcadia* or *The Real Thing* is that going back gets less and less attractive, and means I get less and less time to do new things.

Yes indeed. One of the things I admire most about your work is that you don't do the same thing again.
I think that *Night and Day* disappointed people who would have loved another *Travesties* type of evening. Well, it wasn't that good a play, for a start. But I thought of it recently, funnily enough, because it was done in San Francisco by a theatre which I know very well; so I was over there for a little bit of rehearsal, or technical gen, and, you know, by judicious cutting it worked pretty well, actually.

You were saying at that time, and have gone on saying occasionally since, how nice it would be to do 'a quiet play'.
I always think that. I always think of any play as a sort of overwhelming thing to attempt – a large and complicated thing which is very difficult to do. I often go to the theatre and have a really interesting time with a play that is on such a tiny scale, with so few of what I would think of as being 'problems', that

I think: oh that's a play, I could do one of those!

Whereas you would be inclined to get excited all the time –
And add lots of people, and, you know, naked women on chandeliers!

There are rumours that you're revising The Coast of Utopia.
No. What I am saying to myself, I don't know, some time before the end of this year, is that I'll try and find time and clarity to look at the whole thing, fresh, and see what I can lose, really. I hate the idea that the third play is fifteen minutes longer than the other two; I didn't intend that to be the case. And I also think that, the further you get away from the play, the more time which goes by, the more you see that you don't actually need that bit.

You pay tribute to Trevor Nunn for various changes.
Yes, that's true. I mean, the first time that Trevor read the first play, the last scene of *Voyage* didn't exist, until we were approaching a rehearsal. It ended with the Ginger Cat; and now the last scene is back to Premukhino. And Trevor was desperate for me to bring it back there; he just wanted to go back to Premukhino, he didn't sort of know what was happening; and I did actually try to write a scene . . . In historical fact, Bakunin went back to Premukhino, just before he went to prison; or, sorry, between prison and exile, he had like a day there, so I tried to write a scene of Michael's return to Premukhino, which was very moving because the entire family gathered. He spent most of the time playing draughts with the cook; he couldn't face, you know, the whole thing. So I finally wrote several versions of the Premukhino scene – it was a bit like working for a film director, Trevor kept rejecting them until finally I did it the way he wanted it! I was very grateful to him; he's got terrific perceptiveness.

How early did you show him a script?

I showed it to Trevor very early: you know, before I'd written the other two plays, of course.

You knew it was going to be a trilogy by then, but you'd not actually written the next two. And you'd chosen him as director?
Well, I said I'd like to write about these Russians, and he was in charge of this place. It was somehow implicit that he would direct what I actually said were three plays, which pleased him all the more.

Was that a huge financial anxiety?
No, because everything was budgeted the same. It would have been an anxiety of course, as with anything in this building, if it doesn't get an audience.

And I was quite wrong about the three-in-a-day thing: in fact they sold out quickest, and in a way were the best performances.

And is it going to be done like that in the States?
Don't know yet. It's going to be done there by Jack O'Brien, who's doing *His Girl Friday* here at the moment. He did *Hapgood* in New York, and he did *The Invention of Love* in New York.

And Hapgood *came off better in New York, I gather, than it did in London. Had you changed it a lot?*
Yeah, I simplified it. It was a bit too complicated for its own good. Jack also did *The Invention of Love* in a new production designed by Bob Crowley, which I liked a lot too . . . So, going back to your question about *Utopia*, my feeling is that I should try to trim things a bit, for the New York production. I'm going to Moscow next month, actually, to talk to the Moscow Arts Theatre, because they want to do it. One of the plays has been translated so far. I must say, I'd love it to be done in Russia. I don't generally take much interest in foreign productions, frankly, but in this case . . .

Would you feel a bit like an impostor, writing about Russia for Russians?
No, not an imposter, though they may not find it *persuasive*! I know the play is accurate in its fundamental sense: it's accurate about those Russians. I did have a letter the other day from a historian, saying that the word 'intelligentsia' wasn't in fact in use until about twenty or thirty years after. The fact is, I already knew that, and didn't care! But if I wrote that to him, he'd be so offended . . .

There is a problem with the Russian production . . . The Soviet regime took up Herzen and Belinsky and shoved them down people's throats; so to come up with a play in which they are admired heroic figures goes against the conditioning of now, a time of rejection of the Soviet pantheon. Whimsically or otherwise, because of a fairly casual reference to him in Lenin, Herzen as it were received the imprimatur of Lenin, and therefore there was the Herzen Boulevard and so forth. In the case of Belinsky, he was posthumously adopted as a kind of proto-Bolshevik. In both cases it was quite misleading.

So you'll be resurrecting the true Herzen for Russian audiences?
Yes, and Belinsky too. So I hope that'll happen; it won't happen very quickly, but I'm going over there to meet the director of the Moscow Arts Theatre. I've only been twice, and the first time was back in '77, I think. So I'm just going to go for a few days, really. The translator has been living in London now, a journalist as well as other things, and is going to be the *Financial Times* correspondent in Moscow.

Do you spend maybe half your year writing screenplays?
It doesn't really work like that. If I had half a dozen ideas for plays, I probably would do nothing else. Of course screenplays are work, but they don't *count*, as far as I'm concerned. I mean one tries to do them as well as one can; but since everything in them is dollars, or nearly everything, it's more like a craft, really

. . . But I don't seem to get an idea for a play very often, so it has to be four years between full-length plays, yet I'm not spending four years *writing* them, generally speaking. So, on screenplays, it isn't so much a case of half of my year, more a case of the intervening year. This year I'm doing this Philip Pullman trilogy; I've done one and I guess I'll be asked to do the second; so I'm writing a fantasy film about this twelve-year-old girl.

You like always to have the next thing to be going on with.
I always have something.

And I gather you get called in as a kind of doctor too?
Yes. I now have a lot of friends who work in films, and they send me things.

You've also had periods of adapting other people's plays.
Yes, but never on my own initiative. There's always a director asks me if I'd do this or that, and other things being equal it's a very nice thing to be asked: it's rather enjoyable.

I suppose like so many dramatists you've had the experience of writing screenplays which are then never filmed at all.
Yes. That reminds me, I brought something for you. [*In a characteristic thoughtfulness, he produces the Spring 2003* Areté, *which contains the entire screenplay of* Galileo.] I wrote this screenplay in 1970 but it never got near being done.

Did Craig Raine [editor of Areté] *write to you out of the blue and ask for it?*
Actually he'd heard I'd done a Nabokov film, *Despair*, which was made by Fassbinder – not a very good film. And he said, look, Harold Pinter's let me publish bits of *Lolita* which never got made in that version, and I'd done this other Nabokov. I looked at it, and I had some funny script which Fassbinder had handed me, so I couldn't even remember entirely which bits were his, and I didn't think it amounted to much anyway. So I

said instead, do you want to look at this *Galileo*? – which was something else which wasn't made. And he liked it.

You've expressed your distaste for Brecht at times; did the fact that he did a play about Galileo niggle in your mind?
'Distaste'? I feel a bit mean about that. The fact is that in English Brecht never seems to be as good as you think he's supposed to be. Sometimes you get a production which really satisfies and pleases, but if not, then there's not a lot of compensation . . . Of course he was a man of the theatre; it's just that in translation he doesn't come across as a great writer. He may be one, for all I know; but I've never seen a *Threepenny Opera* which is actually *funny*.

[*We talked briefly of Vaclav Havel.* 'I hope he's all right; I haven't heard anything of him for a while. He's been very unwell.' *Then I mentioned that I was going to see John Tydeman.*]

There's another thing, the last time I wrote for radio was *In the Native State*. I'd like to do another radio play. Tydeman, and Richard Imison who recently died, these are people who would nag me occasionally and I'd say, 'All right, yes, I'll do one'; and then one day it would become an obligation which I'd then try to fulfil. But that doesn't happen any more.

Is there another play lurking?
I wish I could say that there was, and I'd tell you; but there isn't.

The trilogy was a big job.
It was completely draining, actually.

You've been getting in recent years more information about your family, the whole Jewish connection, and going back there. I wonder whether that might lead to something?
Well, it might.

Even a Jewish play.
Absolutely . . . I've been working ten years since *Arcadia* went on, and in those ten years I've only been writing about real people, the Housman play and the trilogy. I don't know whether that's significant or not; I don't know if I've actually run out of plays unless I write about some historical event or person.

One thing about making up your own story is you don't have to do all that research.
Yes. I'd like to avoid getting another idea which requires me to read for two years before I can start! If I worried about these things I would be worried, because if I'm now dependent on my own invention I don't have anything. In the case of Housman and *Utopia*, I was already, you know, on them before the previous one was on; there wasn't really a gap because they both required a long period of research.

When one looks back at the huge amount you've written already –
It doesn't seem that much to me, when you think how many years have gone by. I mean there are people who write a play every eighteen months, and I don't know why I'm not one of them, I'd like to be . . . You know, I don't live what I've always imagined to be the life of a writer, with plenty of time for thought, and reading. My life is too crammed with commitments and engagements. I've now bought a house in France, about five years ago, because I find that's the only way I can actually get out from under. I use the house to work in.

There's no thought of retirement, at least.
What would that mean? Being retired would be like being between plays.

5

Working with Stoppard

The interviews here are all new, for this book. Carl Toms, Stoppard's preferred designer for many years, died before it was envisaged; but most other theatre professionals who worked regularly with him have talked to me, together with some younger artists tackling the plays in revival. Directors are grouped first here, then designers, then actors.

These are not objective witnesses: they discuss Stoppard from the different angles of their own interest. They all agree, however, on the intricate structure which emerges as they work on a Stoppard script; their admiration for his craftsmanship is the praise he would probably value most. And they all feel fortunate to have worked with him; in John Wood's words, 'I've seen glory.'

Peter Wood

In 1958, as a journalist aged twenty-one, Stoppard saw Harold Pinter's The Birthday Party *in its first production, which was directed by Peter Wood. Fourteen years later Stoppard had become a celebrated playwright, but Wood needed persuasion to take on the younger man's new play,* Jumpers. *Before long, however, they became personal friends, and their professional collaboration proved both formative and long-lasting. Peter Wood talked to me in Somerset in the autumn of 2003. He was delighted to recall his long 'love affair' with the playwright, but also unsentimental about it.*

PW: I was in two minds about doing *Jumpers*, because I wanted to be sure just how facetious it was intended to be, and if it was too facetious I didn't wish to do it. If you're Catholic, it seemed a difficult task: I can't be farcical about God. I must say, I was very, very reluctant to do it.

JH: *Not a good starting point for a relationship.*
No; like all love affairs, it started off really badly. Tom wanted (I suspect though I don't know this for a fact) Jonathan Miller. But it seemed likely that I was going to have to do *Jumpers*, though there was a great deal of 'I don't want to' going on: I can do 'I don't want to' better than most people! The McEnery boys were going to do *Rosencrantz*, and I'd worked with Peter and he said to me, 'D'you want to come and do *Rosencrantz* at Nottingham Playhouse?' And I said, 'It's funny you should say that, because I was just going to ask you the same question; if I wasn't pushing myself forward too much, might I come and do it?' Which I did.

So that suited well, because you felt you were getting into the writer. Had you known Tom Stoppard at all before?
No. We eventually met in the most unfortunate circumstances: oh, it was a disaster. Paddy O'Donnell, who at that time was running the happy days of the National – Aquinas Street, the Vic, all the lovely things – Paddy said there was a very good Italian restaurant in Southampton Row. And it turned out to be a greasy spoon of the worst possible kind; so we had a dreadful lunch. Tom fielded a number of questions. I said, 'I know people always ask this question, but what's it meant to be about?' He said, 'It's about a man writing a speech; that's all.' And that was left there . . . He just didn't want me to do it; that was my impression. I walked off down Southampton Row, at the end of the lunch, thinking to myself, 'Well, you were probably right in the first place.' And I rang my friend Peter Shaffer, who happened to be in England at the time, and I said, 'I've just had lunch with Tom, about this play of his; and I don't want to do it.' Peter said, 'You need your head examined: where's the

play?' I said, 'I'll bring it over.' So I took it over, and Peter read it and then said, 'Stop all this nonsense and false modesty rubbish. Press on, ring the National, say you'll do it'; Peter thought it was wonderful – he really did. Yet the opening looked so facetious. It's opaque; it really is a very hard play: every single item . . . Tom has said quite calmly since that he felt it was necessary to have a surprise every few seconds, and of course he did that; but he felt that was his responsibility.

It's a very cluttered set-up on stage.
And to sort everything out, and to get any narrative going at all about Dotty, is a pig; it's really hard. When she gets stuck on the word 'moon', it's very hard to do. Fortunately I did the play so many times, far more than I've ever done anything else, I had to do three productions of it at the National, one in New York, one in Vienna, and then one at the Aldwych in a different way, catering for a sophisticated West End audience.

In Vienna it would be in German?
Yes, I've done a lot of plays for the Burgtheater. That's where all the adaptations come from, because I took up plays from the Burgtheater repertory, starting with *Das weite Land*, which I think is the most wonderful play, and which we did very well, we really did. We did four altogether, we did the Nestroy [*On the Razzle*], with which we had a lot of fun.

Jumpers is quite a serious play, about a serious subject.
Yes, but it was extremely difficult to know how the thing was meant to be slanted where an audience was concerned. The word 'God' in the theatre has never been a rallying cry; and the intellectual climate was powerfully anti-God, in every way shape manner or form. And I must say that at the first preview at the Old Vic I looked along the row and there were nine people asleep, and I thought to myself, 'I was right first time, I shouldn't have done this play, I should never have touched it.' It still needed an enormous amount of rehearsal.

And so what did you do after that preview?
Tom would talk about certain lines where he wanted the meaning to come over. For example, he was very determined that George should say with tremendous force: 'But the rules of tennis can be . . . *changed*'; he always put the breath pause before 'changed'. To begin with – in his doctrinaire period, shall we call it – he had this very strong sense of where he thought the message lay and also the way in which it should be emphasised. The pause before 'changed' doesn't work, of course: you have to say 'the rules of *tennis* . . . can be changed'; the pause is after 'tennis'. So from the very beginning we always had issues like that, and they didn't vanish really until *The Real Thing*. We had terrible trouble with Mageeba in *Night and Day*.

Was Michael Hordern always going to do George?
No. Everybody said no. I was the only person who wanted Michael.

It sounds a tough business being the director, with the author sitting there wanting to change the emphasis.
I thought I would hate it; I thought I would loathe having the writer there. And yet suddenly one day he had to go to the dentist or something, and I felt insulted because he wasn't there, I thought it was cheeky and casual of him not to be there when he was wanted!

So you developed quite early a sort of dialectic relationship, which he clearly came to value very much.
Well, for example: Michael used to say, 'But Professor McFee does not stop to consider such *reductio ad absurdum*, for he has other . . . fish . . . to fry'. And they roared with laughter at the pause, because they could complete the cliché, and of course that gives great satisfaction all round – but Tom leaned to me and said, 'Why are they laughing?' That was what the relationship was like. I'll show you later a charming Grove copy of *Jumpers*, where he has annotated the whole printed

copy; and says at the front, 'I've found this, I think it must be your copy'; it's full of despairing comments: 'This will never do, this is dreadful, cut that!' – he'd gone to the trouble of going through the entire book, messages all the way through. He was wonderful; I mean, really wonderful.

You not only had him there, you had Kenneth Tynan breathing over your shoulder?
Oh, to begin with, and that was really awful. I mean it was so laborious. Tynan was an extremely witty journalist, but he had no idea what was a funny line in the theatre . . . Tynan was totally wrong in his judgement of the play and indeed what would happen to it.

There was a dispute later about cuts in the play, and whether Tynan had imposed them.
Yes, and also a suggestion that the best lines were Tynan's! – which was cheeky. No, I'd liked him up to that time; but we went round to South Kensington to see him, and sat on the edge of his very large bed with the tilted mirror (he was very keen on all that) and I thought to myself, 'What are we doing here?'

There was also Olivier lurking in the background as well.
Ah, but I loved him, and he was, thank God, very fond of me and always voted for me whatever happened. Larry would always say about the Coda, about Dotty coming in on the moon, 'Well, goodness, it's a good *coup*, but she needs a big *scene*, she needs a big *speech* to end the play, something to make our hearts beat!' – and off he'd go. He blamed me for that: 'Why didn't she have that, surely you could prevail upon Tom to put a speech in . . .?'

Jumpers didn't go all that well in New York, is that right?
It was full of difficulty . . . It has to be said of New York that there's a particular form of hysteria which is common to the entire entertainment business.

In England, you realised you'd got a big success. Everyone was talking about Jumpers, *I remember vividly.*
Yes, it got taken up even by the opening night. You could see it in the demeanour in the stalls of the Vic, between the first preview and the last.

Nowadays there seem to be more previews?
That's because touring's now so expensive. You have to remember, the standard trial period was a good six weeks in the provinces.

So by the time Jumpers *was well going, did you get a sense that you might be working with this writer again? Rather hoping to, perhaps?*
No, quite the opposite. But we were playing *Jumpers* in Washington, staying at the Watergate, and he flew in and said, 'Trevor [*Nunn*]'s going to take a year's sabbatical, will you read that?' *Travesties* had been going to be Trevor's.

You were pleased?
No. Once again I was extremely daunted and cagey. Where work is concerned I don't have a lot of confidence; I'm more inclined to say 'I don't think I'll do this very well' than 'I'll kill to do it'. But eventually I became extremely fond of *Travesties* because unlike *Jumpers* it was the most wonderful knitting. We corrected one mistake, which was the business of there being no great speech for Joyce. Our relationship really came to life when about ten days into rehearsal I said to him, 'Listen, you love Joyce; you loved that book [*Ellmann's life of Joyce*], the reason why you're doing the play is because of Ellmann: you adored that book, and now look how you've served him! Don't do to Joyce what you did to Dotty.' And he was very good about it. I thought to myself afterwards, you ass, the man's a brilliant talent, don't tell him what to do. But he went away, for about a week, and he came back with this huge speech – which Tom Bell in the end wouldn't learn! He learned the first half,

the Ulysses half, but the part beginning 'My father once met a man with a glass eye' – I'll show it you in a minute, it's the most wonderful speech – Tom Bell wouldn't learn it; politely refused, in fact. 'I'll never be able to do it.'

Then there was the Cecily problem, the long speech which was shortened –
Thank God, is all I can say. Tom makes jokes about it, about how the big speech was a tremendous success in Paris because the lady was naked: that's Tom all the way through. But no; lots of reasons: it was too didactic, well it was out of a book! But after all's said and done, when we came to the piece about the Beethoven sonata the audience was totally rapt. They really were, it was amazing. What's more it's one of the most moving bits of the play.

I love *Travesties*. It's bolstered by all our favourite lines: 'Rise, sir, from this semi-recumbent posture' and things like that. We did *Travesties* in the Aldwych, which it suited tremendously well, oddly enough. The Vic is a smaller theatre, yet the Aldwych is a very intimate place.

Did you get a different audience?
I thought so. I think the audience in the Vic read the *Telegraph,* the audience in the Aldwych read the *Guardian.* It's not a Haymarket audience, the Vic, but it's jolly near it: it's a small house and it was hard to get in . . . The Aldwych wasn't, and that was much to the advantage of *Travesties*, because of the way the play moved, through various forms of comedy and various forms of address, such as Carr's huge speech with that wonderful stage direction that his mind is like a toy train which keeps getting derailed.

Was that written specifically for John Wood? Not many could do it.
It was, it was. John had played Rosencrantz in New York, and defined himself as a Stoppard actor. He really could do

those speeches, for real; it was that sort of talent.

My working relationship with Tom was always this strange contradiction. I was having lunch with him in London, while *Night and Day* was running in New York, when he suddenly said that he thought he should direct the new play [*The Real Thing*] himself. He virtually said it was about his own marriage. That it was 'the real thing', you see.

You must have been aghast?
You win some, you lose some. It's in the bran tub, all of it, just depends what you fish out.

Yet by that time you'd done many good things with him.
We'd become a very successful team. You couldn't get into anything – *Jumpers, Travesties* . . . We sent *Night and Day* to the Phoenix and it ran there for nearly two years, which is staggering . . .

Yet it got mixed reactions from many.
David Hare hated it. He hated it because *Pravda* was going to be done at the National after *Night and Day* – which he thought was a very superficial piece indeed. Before we did it in New York, Maggie [*Smith*] came; she took over from Diana [*Rigg*], and asked to play it in London before she went to New York. The one great difference it made, and I knew it would because I'd worked with Maggie a lot, was the fantasy scene which began Act Two with Jacob. Tom would ring up in the middle of the night, in despair, 'I've written this great speech for someone who's already dead, what am I going to do?' – and he had! And then he had this brilliant idea that the beginning of Act Two was an extended fantasy, a wonderful idea, and the tree – I mean the tree in the middle of the stage was a cheek, but it worked.

By this time he was ringing you up while he was writing. You were almost working together.

The symbolic moment came when he gave me the worksheets for the Joyce speech. Because of that biography. It was just the same over Wilde. He fell in love with that biography, deeply in love with the Ellmann and of course the Wilde was the same; and I said to him, 'Where's Joyce?' – he comes on, does the soft-shoe shuffle and does limericks and all this (he's always writing verse, you see, spends a lot of time writing verse), but no . . . There you are [*showing the scripts*] that's a wonderful example of Tom trying to write a speech. He gave these to me. He was given to great gifts and charm; as in the dedication to the book [Jumpers '*approbation*'].

D'you recognise [in the mock-annotated Jumpers] *things you had suggested?*
No, they're wicked parodies of me, such as my desire to go and buy something new to wear to go to rehearsal, because I just felt old and stale and useless . . . It was an unexampled working relationship.

Though you hadn't begun it with any enthusiasm.
Yes, but that was half the wonder of it. You got past the barbed wire and machine-gun emplacements and finally found yourself on a great green lawn.

He came to trust you, and to try things out on you.
Rewrites were always shown to me, whenever he added anything – he usually was a great one for the extra line or two. Mostly, as he says himself, I accused him of obscurantism. I looked forward to a time when without doubt the plays would be part of a syllabus; and I always thought (and I wouldn't say this readily) my responsibility was to make sure that when they *were* part of a syllabus they would be understood by an intelligent young audience.

I suppose one could safely say that by the time we got to *The Real Thing*, he'd decided that I should direct it; but we've always been in this situation where 'Is it going to be me again, or what?' Where we got into difficulty was over *Hapgood*. The great idea – that the spy-plot, the le Carré plot, should mirror the behaviour of the actual bodies involved in the atom – 'one to be there, and one to stop being here' – which of course was the twins that Ridley represented – that idea never worked. You couldn't yoke it, you couldn't tie it in, which was a great shame. We should have been told that Ridley was very, very well versed in the whole subject of the nucleus, because of course he was. Kerner in the great big scene in Act One describes the size of the things you're dealing with: the nucleus inside the atom was like a moth in a cathedral, as far as I remember. We should have always known that Ridley was the problem; then the play would have worked – couldn't fail to work.

You need to take the audience into your confidence more.
Absolutely; right from the start. But the characters must not know: *we* must know. I said to him, 'We've got to know what Hapgood doesn't know.' But the day had passed when he listened. A lot to do with hard work, because by that time he was working fiendishly hard; we both were, I was doing about four productions at once, one in Europe somewhere.

Do you think the play wasn't thought through theatrically enough?
Hapgood didn't have any construct at all; and therefore it had no situation. And yet there has to be one; it's not enough to show you Hapgood's relationship with the two men.

What I remember most is the lighting effects at the beginning.
This is what Trevor said! He said in a letter to me that the misfortune of the production was that you could never live up to what you did at the opening, with all these increasingly large images and the A-to-Z and so on.

But after Hapgood *you went on together? You did* Indian Ink, *though that was really a radio play turned into theatre.*

Yes, well, then it came down to what was to happen when *Indian Ink* and *Arcadia* clashed with one another; because the original intention was that both plays should be in the National. I think it's very important, *Indian Ink*, because it allowed him to be a poet, to write verse; he'd always wanted to push his way past dramatic prose, to verse, and the wonderful thing about *Indian Ink* as far as he was concerned was that he wrote those poems. I did think they were pretty good.

I didn't do the first production of *Arcadia*, I was doing *Indian Ink* instead. But it was the one I most wanted to do [*he directed the second production, in Zurich*] because it was the one I knew most about, through my own interest in landscape and the whole garden development of the eighteenth century. That's what all this [*pointing to his house*] is about; and you have to remember that things like the Red Book are easily available to look at, at Longleat [*nearby*] where there is a beautiful copy . . . I found *Arcadia* downright incomprehensible in the second half. I did two or three things to it. There was terrible trouble about the plant, the dahlia. If you remember, it's on the stage, and it always seemed to me that it's the most important object *on* the stage, and he gave me an extra line or two, bless his heart, I dragged him out and took him out to lunch, and he gave me a few extra lines.

It has the best story.
It's wonderful in that it's a detective story, and the audience has the book; you know what is happening. Because *Arcadia* is about discovery of documents, and details of the period. It's hung on somebody else's work.

And research of the past. That does lead on to the Housman play as well, because we've got the full interaction on stage of the older and the younger character, which is very moving.
I thought that play deserved the Lyttelton and not the Cottesloe. It's a big Stoppard play; I thought it just needed more room to breathe.

It's not an expansive play, though; it's more claustrophobic textually, too.
All the plays owe a great deal to Tom's reading; the trouble with *The Invention of Love* is that it never *escapes* from his reading. And the Russian trilogy – all of a sudden, whatever the disease was in *Invention*, it was galloping. He's just eaten by his own reading.

Is there a difference between the senior eminent dramatist and the youngster who was working with you on Jumpers *in 1972?*
The whole thing to him then was stolen-apple time. The moment the knighthood looms, and then the OM on top of that, you become automatically elected to the Grand Old Man.

Do you think you'll direct Stoppard again?
No. It's been a very long innings: enough!

John Tydeman

Starting as early as 1964, John Tydeman directed most of Stoppard's original radio plays, together with radio adaptations of his other work. He talked to me in London in May 2003.

JH: *You and I and Tom Stoppard grew up when radio drama was a family entertainment, and there are things we take for granted which are not familiar to younger people today.*
JT: Radio drama was enormous – still is, actually, because television has more or less given up on the single play. And Radio 3 was like fringe theatre.

It had a big tradition, because of all those poetic dramas.
Yes, the Louis MacNeices, and all the not-known Jacobean plays, and so on. Because radio's relatively cheap, and because there's so much of it, it all got done for a specialist audience. Then in the late fifties there was this upsurge of new and different writing: the Absurdists were writing – Beckett, Ionesco

and Arrabal and Adamov – they'd all been discovered and were all being done on radio . . .

There was a thing at that time called *Just Before Midnight*, and every night it went out at quarter to midnight, five fifteen-minute plays a week, and that's where '*M*' *is for Moon Among Other Things* was done, and also *The Dissolution of Dominic Boot*, which is a kind of epic play in so far as it's the story of this chap with the taxi and as he's trying to get more money so of course the taxi meter mounts up. A lovely idea: it was later made into a film, but I don't think that it worked, because the great thing about it was its brevity. It's a remarkable little piece; you observe all the rules, you know exactly where you are and what's what; when I lecture I use that as a model, of a good radio play.

Radio was a good place for new writers to go to, and natural for someone who was writing something that tickled the mind before it tickled the heart – Tom's very much of the mind, I think, in his wonderful use of language. And you've got to take duration into account. The good thing about radio is that you don't have to write too much: the best radio isn't, by and large, the long play.

He'd done some apprentice work, like writing scripts for the Dales.
Yes. He also had an idea of doing an ongoing five-minute serial which was called *Mr Masapust*. We had the idea that this should be a five-minute serial every day, and Tom's idea was, rather like *Kind Hearts and Coronets*, that there was someone who was like fifty-millionth in succession to the throne, so had to get rid of every intervening person – so it really was ongoing! It never happened, but I think he might have written one or two scripts for it; I can remember we talked about it.

Albert's Bridge I think came in unsolicited, and much longer than it subsequently became. I seem to recall that the first script needed quite a bit doing to it. Tom's plays need minimal rewriting; that was an early play, but subsequent plays, one or two little tiny tickles here and there, but very, very few: they'd come nearly always ready to be performed. He would say that when he was writing for a specific medium, he thought in terms of that medium, and that's the way he would do it. That wonderful play *Glad/Frank* is pure radio. I think that might have been commissioned, or at least I asked him to write it.

He says that standing in the corridor of the BBC he was told there was going to be a series about different jobs, and he immediately said, 'I'll do the speaking clock.'
It's a lovely, lovely Absurdist idea: the talking clock has a nervous breakdown, and then she has to be talked back to the correct time. He's always had this fascination with time. Time and unicorns. And Moon, as a name and as an object.

In terms of money, presumably the BBC couldn't offer –
Oh, even quite late on, when he was relatively well known, the time of *Jumpers* and so on, he said that he earned more from radio than he earned from any other medium, because he had an international appeal. And if you think of the number of radio organisations that there are, certainly during the sixties and seventies, he earned far more money from radio than he got from runs in the theatre, because his runs in the theatre at the time weren't long runs, though of course they exist for all time. Radio plays by and large don't receive more than one production, the exception in Tom's case being *Dominic Boot*, which had two, and also, the schools one, *Where Are They Now?* – lovely little play; that was originally written for the BBC World Service, and then I produced it for Radio 3.

In the theatre you've got the natural response of the audience laughing. In radio sit-com they would put in canned laughter, but with Stoppard that would obviously have been anathema?
It's a different form of comedy. Take a play of Alan Ayckbourn's which is I think one of his funniest, *Third Person Singular*, where there's that woman who tries to kill herself in

about twelve different ways: you know, she's about to cut herself with a knife, and says, 'Oh, thank you for the knife,' and to gas herself and somebody's cleaning the gas oven, and every time she's just thwarted. In the theatre it is absolutely hysterical; on radio, because you haven't got present laughter, it's very black; and a lot of Ayckbourn comes across as black comedy. It affects the timing: the writers sometimes change gear under a laugh that they know they're going to get. So when you do write for radio, you obviously have – someone like Tom has – the medium in the head, and you write in a certain way which is slightly different . . .

There are some restrictions on radio, but in other ways it's enormously free.
Yes. Really, you can do anything on radio.

Except a purely visual gag?
Well, you can't do a purely visual gag; but that of course is why Tom, the lover of paradox, could do things on radio. In *Artist Descending a Staircase*, which in my opinion is still his best play – very much of a piece, there's not much flab on it – there's a brilliant moment where two characters are going together down a road in France, apparently on a horse, clip-clop clip-clop, but in fact one of them is knocking together coconut shells.

A parody of radio.
In a sense, yes. And other things, like the sound of a ping-pong ball . . . The play has been done onstage; so has *If You're Glad I'll be Frank*, which was very much a radiophonic play; that was done even in the West End –

But that then becomes very prosaic in the theatre, because you can see.
It takes away any ambiguity. And the essence of *Artist* is in ambiguity, and the mistaking of things. There's a hinge through

the plot, as I recall, about a painting, which was either of a white fence against a dark sky or was it of a black fence against a snowfield?

Sophie to me is one of the bits of parodic radio. One of the clichés of radio drama used to be that you had to have a blind person in your play to do the interpreting. Sophie is blind, but she doesn't interpret for the listener at all: she only has one speech on her own, which is just before she kills herself.
I think that's the first time really that he got blood coursing through the veins of a character. If I have a criticism of Tom it is that his characters tend to have heads and mouths but don't always have hearts. And I think that was the first character that he wrote that was a human being.

He recently said that he now realised how much of the human-ity in the early plays had to be provided by the actors. I think he feels he's changed. And perhaps you see Artist *as a moment at which that was happening?*
I think that is the first play that had real flesh and blood. I think a lot of the others were a sort of working out of ideas.

It's still a cartoony sort of play in some ways, isn't it? It has this inverted structure, and an allusive title; whereas In the Native State, *ten years later, is a much more realist play.*
Yes. And a very moving one. It made me cry when I read it, and I still find it moving on radio.

It's got the only real eroticism in Stoppard.
Oh, glorious, yes.

That scene in the shower . . .
Yes. Works very well on radio; whereas of course in the theatre it was seen through many gauzes. And in the radio play, all those bits of poetry, I mean you're right *there*, she's breathing. I think in the theatre it does reveal its radio origins.

He says you sent him postcards every now and again.
Oh too right; it was very late. And I'd say, 'What's it about?'
And he'd say, 'I think it's going to be about India'; and we waited and we waited. What was commissioned was an hour-long
play; all the plays were commissioned, from a whole lot of
famous writers, and Tom didn't actually deliver; he didn't like
having the pressure of a commission. At long last it came in.
You get a script from Tom and you put everything aside and
read it straight away, and I thought it was marvellous. So we
met and he said, 'Have you thought about the casting?' and I
said, 'Well yes I have: I'm afraid that my casting is awfully
clichéd, because the name that first came to mind for the girl
was Felicity Kendal.' I didn't know at the time that this was the
beginning of their affair. So he said, 'Funnily enough I wrote it
with Felicity in mind.' And then for the other female lead I said,
'Well I know it's a cliché because of *Jewel in the Crown*, but –
Peggy Ashcroft.'

Stoppard spent a bit of his childhood in India.
The amazing thing is that he hadn't been back, since babyhood
almost: he went back afterwards. He asked me if I would have
it checked for authenticity; and I sent it to someone in Bush
House who had been recommended to me, who said, 'I can't
believe he hasn't been back, everything's right except there's
something about the rainy season, it doesn't happen then,' and
he'd got a date wrong about something. But anyhow I sent the
script to Peggy; and when we came to read through the play it
flashes back to the character that she plays as an eighty-year-
old, and she becomes Nell, the girl. And it so happened that the
girl I had cast for Nell wasn't at the read-through, so Peggy
read it – very nicely, but I said, 'Yes, of course Emma will be
doing it.' And Peggy said, 'Oh, but I thought I was going to do
that? After all it is radio, they can't see me.' [*Dame Peggy
Ashcroft was eighty-three, and died later that year, 1991.*]

I said, 'Yes but Peggy, you know, you can't sound nineteen.'
And she said, 'That was why I took the part, because I knew

that I was going to play both.' So I said to Tom, 'This is getting a bit tricky,' and to Peggy I said, 'All right, have a go.' I mean, I knew she couldn't do it, yet I just kick myself that I never kept it – she performed the scene absolutely beautifully, and she sounded, say, thirty-five. But not a girl. I said, 'It won't do, Tom,' and he said, 'Of course it won't do.' I said, 'I shall have to tell her'; and he said, 'Let's both go in and tell her.' And he said to Peggy, 'When I wrote it I had two actors in mind.' And she took it very well.

It's very interesting, which plays transfer from one medium to another. *Professional Foul*, which was a wonderful TV play; that transferred very well to radio. And nearly all the plays do transfer. The one that's a bit tricky is the one with the two detectives: *The Real Inspector Hound*.

That's very much for theatre. I'm also not sure whether Jumpers *or* Travesties *would translate to radio. They're very complicated.*
Jumpers has never been done, as far as I know. I don't think *Travesties* has, either. *Rosencrantz* has been; he wrote a new scene, it helped explain the game really, and there's a few bits with actors cavorting round and killing each other, which are harder to do on radio . . . I thought it was wonderful as a film, which Tom himself directed. I loved the way that *Hamlet* was happening all the time in the background. I think it's a very good film, that Tom should be proud of. Another one, a film script which didn't get made, but which he turned into a radio script, was *Three Men in a Boat*. You can see why that appealed to him, you know, the humour and paradoxes and all that.

He brings Jerome into the Housman play.
Including the dog, yes. Now the Housman play was I think much better as a radio play. I did it there, and I have to say that I much prefer it to the stage version. To me it was too long in the theatre, and he put certain things in really just to top it up,

I mean like the croquet game, which we didn't have in the radio play because it's not really necessary, it just sort of gave it a bit of movement. But it's very much a play of words, and the whole thing of moving about, and moving back to Hell, and so on, that works very well on radio.

Adapting a play for radio, would you pick up the theatre script and yourself adjust it slightly, or would you ask Tom to do it? Or get somebody else in to –
Oh, no, I wouldn't get someone else in. Either one would do it oneself and show it to him for his agreement, or ask him to do it. By and large I think he'd say, 'I'll leave it to you.' Happily we had a very good relationship. He was wonderful to have in the studio, because he always said, 'No, no, I trust the director,' I mean providing he *does* trust you: if not, you know, he hangs about. His presence was extremely useful.

Sir Trevor Nunn

Trevor Nunn is one of the most successful and versatile direc-tors of the last forty years. He has at different times been the artistic director of both the Royal Shakespeare Company and the National Theatre, and also directed the original produc-tions of many hugely successful musicals, including Cats, Nicholas Nickleby, *and* Les Misérables. *He talked to me in London early in 2004.*

TN: My career in theatre has been inextricably entwined with Tom Stoppard, to my delight and great benefit. Our first con-tact came about somewhat haphazardly in 1965. As an emer-gent RSC director, I was given an important task by Peter Hall, or perhaps I should say, test. It was to set up and run a short season of new plays in a small theatre in London – just as Peter himself had done several years before when he used the Arts Theatre as an adjunct to the Aldwych. He handed over a pile of thirty or forty scripts which had been received by the RSC unsolicited and instructed me to choose four from that seemingly enormous library.

I waded my way through every one of them, which was, I recall, a numbing process; but one script immediately bowled me over. It was called *Rosencrantz and Guildenstern* (no *Are Dead*, as I remember) and tantalisingly, it was missing a last scene. A note at the end promised that a final act would follow. The quality of invention and wit was astonishing, as the unknown writer examined how the world of *Hamlet* looked from the viewpoint of two of its minor characters, used and gobbled up by Shakespeare's plot.

I chose this play to open my season, I urged the RSC to find a small subvention to help the writer to finish it, and I telephoned this Tom Stoppard to explain what was going on. He seemed perplexed and excited in equal measure.

I set about casting the play to make an exact jigsaw fit with the revival just under way of Peter Hall's production of *Hamlet* with David Warner. I persuaded David to make the brief appearances as Hamlet, and Janet Suzman to contribute her Ophelia (which by then she was rehearsing in *Hamlet*) and was overjoyed to clinch Paul Rogers as the First Player, and two brilliant young RSC actors, Michael Williams and Robert Lloyd, for the eponymous pair.

Then came the dire news from Peter Hall that the new play season must be cancelled. The Aldwych operation was in bad financial trouble, and the fund earmarked for the four plays, which would have been presented at the Jeanetta Cochrane Theatre in Holborn, had to be diverted to plug the breach. I had the task of writing to the young and not-so-young hopefuls to say that their plays would not be produced after all. That was a low point.

About nine months later, Peter, who never gave up on new writing, told me that he could afford a small-cast new play to start the next Aldwych season. Alas *Rosencrantz* did not qualify even as a medium-cast play, so my imploring on its behalf was doomed. Instead, I did an excellent Polish play by Mrozek called *Tango*. I remember saying, 'If I can't do *Rosencrantz*, can I employ Tom Stoppard to do the version of *Tango*?' And that's when I *met* Tom. By then he was living in London and I went to see him at his very small flat, surrounded by the domestic paraphernalia of laundry and toddlers, and commissioned him. He finished the work in record time, it was a brilliant vigorous contribution; I directed the play (ended up playing the leading part too, but that's another story) and that was Tom's London theatre debut. His name was in a West End programme, even if it was as an adapter.

But then something happened in our continuing story that was more career-defining and probably life-changing. The dramaturg at the RSC, Jeremy Brooks, told me he had been sent a begging letter from the Oxford University Experimental Theatre Company. Every year they had gone to the Edinburgh Festival with a new play, but they had been let down and were without a project. So they were asking the RSC if we had anything in our cupboard. And of course I said, 'We must give them *Rosencrantz*. It would be a perfect play for a student company, and then we can go up to Edinburgh and take a look at the try-out. And it gives Tom a production.'

JH: *Which made him, of course.*

Yes but in an extraordinary way. Ronald Bryden, then the theatre critic of the *Observer*, wrote a review of the play. I think, truth to tell, Ron was trying to find another show on the Fringe and got lost, and so he went to see this student production instead. Whatever, he wrote that review, beginning, 'This is the most exciting debut of a dramatist since Samuel Beckett.' He telephoned his copy to the *Observer*, as you did in those days, and it was typed up. Now . . . Kenneth Tynan, previously the *Observer*'s great theatre critic, was moonlighting as their film critic while doing his day job as dramaturg for Olivier at the National. So he was in the *Observer* office; and wondering what Bryden was up to in Edinburgh he read the review as it came in. He wasted no time, found Stoppard's agent and bought the rights for the National Theatre the next morning. And indeed, why would Tom and his agent be anything other than overjoyed?

So you'd lost him, after all that.
Tom became a National Theatre writer and I didn't get to direct the play.

And for the same reason, you didn't get Jumpers.
Yes, because of course Tom had to go on delivering his new work to his new employers, who had put him on the platform of international fame.

But the RSC did get Travesties.
Tom is both loyal and highly moral. He gives himself a hard time if he feels he is not being entirely even-handed. He and I continued to talk and meet socially. At one point, after I had become Artistic Director of the RSC, I said to him, 'Why don't you write a play about exile?' He was nonplussed, but I said, 'Because you are one really, aren't you? Like Conrad, you're a master of the English language but actually you grew up with different perceptions, different mores and traditions.' He thought about it and said, 'That's bollocks. Yes, I lived in India and only came to this country as a schoolboy but I don't feel I am an exile at all.'

But about eighteen months after that brief exchange, he phoned me and said, 'I think I must give the RSC my next play.' I was ecstatic but disbelieving. 'How can this be?' He explained that it was to be a play about three revolutionary people living in exile – Lenin, James Joyce and the Dadaist Tristan Tzara – and therefore because we had once discussed the subject of exile, then he could say, hand on heart, that the work belonged in my theatre. As I was later to discover, the play really owed nothing to our conversation, but I think Tom felt, in a general sense, a debt of honour towards the RSC and to some extent to me.

He'd also spotted that John Wood was in the RSC.

Ironically enough, in a play by James Joyce called *Exiles*. I had transferred Harold Pinter's production of that rarity from the Mermaid to the Aldwych, so perhaps therein was a more attributable influence on Tom's play. The conversation about Lenin, Joyce and Tzara led him to be yet more specific about possible casting. Tom was fully aware that John Wood was next going to tackle Brutus in my production of *Julius Caesar* in Stratford, and that Cassius would be played by Patrick Stewart. 'If anyone was born to play Lenin it was him,' was Tom's observation. Needing, as ever, bait and blandishment to keep my ensemble together, I asked Tom if I had his permission to tell the two of them that there was a new Stoppard currently being tailored specifically for them. 'Please talk to them,' Tom insisted; 'don't let them escape into anything else.' So I sold the idea to John and Pat and they quietly salivated at the thought of being Joyce and Lenin respectively, in exile in Zurich, exchanging crushing epigrammatic wit.

Several months later, Tom called me to say he was ready to bring me the play. We met in my office high above the ceaseless traffic of the Aldwych. That evening is indelible in my memory. Tom opened a brown leather satchel and brought forth the play . . . in manuscript. He explained that his writing was so illegible (an understatement) that there was no point in my trying to read it. 'In the time-honoured tradition,' he said, 'I shall read it to you.' And he did. He read the whole play to me. He offered me occasional explanatory footnotes and, I might add, very little by way of characterisation.

I realised it was an immensely witty intellectual farce, based on the structure of Wilde's *Importance of Being Earnest* and that there was a dazzling leading role of a vainglorious British minor official called Henry Carr. James Joyce was a good part. Vladimir Ilych Lenin, by any stretch of the imagination, was not.

The end of the reading was an occasion of great celebration, but I couldn't help asking, 'What happened to Lenin?' 'Oh,' said Tom, 'it didn't really work out for Lenin.' It was clear that Tom had created Henry Carr for John Wood – who went on to deliver one of the very greatest performances of our time in that role – but it was also clear that I had to go to Stratford to explain to Patrick that Lenin hadn't 'worked out'. The highs and lows of being an artistic director.

You didn't direct the play, though?
That was the final part of the indelible evening. I confess I had allowed my excited anticipation to run ahead of me, and so it felt like a pie pushed in my face when Tom said, 'The Aldwych is the perfect theatre for it, and my dear friend Peter Wood is the perfect director.' I remember swallowing very hard while clamorously agreeing. And I was right to agree. Peter did a magnificent production that conquered both London and New York. So it wasn't until *Every Good Boy Deserves Favour* that I got my first Stoppard to direct – and then I got all the actors I was hoping for: John Wood as Ivanov, Ian McKellen as Alexander *and* Patrick Stewart as the Doctor.

And with Previn involved as well.
I knew André well by then because both the RSC and the LSO were moving into the Barbican as our new headquarters; André was principal conductor of the LSO and we had shared several policy meetings. At the same time his wife, Mia Farrow, had played superbly in the company at the Aldwych and André was a fan of what the RSC did. But he and Tom were best friends and I had also met up with them socially. It was a very happy time. I loved being with them, and the play/entertainment they were creating was provocative, brave and extremely topical. We didn't have long to rehearse, and even though it was not a long text, it was a race against time, knowing that when we arrived in the Royal Festival Hall (where the actors were literally surrounded by one of the world's great orchestras) we must be ready and we could not intrude on orchestra rehearsal time by even five minutes.

But then it was clear that Stoppard had different concerns, more about the real world today . . .

I think, for a while, there was a seismic shift in Tom's work. The television play *Professional Foul* and *Every Good Boy* were very different in stance from his previous work. These two plays are political critiques and moral outcries – fuelled by an almost militant anger. There is still the patina of his scintillating comedy of ideas, but the writer is now visibly wanting his theatre to bring about change.

But it wasn't until Arcadia *that you got your big chance with a new Stoppard. He'd been promising you a play for ages.*

In a jocular way he had suggested that one day it would be my turn. When I saw *The Real Thing* I was very jealous. I would have given anything to be involved with that play. But then I directed Felicity Kendal in Shaw's *Heartbreak House*. She and Tom were very close, and Felicity, who I had known for years, became a supporter of mine because we got on so well in rehearsal.

Clearly Tom likes to write with an actor in mind, and Hannah was very much created for Felicity. I suspect that she urged or even demanded that I direct the play. I suspect Richard [*Eyre*] must have gone through exactly the same sensations that I did all those years before, being given *Travesties* for the RSC. Delight that the National had a major new Stoppard, and deep disappointment that he wasn't required personally as director.

He was very gracious about it when I spoke to him.

Richard *is* gracious, and he was generous to me in the situation. The roles were reversed next time around. I had worked in very close harmony with Tom on *Arcadia*, which was immensely successful, transferring both to the West End and New York. We spent all our spare time together in New York and Tom asked one evening if he could talk to me about his *new* play. I learned from him about Housman and his background, and gradually, as time passed, Tom would show me completed sections and question me about whether or not his ideas were landing. I felt very privileged and took my role as talking-post very seriously. After several months, Tom sent me the finished play and asked if we could meet to discuss it. Naturally I was excited enough to believe that the previous months were a prelude to Tom popping the question. When we finished our 'no holds barred' analysis of the play, I waited for Tom to ask me if I would like to direct it. 'It's been so enjoyable talking this play through with you,' he said, 'and I thank you for your help. But I hope you understand I feel I must give this one to Richard.' I hope *I* was gracious too . . . well I'm certain I was, but the sense of loss, rather like grieving, remained with me for weeks.

Nevertheless, I may have exerted some influence on the finished form of *Invention*. To my surprise, Tom wanted my services as talking post and sounding board to continue, and so we met several times to discuss the latest draft or variant, even after it had been scheduled at the National. At one meeting Tom said he was unhappy with his second act to the point where he felt like the play was in crisis. His answer was typically Stoppardian. 'I know what the answer is to Act Two. I have just realised that I've already written it, and it's called Act One! It's a new *Act One* that I have to write.' I expressed considerable doubt, but reminded myself that you don't dissuade a genius to abandon his perception of Eureka. He duly did a draft of his new idea, and of course the wonderful climactic young Housman/old Housman scene disappeared from the play.

The best thing in the play.
Exactly, he was throwing out baby, bath, if not bathroom. So I begged him to think again, while itemising the losses the play would sustain in its newest form. Happily Act Two returned in an improved form and Act One went back to where it most emphatically and immovably belonged.

As a footnote to the story, I should explain that I was by then

Director of the National Theatre elect, and I occupied an office next door to Richard's office – the two spaces separated by a paper-thin wall. I often sat at my desk, ostensibly reading scripts, but unable to avoid listening to discussions about *Invention of Love* design, casting and meaning – discussions of a play I knew by heart, back to front. Now that *was* hard.

How much did you hear about Arcadia *before you got the script?*
Not a great deal. My impression was that it was going to be a comedy about the biography business, which in one sense it is, but when the script arrived, I knew instantly that I would have to educate myself in the mathematical and theoretical strand – which was way over my head. I knew a little about chaos theory and quantum, but nothing sufficiently substantial to allow me to control rehearsals and exposit the text.

My guess is that Arcadia *may have arrived in a more finished form than earlier Stoppard scripts.*
Well, it had a final scene . . . Indeed, I first saw a well-presented bound playscript, and not a work in manuscript as I had twice before. But I don't think Tom was ever part of that seventies and eighties fashion of writers leaving their work unrevised because 'heh, man, we will finish the play as part of the rehearsal work'. I think with some, that rapidly became an excuse for slipshod unresolved writing. Tom's plays are so linguistically precise, and are so brimful of cross-reference and interconnection, scene to scene, speech to speech, that relatively little in the writing will change between the first and last day of rehearsal. His plays are very difficult to cut because ideas and phrases planted in one scene are paid off, directly and obliquely in many others. So a Stoppard director would say 'Let's kick this script around in rehearsal' at his peril. We did make changes to the text of *Arcadia* during rehearsals, but invariably in the name of achieving greater clarity in the areas where I felt the audience would need more help.

That was where Peter Wood says he tended to intervene.
Tom sets the bar very high. He is very demanding of his audience's concentration and learning. But when he sets the bar too high, so that even his aficionado audience can't make the leap, then we practitioners have to beg him to bring the cleverness back within range.

Did you see Hapgood?
I did. Twice. I certainly felt I'd got it the second time. But I confess I was in the midst of an audience that hadn't. I had a similar experience recently at *Jumpers* in the West End. There were pockets of reaction but not that certainty that everybody was equally au fait with what was going on. Perhaps this is a heresy, but audiences are different in the West End as compared with the National or the RSC. We could *rely* on certain reactions in *Arcadia* at the National that became more sporadic when we moved to the Haymarket.

In casting, I guess a lot of actors are ruled out because of the articulateness of the scripts.
Just as for Shakespeare or Sheridan, Stoppard actors need to delight in language, and be possessed of immense verbal dexterity. But they must also be actors with heart and emotional openness. Self-congratulatory dazzle with no humanity equals bad Stoppard.

Casting Arcadia *must have been quite a challenge.*
Three challenges. I cast the National production, the West End production and the second Haymarket cast which also toured. Oh – four challenges, because we then did it all over again, with an American cast in New York. 'Discovering' Rufus Sewell and Emma Fielding was exciting in London, just as discovering Billy Crudup was thrilling in New York. I mean it's very encouraging to realise that flamboyant skills with language do continue from generation to generation – and if Stoppard is safe in the hands of youngsters, so is Shakespeare.

As director you would choose the designer and lighting designer.
Well, these choices are in the director's gift, but I felt it was important for Tom to be included, and to be involved in assessing the design solution from an early stage.

Arcadia was an interesting problem, a single set for two eras. Can you remember discussions with the designer about that?
Yes. *Arcadia* is based on the Plaza Suite principle – the same room witnessing different people in different crises over many years – the room is essentially the constant. Making a beautiful room was simple enough, though Mark Thompson's semicircular space suggesting a rotunda was in itself exquisite. But I fear I became responsible for the most contentious area of the design. I urged Mark to reveal some element of nature beyond the windows.

Something of the Arcadian landscape.
But Tom feared, with so many references to the *changing* styles of landscape gardening in the grounds of the house, that any depiction of nature would confuse or even refute his intentions. I argued that a windowless room, or a room of clerestory windows only, would be an arid debating chamber, a lecture theatre devoid of the vernal Arcadia that was one of the references of the title. I urged that the middle distance could remain unseen, but some huge foreground greenery and a tree-lined distant horizon would not in any way compromise the references within the play. Tom was persuaded and eventually became completely converted and thought the design was perfect.

Arcadia did change to some extent during the rehearsal period?
It's very important to Tom to be in the rehearsal room throughout, and of course it's equally important for the director to be, and be seen to be, in charge. So it's vital that no wedge can be driven between writer and director, which in turn means that

together they have to do careful preparation to be sure that they are in agreement about meaning and priorities.

After an introductory exposition to the company from Tom, I took on the task of explanation and analysis – and every now and then in front of the company, I would ask him, 'How am I doing?' as he sat observing us from the furthermost corner of the room. He was always encouraging and rarely had much to add. But of course there were occasions when an adjudication was necessary and we would all turn to Tom as the arbiter. Gradually the actors got used to asking him, 'Is that what you meant?' and then later on, 'Did you write it with the stress on *this* word or *that* word?' At which point, I noticed he started to be less diffident and more inclined to make precise instructions about the delivery of a line.

After three weeks of rehearsal, he proposed going away for a couple of days to accomplish the rewriting of passages we had collectively decided needed greater clarification. I remember deciding to grasp the nettle and saying, 'Do you think a couple of days or perhaps you need more like seven?' He took the point instantly – that the actors in particular and the production in general needed to breathe, discover itself and make mistakes, blunders and wrong turnings. Somehow the density and richness that scenes acquire during rehearsals is thinned out if the possibilities that *weren't* necessarily the writer's intention are not tried – perhaps to be discarded. If there is only 'one way' of doing it, the work runs the risk of being short of a dimension.

Tom went off, I think for ten days in the end, and in essence, I suppose I'm saying, 'The trick worked.' He was delighted with how alive and unexpected the show had become during the time of his absence. Of course his presence was vital during the final stages of rehearsals, but the texture of something living and breathing and spontaneous had been achieved, and so it was time for authorial authority again.

One actor did say to me he sometimes rather wished Stoppard wasn't there.

Oh, I would never minimise the importance of the writer's benediction in rehearsal, but with a writer as famous and acute as Tom, the idea of winning his approval can be daunting for actors.

We certainly all needed the writer to be there on *The Coast of Utopia*. Once again, we balanced things so that there were brief periods when the omniscient author was not around, but his insight was vital to our work from beginning to end of that extended rehearsal period when we kept three plays moving forward simultaneously.

He did quite a lot of rewriting there.
A great deal, honing, refining, clarifying, cutting, amplifying . . . it was a privilege that all the actors and myself were perpetually aware of, that we were witnessing how a great writer operated, and at very close quarters.

Years ago, I asked Tom about his method, how did he arrive at such unexpected juxtapositions of ideas. His reply was, I thought, very revealing. 'I begin the play I think I want to write. And then quite early on in the process, I discover that there is a quite different play I want to write, about a different set of ideas. So I write both of them and I allow them to collide – or even smash into each other like two trains meeting head-on.' So I think often the structure of his work, which is seemingly fragmented and very rarely linear, arises out of his delight in creating controlled accidents. The wreckage spreads far and wide and he discovers altogether unpredictable juxtapositions, relationships, reflections and contrasts between all the pieces, as they land.

It's a characteristic of this particular dramatist that so often, things that seem chaotic and angular turn out to have an explanation.
Partly because he and he alone knows where all the chaotic pieces came from. Partly because, as a theatrical conjuror of genius, he is uniquely able to tie up all the ends, he 'pays off'

everything he has planted. Repeatedly on *The Coast of Utopia* he would say, 'I know the last scene in this sequence has got to pay off this and this and this' – and he would list key ideas or phrases or running jokes. The pay-off might be ironic, or a comic twist, or an inversion, or sometimes an emotional delivery.

The Coast of Utopia *is a hugely different work from anything else he's done I think . . . It became three plays. It was going to be one originally; he was keeping you informed as he was writing?*
He was. And indeed the nature of the project changed a number of times. Actually Herzen didn't figure in the original format. Tom talked about Bakunin and Turgenev and suggested there would be a flavour of Chekhov to begin with. So in every sense, it was going to be his Russian play. I think he had been strongly influenced by writing a version of *The Seagull*, and equally, if not more, by the production of Gorky's *Summerfolk* I did at the Olivier.

Then he told me his new play had become two plays. And eventually, a couple of months later, the word 'trilogy' was used for the first time. At that stage Tom defined play one as an Olivier theatre play, the second, more talking and probably best in the Lyttelton Theatre, and the third, a conversation piece that would have to be in the Cottesloe Theatre. I felt it incumbent on me to point out that selling a trilogy in three different-sized theatres was impossible for the box office, and something of a contradiction in terms. I remember Tom was genuinely surprised that his embryonic three plays could ever be sold as a trilogy, even though he was planning for some characters to go through all three plays.

Most trilogies have a gap between them – they're written a year or two apart.
Tom knew a year before the completion of the work that he wanted to write the three plays together.

So you persuaded him to make them all for the Olivier.
Not really. I was perfectly happy to do them all in the Cottesloe, where I had directed *The Cherry Orchard* and had loved the freedom of *unprojected* Chekhov – the intimate theatre allowing real people to talk, in real time. But I was equally happy for Tom to nominate the Lyttelton (a proscenium theatre) or the Olivier, our vast open-stage amphitheatre. Tom knew his first play had to be in the Olivier – as *Summerfolk* was – and then he acknowledged that the scope and scale of the second play – Russia, Paris, Nice, the forty-eight revolution – was to be the same as play one. Finally Tom confessed that play three was no longer a conversation piece, and no longer predominantly about Turgenev. Indeed the central figure linking the trilogy together was to be Alexander Herzen.

He would be confident in you for the project because you'd done a lot of huge stage productions.
I suppose he concluded that if I could stage the eight and a half hours of *Nicholas Nickleby* then I could probably get his nine-hour epic on. It was certainly the biggest project I have ever undertaken. Nevertheless, I thought it would be ill-advised to make the rehearsal period too long. Seven weeks on each play, technicals and previews, would amount to more than six months' rehearsal, and I feared during such a long time, everyone's head would drop. So each play ended up with only four weeks' rehearsal. Of course the plays interrelated, characters continued and developed, themes continued and developed, so neither play two nor play three had to start from scratch.

But it was still a huge scramble.
I won't deny it was a challenge, real North Face of the Eiger. It was to the glory of the National Theatre – staff, stage management, crew, technical departments – that every target on our phenomenally complex and burdensome schedule was hit exactly. We were precisely on time, doing every rehearsal-room run-through, every first day of technical, every dress rehearsal,

every first preview, every first night. It's the sort of undertaking that can go catastrophically wrong, so it was something of a miracle that we came through untrammelled. More especially because Bill Dudley, the designer, and I were in totally unexplored new territory, beyond the frontier of tried and tested technology. We were making a film onstage, and what was achieved has had an enormous impact, with many people saying that theatre design has taken a quantum leap and can never again be as it was before.

Stoppard told me it was your idea to use the whole Olivier stage for every scene.
I fear you could never involve the big, far-flung amphitheatre audience of the Olivier by subdividing the stage into little pockets of action. The staging in the Olivier has to be coherent and unifying for the whole audience.

And in fact I still wonder if there aren't too many short scenes. The plays certainly whirl you about. Intentionally – as they capture the scattered fragments of thought that became a ferment of European revolution.

I did sense something of the film about it. If, today, we had the kind of television we had twenty or thirty years ago, it might have become a television series of six instalments or so.
It's the great sadness of my happy time at the National Theatre that I was unable to persuade the BBC to record *The Coast of Utopia*. I offered to break the habit of a lifetime and instead of insisting on studio conditions, said I would agree to filming the work onstage. I particularly urged the new cultural channel, BBC4, to make it as both a landmark play and production, but also, material that could be given the series or serial format, or an educational format.

Did you ever feel, at the back of your mind, that this might be a one-off?

Utopia was a unique and utterly stimulating project, so one-off or not, I have only pleasure in having been part of creating it. But I do hope the plays are done again, in New York, in Moscow and throughout Europe; and I hope at some future point the plays will be revived here. The disappointment was the behaviour of the press. For the previous two years, they had often cajoled me for selecting a repertoire that was too populist – insufficiently challenging. Yet faced with *The Coast of Utopia*, many intelligent writers just said, 'Too difficult'! Frankly, I thought the response in these cases was pathetic. Audiences were following, laughing and cheering the plays, they weren't 'too difficult' for them.

It's been a remarkably long, continually successful career. Richard Eyre describes Stoppard as an exception to a general rule that dramatists grow old and grumpy.
I am sure there must be wells of irascibility underneath, but Tom is meticulous in his decorum, unfailingly polite and has a natural tendency towards generosity. And I should know, having observed him at countless National Theatre Board meetings! He really likes actors, and he loves the whole playmaking process. He is invariably present in rehearsals of revivals of his plays, and he is deferential and patient with people who have somehow got hold of the wrong end of the stick. I would say he is almost saintly in relation to his work, as he hands over his innermost perceptions to be made flesh by others.

What would you say to a young actor or young director who was sceptical about Stoppard: partly perhaps for political reasons, wanting something more left-wing, but also worried that it's all for the chattering classes of a metropolitan kind?
Specifically to anybody uneasy about Stoppard's political grasp, I would say read *The Coast of Utopia* – again and again. It's a seminal treatise about revolutionary thought and revolution in practice. It reveals a writer profoundly seeking change while rejecting all the solutions of human engineering demand-

ing bloodshed and destruction. And he also rejects the babel of chattering as represented by the daily outpouring of the media who feel no responsibility for anything they say.

But to these young people I would say, there are many different kinds of writers – thank the Lord – and what a very dull theatrical landscape it would be if everybody wrote social realism or political polemic. Theatre must offer diversity above all else. I would tell the young that Stoppard is a great original, but he is also in a great tradition that flows through the heightened language of Shakespeare's comedies, the cadenced prose of Wycherley, Congreve, Sheridan, the self-congratulation and scorn of Oscar Wilde and the dramatisation of ideas of Shaw – the tradition is glittering, but throughout its development there is a seriousness and humanity below the surface. Tom's work acknowledges and celebrates this tradition in pursuit of his unique creation, the intellectual farce, but if we, his interpreters leave out, or understate his emotional engagement with his characters, we fail him, and devalue his achievement.

I am convinced that, unlike much of the gritty, 'tell it like it is' drama of the late twentieth century, Stoppard's plays will be performed a hundred years from now and when they are, their philosophic and poetic wit will stand the test of time.

Sir Richard Eyre

Richard Eyre was director of the National Theatre from 1987 to 1997; his diary of the period is published as National Service. *He has vast experience of directing plays, television films, musicals and occasionally opera. His survey of twentieth-century theatre,* Changing Stages, *written jointly with Nicholas Wright, includes the following elegant comments on Stoppard:*

England was the floor on which he laid his sleeping-bag with all the determined masterfulness of the new arrival. He learned the rules and studied the small print. His attachment to British free speech was fierce and foreign, like an enlightened explorer seeing the value of a native tradition long after the actual natives had forgotten the point of it . . .

What other playwright, after four fantastically productive decades, has entered mellow greatness? [It seems that] stardom, sustained over year after year of hard work, gives you at least a partial invulnerability to the darts and dents of disappointment. Whatever the reason, no modern playwright since Ibsen has made such sense of late middle age.

Richard Eyre talked to me in his London home in autumn 2003.

JH: *Can you remember when Tom Stoppard first came to your notice, presumably way back, and did you feel, as a lot of people did, slightly antipathetic to this kind of dramatist?*
RE: I think the DNA of British comedy is found in *The Goon Show* and Tom Stoppard. If you trace the genealogy of, let's say, *Blackadder*, it goes straight back to *Rosencrantz and Guildenstern*. And I did think it was dazzling, and I thought the jokes were wonderful. I did feel it's a slightly rich conceit to make a play which is based on your knowledge of another play, but I wouldn't say that really interfered with my pleasure. I was slightly alienated by *Jumpers*; I did think at the time it was too clever by half. So I would say, my increasing love of Tom's work – and I would put it that strongly, certainly in the case of *The Invention of Love* – was actually paralleled by Tom putting his heart on his sleeve, more and more. And I was very struck by a television play he did, *Professional Foul*, which I thought was a wonderful, wonderful piece of work.

Before that some people felt a political anxiety.
Yes. To some extent, because I'm a child of the seventies – I was running a theatre in the seventies where my house writers were David Hare, Howard Brenton, Trevor Griffiths, Ken Campbell: sort of lefty anarchist – so, yes, we thought Tom was . . . I don't

know that we politicised him as a right-wing writer, but we saw him as not engaged.

The usual left-wing argument was that if you're not engaged, you're automatically right-wing, by default.
And one of the things that I admire and like about Tom is his absolute unwillingness to appease any faction. Finally he will say: 'Well, look, that is what I think. I think this for the following reasons; take it or leave it.' And of course the fact is that at the time, when Tom was being vilified in some quarters as being a right-wing toady, he was actually active in a number of organisations, not least Index and Charter 77, which were extremely important, and a lot more actively engaged than most 'political' writers.

In the eighties I was appealed to by the widow of a Czech Charter 77 activist, who was in London and looking for a job and indeed somewhere to live, and I couldn't help personally but I wrote to Stoppard. I didn't hear anything for three weeks and then he wrote to say, yes, he'd found her both. That was the kind of entirely unpublicised thing which would go on.
Also unpublicised is the fact that Tom has a Trust, and he invariably gives money to people who write, for a good cause.

So, you began to feel the heart was there. But you perhaps never expected to direct for him?
He was very loyal to Peter Wood, for years and years and years. And in a sense he was also very loyal to Trevor: *Arcadia*, in Tom's mind, was the play he had promised Trevor fifteen years before.

You were director of the National at the time of Arcadia.
Yes, I was, and for about five minutes I thought I was going to direct it. Generously, Tom said to me, 'Oh you know, it should be either you or Trevor,' and then somehow I heard that he was saying that 'maybe Trevor should direct it but I'd

like you to do it', and I thought, 'Great, I'm going to direct *Arcadia*.'

You'd read the script?
I had read the script and I was very excited by it. Not least because when I first read it I was in New York, and I was staying in the Hotel Morgan, which is next to the Pierpont Morgan Library, and in the library there was an exhibition at the time of landscape drawings by Humphrey Repton, and I just thought this all had great felicity. Then Tom said, actually, he was mortified, sorry, but he felt he owed the play to Trevor. Which was fine, and Trevor did it brilliantly.

But you were naturally disappointed.
Well, I was, because I just thought it was such a wonderful play. A glorious play, that attracted me on a number of different levels. In so far as I have any academic qualifications at all, I started as a mathematician, so I understood the mathematics.

Stoppard joined the Board of the National round about the time that you became Director. Did you have anything to do with that?
I think I did, actually . . . In my day, the Board used to be essentially appointed by the Queen. In other words, appointed by the Arts Minister of the day. In time-honoured British fashion, the Permanent Secretary would call me, and the Chairman, and say, 'Who do you think we should put on the Board?' And I said, 'Well, why not ask Tom Stoppard?'

And would you look to him for a certain sort of contribution, a certain line? Would he be perhaps pushing continental dramatists?
Not at all. No, no. Tom would never push a dramaturgical agenda at all. He would engage in philosophical questions, what the National Theatre existed for, what we were doing, did it fulfil our remit, what was our remit, and he would talk on

what I can loosely describe as moral issues. It's always a question of should we take sponsorship, or how much on the front foot should we go on sponsorship, and were we prepared to call the National Theatre the Disney National Theatre, that sort of issue. Tom was always the voice on the Board that people would turn to – I think sometimes to Tom's astonishment; they would expect oracular wisdom to pour out of him, and he would say, 'Well, look, I'm just thinking out loud.' I'd be sitting next to one of the great minds of our time, thinking [*laughs*], 'Where are you going with this, Tom?'

[*Eyre emphasises that in his time the NT Board was never allowed to act as 'a play committee', and contrasts the difficulties of the Royal Opera House as 'ghastly dilettante intervention'.*]

Having failed to get Arcadia, *perhaps the next play was morally promised to you?*
Yes, it was, actually. Tom said, 'If I write a next, that one is for you.'

And can you tell me how you came to hear about it?
He said he was writing a play about Housman. Um . . . I mean, I knew *A Shropshire Lad*. I knew that Housman was a classical scholar. I think I also knew that he was responsible for introducing crème brûlée to the English dinner table . . . So I guess I knew very little. I think I might have had a sense that it was about romantic love.

Perhaps it didn't have a title, at that stage?
I'm pretty certain it didn't have a title. [*He turns to* National Service.] 'Letter from Tom.' He hoped to write the Housman play this summer – this is August '95. He's written the first couple of pages – 'which would normally mean that I'm over the hump', he says. But he's not despairing: the summer's achievement is to recognise the unwritten play.

Then it comes through in typescript. Some directors make suggestions at that stage for changes.

Well, I didn't have a very clear understanding of the play. But I had a very, very powerful response to two things. One was the sense of the unconsummated love – that I found incredibly moving; that came through very, very clearly. And the other thing was the originality, and the beauty, I mean the poetic beauty in theatrical terms, of the scene between the old Housman and the young Housman. But I was surely intimidated by the length of it. And also by what seemed the intractability of the play; I mean that was the first draft. And then there was a period where Tom was doing a lot of thinking out loud about whether he should change the structure of the play, and whether he should reverse the acts and tell the story in almost reverse order. And instinctively I thought it was better as it was . . .

When you say 'intractable': it's very talky, and very Latin, at times.

Well, I think one's first response to a play is generally the most important. And what I first took from it, as I say, was the story of romantic love and the beauty of that theatrical device. But along with that were the thickets of the classical scholarship and the Oxford world. And the three men in a boat, the sort of coincidence and circumstantial connections. When I'd read it half a dozen times I could see that the whole thing was an extremely complicated structure. It's like a piece of architecture with a number of buttresses, where at first sight you might think that you could just remove a buttress and that the building would stand, only to discover that everything linked in, and that it was astonishingly difficult to. And I thought oh, it's probably over-length, and we could take that out; and then you started to see that you did diminish the piece if you did that. It took me some time to understand the theatrical imagination of the piece and kind of give Tom the credit, after writing for the theatre for thirty-plus years, of knowing exactly what he was doing!

Was he nevertheless ready to make changes?
No, I think he was pretty – I wouldn't say stubborn, but certain that if we started to take out lumps then it would crumble. And I started to see that what I'd initially seen as rather dry and dusty, and unintelligible stuff, was as accessible, and as passionate, and as moving, as the romantic story. The story of the importance of classical scholarship is a metaphor for the importance of knowledge and education and curiosity and truth. And I wanted to shove the play in the face of that fool, Charles Clarke [*Secretary of State for Education*], going on about unnecessary classical education.

The play tends to appear to be written for an elite who can pick up the references. 'How would it play in Peoria?' is a problem with Stoppard generally, but perhaps more with this play.
That's what I thought, when we were rehearsing it. But actually the play carries its own information. It is possible to understand the play without knowing any Latin; you don't need to know anything about any of the worlds, because the play carries its own manual with it.

I was thinking particularly of Stead, Labouchère, Harris.
Yes, the Labouchère scene is the only area where I always felt the play teetered on the edge of inaccessibility; because although the arc of it was finally taking you round to Wilde and to the whole discussion of romantic love, and homosexuality, it kind of bent the arc at that point.

When it came to casting: John Wood had been associated with Stoppard, although not for a while; he had been important in Travesties *and other work. Did Stoppard push for John Wood?*
Tom said early on, 'There are only two people I can think of who could play the part: John Wood and Ian McKellen.' It's a part for people who can take a deep breath and be unintimidated by a fifteen-minute speech, and who indeed can welcome it. I think there are very few, and of a generation, who have that

sort of dexterity: Nigel Hawthorne would have been another. I'd never worked with John, and I loved working with him and I regretted the fact that it had taken me so long to do it.

Did you take it to New York?
No, I didn't do it in New York. It was done, by the Lincoln Center, very successfully.

Were you interested by any changes they made?
I don't think they made many changes, actually. We made a few changes when we did it in the West End. Just a nip and tuck here and there.

It started in the Cottesloe and then went to the Lyttelton. That's quite a change, isn't it? – did you have that in mind always?
No. I hadn't had that in mind; in fact it coincided that the opening night of *The Invention of Love* was the last night I spent at the National as Director. So in fact it was Trevor's decision to transfer it to the Lyttelton. But you could say it exemplified the Stoppard thesis: get your reviews in the small theatre and then transfer to the big one. It's a pretty inviolable truth!

Arguably most plays are best done in a small theatre.
I'm absolutely sure of that. That intensity, sharing the same space with language and touch, and passionate distillation.

How did you find the trilogy, The Coast of Utopia?
Well. I had a pretty good day. I thought the first play was really thrilling; but then there was definitely a sense of the energy in the writing, and the energy in the performance, just being dissipated throughout the day. And I did feel – and I don't know if he will – that with hindsight Tom might have found a way of distilling all that information into one play. Because essentially it's the same themes being examined over three plays.

I think he'll resist that idea.
I don't know if he'll resist the idea of reducing it to two plays.

It took up themes from earlier work, but it did seem a bit joke-free.
Yes. And the jokes rather sat there; they were rather sprinkled like slivers of lemon peel as decoration on a piece of meat.

Taking an overview: you wrote beautifully about Stoppard in Changing Stages, *and particularly about the mellowing in late middle age, with* Arcadia *and* The Invention of Love, *and perhaps* The Coast of Utopia. *Of course we hope he'll write more; but are we going to see him in the end as a kind of sport or off-shoot or siding in British theatre? Do you think there's anything that young dramatists today can take from him?*
Oh yes. Tom is one of those great emancipating figures. When I interviewed Tom for the TV programme, I was asking him about Beckett; and he told this wonderful story about going to see this production of *Waiting for Godot* with one of his sons; and his son said, 'Y'know, Dad, this bloke writes a bit like you.' Seeing *Waiting for Godot* emancipated Tom; he saw that he could write anything; you could put anything on a stage. And I think that in the British theatre tradition there are two great, well perhaps three . . . Shakespeare is the DNA of British theatre: he's a fantastic liberator, because every time you think, 'Oh, these plays have to be in rooms about families,' he makes you think, 'Hang on a minute!' And Brecht had a similar effect, not as far as the public was concerned but on the thinking, such as it is, in British theatre, of finding a sort of twentieth-century Shakespearianism, that you can put worlds on stage. And in some way I think Tom has sort of taken Brecht – with whom he has no sympathy at all – and Beckett, and has simply seen, 'Yeah, this medium: you can expand and contract, it's a poetic medium that is fantastically flexible; you can throw your imagination at it and it'll bounce back and amplify it.'

And you can throw your language at it. It doesn't have to be in verse to be poetic.

Yeah, exactly. It's essentially the thing about theatre that everything there is unreal, and the audience knows it's unreal. It's all metaphor; whereas with film it's all literal, it's very hard to make film poetic. So I think Tom will always be that sort of fantastic exemplary figure who demonstrates that the medium is capable of anything, and is so alive. So I think he's an inspiration. I don't think anybody's going to set up a sort of neo-Stoppardian school of playwriting, but if you watch Tom's plays with any degree of curiosity and engagement, then you can't fail to be entranced by the imagination of the work, and the wit, and, latterly, I think, the passion.

Vicki Mortimer

Theatre designer Vicki Mortimer, who has worked extensively with the RSC and the National Theatre, designed two very successful Stoppard revivals: the 1999 Donmar Warehouse The Real Thing *and the 2003 National Theatre* Jumpers. *The director of both was David Leveaux, with whom she has also worked regularly in Japan. (For Leveaux on* The Real Thing, *see p. 156ff.) This 'interview' was conducted by e-mail.*

JH: *Before commenting on Stoppard specifically, what would you say about the basic relationship between director and designer?*

VM: The theatre decides who should direct the play, and he or she then chooses the rest of the team. I have a long track record of working with David Leveaux, and usually find it very rewarding – he is very confident with visual language and is not afraid of re-inventing ingredients, particularly at technical rehearsals, where he is a fabulous improviser. At design stage, I really cannot move independently of the director – we have to be discovering the play alongside each other. If we get stuck, I try to bring along images that nudge us to the next step.

And the lighting designer?
Lighting designers are crucial, and can make or break a set design. Mark Henderson (*The Real Thing*) knows the Donmar space incredibly well, and was great for the show – very flexible and articulate. Paule Constable is a designer I have a very strong working relationship with, and I think I suggested her to David for *Jumpers*. Her language of practicals was a key to the audience's understanding of the geography of the space.

Stoppard is known for being present at revivals of his work. How much was he involved in your decisions?
For *The Real Thing*, circumstances meant that David and I did much of the design work in New York, so we didn't involve Tom at that stage. It was early days in our relationship with him and we were working independently. Once rehearsals began, Tom did show a quiet need to be convinced of the staging solutions, which were very fluid and demanded a relaxation from the audience in terms of their expectations for any consistent literal setting. He was incredibly supportive and trusting of David from the outset.

For *Jumpers*, we presumed early on in the design process that we would again re-invent Tom's stage directions! But this time, because we had worked with him, and because the staging demands were much more of a puzzle, we went to him to discuss the design when our ideas were still embryonic. Tom has a great understanding of allowing the pace of the design process to be set by the team concerned – and the delicacy of the terms of reference. He was very generous and open. We talked about the party scene – he wanted it to take place in empty space as described in the script, but for it not to feel like a 'hangar'. I remember him laughing delightfully at the memory of being teased by Peter Wood about his stage direction 'the bedroom assembles around her' – as if it were that easy!

Did you ever feel him clinging to the original Carl Toms conceptions?

Tom never really alluded to the other productions of *Jumpers* except when trying to help us out with solutions to the practical demands of the play – the body in the cupboard, the goldfish etc. He's quite interested in the mechanics of how a play is staged, and likes stage magic very much. His stage directions try to make rather conventional sense – one gets the feeling he is trying to be helpful and take responsibility a bit for what he is demanding. Despite this, both *The Real Thing* and *Jumpers* lend themselves to deconstruction – environments which contain the ache, so to speak: in *The Real Thing*, Henry's unwitting descent into self-isolation, in *Jumpers* the loss of Dotty into some kind of madness, and the ever-retreating 'answer' to George's enquiries.

How much does theatre space dictate design?
For *The Real Thing*, the shape of the Donmar stage almost enforced the fluidity of staging between multiple locations. We drew out an arc of stripping away domesticity during the play until Henry waited to confront Annie in a single armchair – the furnished ease of his married life reduced to this simple picture. It was the beginning of David and I using screen language as an architectural wipe, a dispassionate divider of scenes and people: cool, objective, part of the psychological jigsaw. We used screens to fracture and dislocate the space as the play went on, becoming more austere and unforgiving; as if they worked as an objective interruption of a mental state.

In *Jumpers*, the screens found a further function as a non-literal projection surface. The projections on the screens were not only illustration: the images transformed depending on which character controlled them – Dotty's images jump-cutting abruptly and chaotically; for Bones, a moonscape became a romantic horizon; for Archie, a scientific diagram looking remarkably like an erotic painting. They were also a semi-permeable barrier between George and Dotty.

Jumpers is a difficult play to stage. It's very cluttered.

The play contains so much, it's a real problem to decide where to prioritise. There's the theatrical thread through the play, and, of course, the *relationship* in the middle of it all – we had to somehow understand that George and Dotty actually do have a life together with kitchens and front doors (and that this life is one which is under threat of annihilation at the point when we meet them). And then there are the practical staging requirements, which are incredibly complicated. Conceptual content had to be partnered by solving the physical problems set by Stoppard.

I led us up the garden path rather, with over-literal references to a dusty art deco ballroom . . . meanwhile, David was countering with the room as a spiral with no doors, which ended up looking like an idea for an opera. He was very keen from the beginning to keep away from orthodox naturalism, wanting to let the audience in on the collision course steered between dream and reality in the play. He was strong on all the moon imagery – coincidentally he has always been fascinated by the moon landings, and a key book (although not directly used) was the then recently published *Full Moon*, a collection of incredibly beautiful and moving photographs taken on the Apollo missions.

The night-sky walls were a photographic image printed onto a vinyl which is then applied to the scenery with adhesive. It always seemed important to me that the galaxy should have a reality in order to supply the magical impossibility of the Milky Way being the architecture – had it been an image interpreted by a painter, it would have lost its surreal edge, and, perhaps, some of its romance.

The key idea was that of orbit – we attempted to make a space in which the turntable did not operate in the conventional way of concealing one set when the other was in use, but where the objects and people were acknowledged to be orbiting each other, where the spaces were fluid and shifting, and where the characters were on shifting ground. We wanted a rim revolve, or two revolves: David always wanted the Secretary to revolve continually throughout the main action.

The other key decision was deciding to elide a couple of references in the play to where George and Dotty live – we chose to encase the whole show in the ballroom, band and all, so that Dotty's world maintained as strong a hand as George's, and the latent possibility of escape into fantasy was always supported. This also made it possible for the opening sequence to be genuinely magical and theatrical, whilst still in some kind of space that remained present in the rest of the play. What we called the 'mini-stage', where the band are, became one of my favourite elements in the show – a self-conscious admission of how an audience is drawn into a show, and how amazing to have three lovely jazz musicians supplying spontaneous mood music for the low points in the technical rehearsal!

Dotty's room was inspired by everything that is romantic but vulnerable and innocent about the early days of variety in England. Having said that, one of the key visual triggers was the photography of James Abbe, who took pictures backstage at the *Folies Bergère* in the twenties, and in Hollywood in the thirties – his work has an amazingly nostalgic, aspirational quality, perfect for the damaged Dotty. I also felt her room should have the props of a stage creature: the mirrors, the lighting, all contributing to a kind of brittle artifice, as well as a seductive glamour.

We were much restricted by the repertory at the National; it included *Jerry Springer, the Musical*, which occupied almost every flying position in the Lyttelton – not helpful when programming a play which requires at the very least a trapeze act somewhere downstage. The trapeze in London was a somewhat complicated system of tracks whereby we tried to control the speed and curve of the Secretary's journey, allowing her time to strip off each piece of clothing in a hiatus at each end. It never quite worked, and for me, never quite convincingly looked like she was just swinging from the chandelier. Luckily, in New York David Benken was sure we could achieve everything with a simple pendulum . . . and thankfully he was right! It meant we didn't have much flexibility with the speed of travel, but it worked, and looked so much more surprising and exciting. I think the final design at the National was an uneasy marriage between the two instincts (both essential for the play in some form) which then found its real form in New York.

The fluidity I mentioned earlier meant that although we had been quite diligent in working out roughly how each sequence might go, it was by no means concrete . . . This meant that rehearsals were incredibly nerve-racking for David – it might never have worked! Luckily he is a director who flourishes in the technical rehearsals, and comes up with the most amazing language combining all the technical elements. The opening sequence took a very long time to rehearse on stage for the first time because what Tom demands in the first few minutes is worthy of a substantial musical.

How much are you yourself around for rehearsals and previews?
As a rule of thumb, I try to be around a lot during rehearsals. In reality, this is very hard to achieve, particularly if one is designing costumes as well as set; fittings are very time-consuming, no matter how wonderful the costume supervisor may be (and I had a great one, Irene Bohan, on *The Real Thing*). With *Jumpers*, I wasn't designing costumes, but I had a prior commitment to an opera which kept me away from rehearsals – David had been quite accepting of this in advance, but come the reality of the rehearsal, and the difficulty of the way we had decided to stage the piece, it was deadly: it took us until New York to recover!

As for previews, I would usually try to see all of them – really, there aren't many, and ideas are always developing. With *Jumpers*, we made the first preview by the skin of our teeth, and barely respectably, so previews were key working time. It was a punishing time, with David getting very frustrated as we tried to bring to reality the show as he saw it. The play is really technically demanding as so-called straight plays go. For *The Real Thing* the previews were more about acting and small refinements in the language of the production.

Both productions were successful and eventually moved to different theatres, or tour, or New York. How involved were you at that stage? Could you make changes, or did you in practice lose control?

When a play moves to the West End or to New York, the expectation is that the designers will be as involved as possible – and it is in one's interest to be so. Changes of venue can affect the design in unpredictable ways, not just proportion. With *The Real Thing* and *Jumpers*, I really welcomed the opportunity to re-address choices we had made and to develop ideas where they had more to give. With *The Real Thing*, Tom gave his blessing to expand the use of the screens we had for transitions, and their impassive presence became a much more potent ingredient in the erosion of Henry's certainties. As for *Jumpers*, the transfer to the West End was an exercise in gritting our teeth – there was no money to make improvements and the timing was such that neither myself nor Paule Constable, the lighting designer, were available to look after the show as it went in. It was a huge relief to get our hands on it in New York and have a second chance! The commercial set-up in New York includes the provision of a set design associate who manages, with the production manager, the technical aspects of the changes, draws up the show to be built, etc. If you have a good team, it is a very enjoyable and supportive way of working.

Re-visiting a show is always rewarding, as, in the light of the bigger picture, the scope of nasty surprises is narrower, and there is an ease in the dialogue due to the pre-existence of a shared language – good ideas can be built on, bad ones jettisoned.

David Hersey

The lighting designer David Hersey, American born, settled in England in the late 1960s and has become a senior figure of British theatre in his field. Soon after arriving in England, he worked as assistant lighting director on a tour of Rosencrantz.

'I was really quite taken with the play.' Having seen the original production of Jumpers, *he lit the 1985 revival. He also lit the first productions of* Hapgood *in 1988 and* The Coast of Utopia *in 2002.*

We met at the National Theatre early in 2004. David Hersey explained that the director tends to choose the designer and the lighting designer; occasionally a producer is involved as well. Usually the set designer is appointed before the lighting designer, whose job is to serve the purposes of the play and the design.

DH: You hope to see the designer really early on, in the hope that you can help to ensure that his ideas are achievable. In the case of Carl Toms, who worked very often with Peter Wood, obviously we would discuss – when a model was there we'd look at the model and try to bring in some of the realities, and make adjustments here and there to make things possible. So that involvement is very helpful. And of course the director will have a certain amount to say about what he thinks about light. But I find over the years that watching rehearsal is the best way.

JH: *The opening of the original production of* Hapgood *featured a striking lighting effect which some even found the most memorable bit of the play. I recall that we followed cars round a blown-up map, projected on a screen.*
Yes, with a little laser pointer. Great fun! Sometimes very simple technology can make a big effect. But you don't do effects for their own sake, you just do them when they're needed to help tell the story. Lighting is really a narrative tool. If it doesn't help to develop the story line, it's not doing its job.

Did Peter Wood ask for something special there?
I'm sorry, I don't recall. But, you know, these things don't just happen overnight. It's a process; things grow and they get worked on, you try something and it doesn't work so you try something else, and gradually something emerges. And very

often you wouldn't really know in the beginning how it was going to come out until you had a go at it.

We also talked about the huge difference between small and large theatre spaces. Even within the National, moving a play from the intimate Cottesloe to the vast Olivier requires completely different lighting. In The Coast of Utopia *design and lighting became almost inseparable, because William Dudley decided to use video projected on to a huge curving cyclorama. Hersey remembers many hours of discussion between the two of them. Nothing was straightforward, because sometimes the basic needs of lighting – to see the actors' faces, for example – clashed with the 'needs' of video.*

Overall, Hersey – who has lit big shows such as Nicholas Nickleby *and* Les Misérables *– found the whole* Utopia *project 'up there' with the biggest challenges he has faced. In common with others he also remembered not having enough time to get the trilogy ready; some lighting cues were still being altered after the previews. It would have been easier a play at a time – as indeed trilogies are usually staged. Finally:*

Lighting is a difficult thing to talk about. It's tricky. When you do your best work you're invisible. Although you may think we have a common vocabulary, it's so subjective; I might say one thing and you might think I mean something completely different. So in the end the lighting designer really has to understand what the director and the playwright are trying to achieve; and so really consider the text itself.

John Wood

John Wood, one of Britain's leading classical actors, became the young Stoppard's first choice in the 1960s and 1970s. He was the first New York Guildenstern; Travesties *was to some extent written for him, and he returned as the elder Housman in 1997. He talked with me in Kent early in 2004.*

JH: *Your first experience with Stoppard was a TV play.*
JW: Yes. *Teeth*; that just came out of the blue. But Tom and I got on extremely well, and so I seemed to be more or less an automatic choice for the next one [*Another Moon Called Earth*].

In those days TV plays were done live.
Those were; they were just about the last! We had two weeks' rehearsal.

And was he there then?
Yes, he was. He's extremely good at that. He just sits in a corner, saying, 'My work is done'; but in fact Tom is tremendously adaptable and frequently gets us out of difficulties.

One younger actor has said that he finds the presence slightly daunting; we're now talking about an Eminent Dramatist, a bit of a Grand Old Man.
No, no. He's got a terrific way of not being put-offing; he sits there in a corner and often he's writing, as if he's writing something new. So his presence was always helpful. Almost indulgent, like a father watching his children playing.

Did he suggest you for Guildenstern in New York?
No, I asked for it! I thought straight away, 'This man's a genius; he's much the most important playwright I've ever met or am ever likely to meet, and obviously I'd like to stay close to him in my work.'

You felt that even with those two TV plays – before Rosencrantz?
Rosencrantz opened at the Old Vic in about February of that year. The first night was quite wonderful. It was just the most extraordinary evening; the central joke was just mind-blowing.

He clearly came to feel that you were his actor of preference.

And later he wrote Travesties *for you.*
I was told, many years after the event, that he actually wrote *Jumpers* for me, too. By that time I was at the RSC, and having some respectable success; *Jumpers* had been commissioned by the National, and I believe that Olivier did try to get me.

You would have been a rather young George Moore.
Oh, as an actor I have no age.

Can you put your finger on what in your performances may have appealed to Stoppard?
[*Laughing*] I'm flaky. I'm a fantasist, I'm totally unreliable . . .

I was expecting you to say something about articulation! I'm told that a lot of actors are frightened of long speeches.
Are they? I must admit that Carr's first speech in *Travesties* looked like a nightmare. But then you find your way through it . . . Those long speeches are like huge interlocking curves, aren't they? – of varying radius. As long as you've got that pattern in your head . . . And as long as you treat every single line as if it's the last. You know what I mean? – you don't 'know', once you've finished a long line, that there's another one after it.

Because in real life we don't always know what we're going to say next. So you come to a series of endings, as it were?
No, no: 'endings' would put it on the floor. A lot of American actors tend to do that; they let it bother them. It has to stretch in the air, you have to give the thing its music, at the same time as articulating muddled thought! Henry Carr's a lovely character; he's such an idiot.

And the train keeps jumping the tracks. You keep coming back to where you were before.
Yes. When the play opens, he's clearly dictating his memoirs. There's one absolutely marvellous bit, one scene where the lines don't go the way he thought they ought to . . . Here it is: 'match

233

the carnage / match the carnation . . . God's blood / ox-blood . . . shot and shell / shot-silk . . . graveyard / cravat . . . stench / starched . . . Christ / creased . . . Jesu / just so . . . deserted by simpletons / asserted by a simple pin . . . the damask lapels / they damn us to hell . . . ora pro nobis / or a brown, nobis . . . quick / -cuit . . . no, get me out! / no get me out the . . .'

I didn't bring that out till we were on the road in America, in Boston, at the Colonial Theater, which is gigantic; it was more successful in Boston than anywhere else I ever played it. I managed to get them to *hear* that; they actually heard that it was the same consonants in the same order: the first time, a man in the last hurricane of terror; the next time, deciding what fancy garments he's going to fancifully wear.

Did you do that by slowing down?
No, by *thinking* it. Nothing works unless you think it. You've just got to be thinking it so hard that the audience picks it up.

One of the problems, above all in Henry Carr but also elsewhere in Stoppard, is that there are so many jokes that you can't go for all of them. You couldn't hope to get a laugh on every single one.
No, that would be ghastly and exhausting, just to *allow* the audience to laugh. The trick is to not let them, and not let them, and not let them, and not let them, and then finally bouboum! And often the bou-boum might be the weakest of the sequence.

That's the kind of thing that might change in rehearsal, perhaps?
No, because you don't know in rehearsal where they're going to laugh. The number of times I've worked with a script and thought, 'Oh, there'll be a laugh here'; you get to the theatre and there isn't . . . It's a very mysterious craft.

And it varies night by night as well.

Absolutely. The play is actually made by the aggregate of the people watching.

Did you find American audiences noticeably different from English ones?
New York, yes. 'This seat is costing me fifty dollars . . .'

With a play like *Travesties*, you get out onstage and you start and the play just picks you up. It's like being carried on a wind; it's very hard to put a foot wrong. The same thing happens with Chekhov, and with Ibsen; you read *The Master Builder* and it's almost turgid, and then you do it and you feel what's actually going on. It's electric to do.

The designer – Carl Toms – did the most sensational things. He put the Zurich public library on the stage; the only trouble was that it was black oak! Carl and I knew each other well, and I said to him: 'There's an old tradition in theatre that you *cannot* be funny in front of a black set.' *The Invention of Love* would have been a hundred times funnier if set in the Elysian Fields and not in Hades. Anyway, Carl said, 'Oh,' and when I came in the next morning it was all lined in pale shades. I mean I would imagine that Carl had already been having his doubts . . .

The big difficulty I remember in *Travesties*, and I said it on the very first day, is the problem of getting from a young man to an old man. Stoppard just writes: 'Carr is now a young man, in his drawing room in 1917.' And Peter was saying things like: 'I'll get you these ormolu screens,' and: 'You'll have to shave,' expecting me to be onstage covered in foam, and I thought, 'There's no *time* for all that.' You just do what it says on the page: he was an old man, now he's a young man. I said, 'Look, give me an old dressing gown, and I tell you what I'm doing: I'm watering the window-boxes, it's a sunny day, I've got an old straw hat, and the dressing gown, a cravat, and big carpet slippers that go over shoes, and I'll do it: it'll work.' And Peter Shaffer picked that up in *Amadeus*, exactly the same device.

Stoppard was developing a team around him. You were friends who met occasionally?

I don't know that I really got on very well with Peter Wood, but I've always got on well with Tom. I mean, he thinks I'm a total fool. He told me once that Henry Carr was in fact a portrait of me: well, I was thrilled to bits! If that's my claim to some tiny fragment of immortality, that's fine by me.

It worked the other way round, I think, with Undiscovered Country: *you and Peter Wood were already down to do it, and Stoppard came along and rewrote it.*

I didn't know that. That was another wonderful thing to do; that's a very good play.

Going back to Travesties *for a moment, was there any doubt in your mind about the whole Lenin stuff? Critics did comment that the play stops being funny when Lenin's onstage.*

But that's the intention . . . The question is 'What's art for?' Is it just 'a chit for life'? But there's an occasion, in a letter or something, when someone's playing the slow movement of the Appassionata and Lenin . . . tears begin to come to his eyes; 'human beings . . . so beautiful . . . make this wonderful art . . . it makes me want to pat heads . . . But we mustn't pat heads, we must hit them.' That's the moment when even Lenin actually is moved and transported by art . . . The recording we used of the Appassionata was by Ashkenazy, and at the end on stage I had to join in! Then when we did *Every Good Boy* in Washington, André Previn spoke to the orchestra and said, 'John is himself no mean musician: I have heard him play with Ashkenazy . . .'

I suppose Ivanov in that play was in a sense easy after playing Henry Carr?

Not really. My recollection is that Carr was just go, all the way: getting on a slide, and letting go. Whereas in *Every Good Boy* there's more to be supplied. 'What is your instrument?' – to

make that absolutely new at the time. And also it was technically very difficult, because you were playing in a concert hall.
A lot of vocal technique was required so that everybody could
hear, without slowing it right down to 'Peter and the Wolf'.

*After that there was quite a gap; and then the Housman play
came along. When the script came along, were you immediately excited?*
No. I don't have that sort of mind. It seemed to me a very risky
piece. The idea of just sending two people out for thirty-five to
forty minutes, in the first act, you know . . . But I'd have been
a fool not to do it. With Tom's plays, you don't understand
them the first time you read them, unless you're some sort of
literary critic. Actors don't know that they're going to work;
but, boy, do they.

*And it was the first time Richard Eyre had directed a Stoppard
play. He'd hoped to get* Arcadia.
But Trevor did that. Yes, that was the most amazing idea,
putting people from two different periods on stage.

Which then led on to The Invention of Love. *Isn't it the basis of
the Housman play that you're talking to your younger self?*
But in a dream. He's lying in bed, he's dying, and he dreams
that he's already died. And then at the end of the play he actually dies: the sphincters release. I kept thinking about that,
working it out, and finally I went to Tom and asked, 'Is that
it?' and he [*silent nod*] . . . He's awfully reluctant, you know,
to impose anything on you. He doesn't say, 'I didn't mean that,
I meant that'; he waits for everybody else to catch up. As with
that passage I pointed out to you, in *Travesties*: I didn't notice
that till after the previews, and the script was sitting open on
my dressing-room table, as I was getting ready, and I suddenly saw it. We'd rehearsed for six weeks and I'd never noticed
it.

Yes; one wonders what other things are buried there that none of us has noticed.
I think his attitude is: 'It's there. Doesn't matter if they don't get it now; somebody will see it, one day.' In that sense it's rather like a sacrosanct book.

Yes. Though a man of the theatre, he's also a writer of 'texts'.
If I were that talented, I would rule my world – I would tell everybody what to do next, because I'd be eminently qualified to do so. Tom never does that. That's what's lovely about having him in rehearsals. The perfect director is a kind of father-figure, with the actors as children, someone of judgement who loves you as he listens to what you do. It doesn't matter what you do, he loves it. And later on he might say, 'Look, maybe . . .'; but not in a dictatorial way. And Tom does exactly the same as a playwright. If there's something you just can't quite get right, certain phrasing or something like that, he'll rewrite it.

I'm most fortunate to have worked on these plays: I've seen glory.

Simon Russell Beale

Simon Russell Beale is widely considered the leading classical actor of his generation. He played Guildenstern in a 1995 revival, and I was touched by his recollection of being given a lift home by Stoppard: 'He had a lovely BMW, but it was actually quite scary, because I'd never spent time with Tom alone.' Famous actor overawed by famous playwright; John Wood made a similar comment: 'You feel you don't want to waste his time . . .'

We talked in Beale's dressing room at the National Theatre, in late October 2003. The revival of Jumpers, *in which he played George, had been running for five months and was about to transfer to the West End, and later to New York.*

JH: *Which part did you play in* Rosencrantz?
SRB: I was asked which one I'd like. And I'd done Guildenstern at school, so I said Guildenstern; and in fact that was right, I think, because of his particular type, which is rather pompous, you know, the elder-brother bit.

The two plays are obviously different. But are there general things about acting a Stoppard role which are unlike other dramatists, or trickier? Words-words-words, I suppose?
Well, there is the words-words-words problem. At one point he said, 'If you really listen to the consonants . . .' And of course what he requires from his actors is clarity of utterance; but it is slightly more than that: the consonants give the rhythmic balance to sentences, and once you've got that, you're fine. It's about rhythm, that's what counts. And it's quite a long haul, because you can't – I mean, you could probably do a perfectly decent presentation of a particular person he's written, because they're always articulate, by just speaking clearly. The difficulty is trying to find the emotional heart which I think is there.

He comes to rehearsals. Does he intervene much?
Not very much: we make the joke that he does about six minutes' worth of work a day, of talking; but that's to do with courtesy. I think with two early plays it's different; I imagine if I'd been doing *The Invention of Love* or *Arcadia* it would have been a different experience; he'd be more worried. I mean he did occasionally say, 'My God that's a dreadful joke, you can cut that.' And we changed a couple of things for the sake of clarity. I think he likes visiting the plays as old friends, or an old child.

Jumpers is a classic, according to Richard Eyre's twenty-year rule. But Stoppard himself says that 'Plays tend to go off, like fruit.'
Tend to. When I first read it, I said I think this and this needs to be changed; but I was completely wrong. I thought that the philosophical debate had moved on, and also references to the

particular period, threepenny bits and gramophone records; but of course I was wrong because it is now a period piece, or a piece of its period, so there's no point in changing even 'threepenny bit'.

The philosophers when Jumpers *first appeared said, 'This is about forty years out of date'; but then that's exactly what George says he's hoping to do. You couldn't update it . . . Stoppard has said recently that whereas Essie Davis [Dotty] settled very quickly into her part, you took your time in rehearsal.*

He's quoted as saying roughly, 'Simon looks as if he's doing nothing at all.' I had a sort of mixed response to that; I hope it didn't look as if I was somehow lazy! To do those lectures is an intensely private experience, apart even from the writer and the director, because – I don't want to suggest a one-man show, but – it really wasn't up for discussion. I mean yes, occasionally one would ask for a bit of clarity of the argument, whether one was doing it right or had missed something; or occasionally David [*Leveaux, the director*] would say something like: 'The way you do Tarzan of the Apes, what about if you present it as the most beautiful story in the world, and then demolish it?' – some comic effects. But in fact it's not like rehearsing any other bit of the play; it's your own incredible journey.

Essie is an actress who has a phenomenal ability to access her emotions very quickly; and because Dotty is a more overtly emotional part I think that's probably what was seen. Certainly the greatest amount of work was done on that major scene between the two, that's the most difficult scene in the play.

Richard Eyre told me that not many actors can do the big Stoppard speeches.

It's not easy. In *The Invention of Love* the big speech, if I remember, is a lecture to the audience, who are named students; but in George's case what is written is actually a four-wall drama, and so logically I should not refer to the audience at all. But I decided very early on – and this again is why it was a private thing; and you can't judge it at all, until a new face shows up at rehearsal – I decided very consciously to turn it out. Michael Billington said that was the one mistake. I think he meant that I turned it outwards too early; but it seems to me it came off with the audience.

You want the laughs.
Oh, you need the laughs. And I remember Tom talking about Chekhov and saying that great dramatists very often don't worry about a slight slip in theatrical consistency, such as some speeches in *The Seagull* or *Vanya*. And I *like* direct address.

In all the months of performing it, did you find yourself changing anything?
Yes, there are changes. There are so many aspects of George that it all almost depends on how the audience is reacting. I love his pomposity. I love the fact that this George laughs at his own jokes, jokes which are really rather bad. Also, in his relationship with Dotty, I like playing round with how much he's cool, because of the long term, how much he's careless, how much he's loving . . . Although I said that the hardest scene is the long scene between Dotty and George, the single most difficult *bit* of the play is what Essie and I see as the breakdown of the marriage, where George has the speech about Wittgenstein meeting a friend in the corridor. I ignored a stage direction at my peril for the last few months, which I've just put back in. In the original it says that he stares out of the window 'emotionless'; and I tried it many many ways: I tried it – always direct to Essie – kindly, angry, hurt, all sorts of things. In the end we both decided that actually the best way was to cut off from her completely and go into a completely different world, and I think that's right. Though Tom very often says, 'Oh, forget that stage direction, forget that,' because the script is littered with them. The emotional instructions at the beginning of speeches are the most tricky.

You're about to transfer to the Piccadilly, and then later you're going to Broadway as well: do you think that'll make a difference?
We've had a little test run on tour, playing to bigger houses, so I don't think the bigness of the house is going to be much of a problem. I don't know about the composition of the audience – they are a different audience in the West End.

And in America.
Now that should be fascinating. I've no idea how they're going to react. Sometimes you're aware that there's quite a large composition of Americans in audiences here, but . . . there are things that worry me. If there's any way in which we could prime the audience in the States about the Captain Scott story I'd be grateful. Though God knows whether even people here under thirty know the Captain Scott story; but it's quite essentially important . . .

How long will you be on Broadway for?
Well, I heard that it might be till August next year, which I think is a bit too long. I think I might go earlier.

Is it the longest run you've ever done?
I think it will be, of continuous playing.

You wouldn't go on doing it unless you felt satisfied with it, and enjoy it.
I love doing it, yes. As to 'satisfied', I'm not sure, because there are certain bits that I think still need to be sorted out [*this after six months*].

. . . and Essie Davis

[*Essie Davis joined us, from the next dressing room. I asked her about Peter Wood's comment that Dotty's voice isn't sufficiently heard.*]

ED: Glenn Close played *The Real Thing* in New York, and she said to Tom that it was an unfortunately underwritten part. She said she wasn't able to talk back; and there are times in this play when I wish I could have. But I pride myself on finding, making it have a clear path. I think it's there, I've worked it out.

SRB: Dotty has the most complicated technical speeches. George has, because of the lecture, a voice that you get used to; and I think his carelessness, and, well, simply his desire for some sex, and his inability to express emotion, are all quite clear. But because Dotty is sort of defined as losing her mind, it's a difficult thing to locate, isn't it?

ED: She's defined by all of the men's reactions and treatment of her; and that's really hard therefore, to make your voice heard, above other people's ideas of what your character is.

SRB: I think your performance absolutely solves that problem. I don't think the audience thinks, 'Oh, she's just barking and therefore not worth listening to.' She's genuinely in trouble, more than ever.

ED: I just think it takes a very sensitive audience to actually follow my story, because so much of it is in my mind. I try and put it out there, but I don't know that it's spoken.

JH: *According to Stoppard you worked it out extremely quickly, whereas Simon took his time!*

ED: Oh. I don't think I worked it out *quickly*! I think I'd only worked it out after we came back from our tour.

You said a moment ago that it's 'elliptical'. That's how it should be, isn't it? The dramatist shouldn't know all the answers himself, really, because the actors have still got to find them. Beckett would absolutely refuse to say anything about his characters.

SRB: Yes, I think Tom is a bit like that. Certainly at that section, when Dotty has the long speech about 'local customs' and then I have that line about Wittgenstein, I remember trying at rehearsal, trying about three times to say, 'What precisely is the

Wittgenstein speech about?' and I remember not getting an answer. He's got the Beckettian ability to go quiet there, and say, 'That's your problem to sort out.'

Did you find in the months you've been doing the part that things have changed? You've altered things?

ED: Yeah, definitely. David was very strong in his reining in – we did lots of different ways of playing particularly that long scene, and he was quite determined to make sure that it wasn't too tragic too quickly. And sometimes we will occasionally start on a very tragic black note, and though you might really want to do something vital and joyous and full of love –

SRB: The worst is what we call 'the bitchy start'. If that happens it's almost impossible to pull yourself out of, though if you look behind you they're going: 'No, no, not like that!' It's sort of petty. At least with the really dark version, which sometimes rears its head, at least then you feel sorry for both of them. But it's difficult, because you have to go at such a speed, it's hard to let the air in.

ED: But we *have* let a lot more air in.

Does that mean you've slowed down?

ED: In moments . . . I talked to people who saw the previews [*early June*] and then saw it again last week [*late October*] and I ask them if they think it's changed and they say 'No!' And you go, 'Oh, really?' I think it's changed a lot. Subtly, though.

SRB: There was a very conscious moment in rehearsal, when we found we were playing Strindberg! We said, look this is wrong. It was almost a purely technical thing, because a lot of the groundwork had been done . . . The important thing is that we make each other laugh, not necessarily as Simon and Essie but as George and Dotty. Because right at the base of their relationship is the fact that they –

ED: Adore.

SRB: – adore one another. When Diana [*Rigg*] came, she was extremely generous, loved it, she said, 'The one thing we [*her-*

244

self and Michael Hordern] couldn't really do was to have the potential of a genuinely sexual relationship.' I think that's extremely important.

ED: I do too. But I think that's a direction thing, I really do; it's got nothing to do with age, there's plenty of shaggable older men. It's just a choice, and they decided not to do it. The fact that we've chosen to, and the fact that, like me handling you, and you handling me, is just fine. And I do believe that Dotty isn't having sex with anyone. I honestly do. And yet the amount of reviews that said, 'And Dotty's obviously shagging that Vice-Chancellor' . . . No!

When you'd been going a while, did you have re-rehearsals, with David?
SRB: He's been a bit busy.
ED: We could have done with it. But in fact we're rehearsing a new Archie now, and revisiting it has allowed us to start reworking stuff, and when David comes back next week I'm sure that we'll vastly change at least two scenes, small ones, scenes that I think are lost.
SRB: David is the sort of director who doesn't force his own pace to produce. But I think there'll be lots of changes in New York; we've got a month.

You look forward to that. It'll give you a fresh impetus.
SRB: And also I think things need to be changed. Technical things.
ED: Technical things need to be changed. Also when we went on tour, and took the pressure off ourselves really, it brought out a whole new light.

[*The actors discussed their audiences – some of them disappointingly small – in the English provinces; and how different jokes work for different audiences.*]

SRB: I do think the play's journey is a very moving one. We had to do an education panel and we were all asked: 'Pluck out a favourite moment of the play'; and almost all of us chose as at least one of our favourites the image of the lorry drivers exchanging headlights on a wet night on the A1, and I think that's just brilliant. 'To be ambushed by a trivial moment.'

'Ambushed' was one of Stoppard's words when he was young. He saw himself as having to keep surprising his audience. But underneath the plays, including this apparently very harsh play, there's a tremendous compassion.

SRB: Yes. And it answers the question about whether it's relevant, which is always the dodgy one. There can't be anything more relevant than virtue, or God.

Stephen Dillane

Stephen Dillane played the lead, Alexander Herzen, in the trilogy The Coast of Utopia, *2002; three years earlier he had played Henry in the Donmar Warehouse revival of* The Real Thing. *This 'interview' was conducted by e-mail.*

JH: *Was* The Real Thing *the first time you had acted in a Stoppard play?*
SD: I had played Rosencrantz at school, otherwise it was my first Stoppard.

What was your view of his writing before that? A dramatist you found sympathetic, or did you need some persuasion to take the role?
I wasn't particularly sympathetic towards his work, largely because I imagined his audience to be conservative and self-satisfied, congratulating themselves for understanding the jokes. I was certainly reluctant. It was only by persuading myself that Stoppard was a Czech writer in the middle-European tradition – someone like Milan Kundera – that I was reconciled to his play. Somehow that enabled me to approach its world of

sex and philosophy with less baggage; it all seems a bit silly now, but there it was. My instinctive suspicion of the politics of the play remained throughout the run, but I found the reasoning flawless and surrendered to a greater mind than my own.

Does Stoppard's writing present special problems for the actor? For example, when characters are so articulate, can that get in the way of other elements of drama, such as emotion and interplay? And does his writing present special opportunities?
The rewards of acting are always the same, in my experience – peace, joy, excitement, love and fulfilment. As far as *The Real Thing* is concerned, when we finally got on top of it there was the pleasure of imagining ourselves to be much cleverer and wittier than we actually were, as well as braver in love, more noble in suffering and more profound in forgiveness. For me personally there was the delight in having the means given to me with which I could make people laugh on a regular and reliable basis, as well as take them on an emotional journey of some kind. My experience was that the writing was rigorous and precise and required similar qualities in performance but, unless they were informed by accurate and deeply held conviction, the words could seem detached and the characters disinterested.

I think there is a kind of triangular tension between deep feeling or passionate conviction, intellectual precision, and lightness of touch. I suppose the criticism of Stoppard is often that the first of those is missing. That wasn't my experience of *The Real Thing*, nor – by the way – of *Arcadia*, which I read as a deeply emotional piece of work but when I saw it onstage seemed dry. So perhaps there is something in the writing which militates against the discovery of the deep currents of emotion. It is difficult sometimes to find the subtext when the text itself is so spare and subtle and seductively buoyant and already dense with abstract thought and ideas. Perhaps there simply isn't the time in English rehearsal rooms to examine the whole thing properly.

Stoppard likes to attend rehearsals. How did his presence affect the chemistry?

Yes, Tom was in rehearsals for both *The Real Thing* and *The Coast of Utopia*, and I often wished he wasn't. I think the temptation if the writer is there, especially an eminent one, is for actors to 'show' that they know what they imagine he is getting at long before they're ready to show anything. This often precludes a deeper examination of the play. It's possible too, I suppose, that the writer is unconsciously seeking reassurance that his baby is in good hands. In rehearsals for *Utopia* there were rewrites going on all the time, some major, most minor, and there were many long conversations between Tom and Trevor Nunn about the ideas, the philosophy and the politics of the plays.

Can you describe how Trevor Nunn helped you and the huge cast to get hold of the trilogy? Did he go straight to the text, at early rehearsals, or were there some preliminary team-building or improvisation exercises? When it came to previews, you were performing play one while presumably still rehearsing plays two and three, and thus still learning things about them?

No, there were no team-building exercises: no time. And yes, we were rehearsing two and three while performing one so, yes, previews were really just regarded as rehearsal time, by me at least.

What I enjoyed about playing Herzen, eventually, was being the mouthpiece for Tom's most passionately held beliefs about how a good life is lived, with all its contradictions – home and exile, children, politics, influence and impotence, friendship, money, sex, love and loss and death. And being on watch, as it were, as the fog began to clear and the great shapes of the plays began to emerge like a new landscape.

To my mind *Utopia* was a mismanaged masterpiece. I think, largely through lack of time, we didn't reveal the poetic architecture of the trilogy, but nor did we get anywhere near the necessary complexity of relationship that should have under-pinned the whole thing. I don't think the audience was able to become intimate with anyone, and I believe they should have been intimate with everyone. As a result *Utopia* was judged on its political thought, which I don't think was really the point; it was a strand, for sure, a homage to Herzen and Isaiah Berlin, but the point – if any play has a point – was its poetic reflection on time, vanity, futility, hope and passion (and love).

Felicity Kendal

Felicity Kendal was born and brought up in India; her parents, though English, were travelling players there in the classical tra-dition, constantly touring in performances of Shakespeare, in which she herself took part from infancy onwards. As an adult she came to live in Britain and became one of the country's leading and best-known actors, on both stage and screen. Stoppard has written more for her than for anyone else, and their relationship was personally close during the 1990s. She talked to me in London early in 2004.

FK: I saw *Rosencrantz* soon after I came to this country; it was the season in fact that made me determined to commit to England, seeing Olivier, Ralph Richardson, Paul Scofield, Peggy Ashcroft, Maggie Smith: all these greats on the stage in brilliant productions. I don't know that we've ever had any-thing like it since, quite like that period: you had Michael Gambon carrying a spear, and Anthony Hopkins playing a small part, and Geraldine McEwan and Billie Whitelaw – it was an extraordinary time. I can't say I was any more impressed by *Rosencrantz* than by anything else I saw, because it all seemed excellent. I did of course love *Rosencrantz* because I knew *Hamlet* very well, but then so did a lot of people. Some of the Pinters and Osbornes took a little time for me to get totally comfortable with, because it wasn't the sort of theatre that I had ever seen before or had experience of. But

Rosencrantz was more like the classical plays I knew: much more of a traditional theatrical experience.

JH: *Highly verbal.*
Highly verbal: Shakespeare, Shaw, Stoppard, they're all the voice of the author, and all the characters are feeding that voice – unlike Chekhov, for example, where there are many different voices: he goes into different characters and he's saying, 'On the one hand there's this, and on the other hand there's that' – it's an argument, he's arguing with himself.

Everybody in Stoppard has to be clever.
He poses the same challenge to an actor as for example Shaw does. You have to have the verbal muscle to appear to be thinking at the speed that he wants you to be thinking at, ahead of the speech.

When you first played in Stoppard, you were in a trouser-role, as Christopher in On the Razzle. *I'm not sure whether that was the European tradition?*
Oh yes, in Vienna he was played by a girl: absolutely. I hadn't worked with Peter Wood either, so I got to meet the team, and work with them. And I actually based the character on my son, who was nine at the time – though Tom, having four sons, was way ahead on how boys should be! That was my first getting to know how very closely Peter and Tom worked. In my experience I haven't worked with any other writer and director who work in that fashion; Tom's there at every decision, every day in rehearsal. Writers come and go, usually; but these two were an exceptional team working as one.

Usually in rehearsal the director is the one person you feel safe with, you lose all inhibitions ideally. He is judging you, he'd be the person you're stripping for, in a sense, and then the building up from this sort of naked character the layers of some kind of performance. And then at a dread moment the writer comes in to see part or all of a run-through, and everyone gets very nervous and acts rather badly, and there's a sort of no-man's land where you have to prove that you *do* know what you're saying; and then it settles down and then you get used to him being there. There's a process, and it's always slightly nerve-wracking. Michael Frayn, for instance, is very close and he comes in a lot, but he's not there all the time, so it's always an *event* . . . But because Peter and Tom were always together, and in fact would discuss and argue sometimes over a point of production, there was never any shyness; that immediately went. Because Tom was there, people would either ask him a question or they would ask Peter: it would always be what seemed the most appropriate at the time, but there was no division between them. Not that Tom would *direct*, at any point whatsoever; he would never step over that line.

I've heard of him sitting in a corner, rather a long way away.
Not with Peter. I've got some pictures of them, working on *Jumpers*, and they're both sitting there together . . . *On the Razzle* was very hard work, but a lovely company. And Peter Wood is a wonderful director for that kind of thing – magic is what he does best. His comic talent is superb; and by then he understood a Stoppard script so well. What he had was an understanding of how the audience would react, so that you could time something. He would just go, 'Duh-der, duh-der, *laugh*.' And you'd think, 'There can't be a laugh there, Peter?' But he knew there was. He would read it like a score, and know where the pauses needed to be.

And then you had a new play, The Real Thing.
That was very different; that was with Roger [*Rees*]. There again, the team worked very well: Roger and Peter and Tom made a very good combination. I think it's a great play. And it's a very raw play, for him; he's usually pretty guarded, emotionally. I mean, in his other plays there hardly seems room for emotion, not that it's lacking, there's almost a surfeit of it, but it's not raw emotion.

But that was a play that touched a lot of people's hearts one way or another. It worked brilliantly, and then it went to New York.

Did you do it there?
No. I've never taken anything to New York; every time I think I'm going to – I've only had two sons, but they've always been here, and I've never wanted to leave them for three or four months.

There were bits of rewriting going on, in The Real Thing *rehearsals.*
Rewriting is what he does; he rewrites all the time. One of the dangers of studying his plays is that you could take a portion and say, 'This means this, and clearly this is the root, the most important moment in the piece because I can see that every-thing is leading up to this,' and there will be a production three years later and he will cut the scene! You cannot interpret his work, in one sense; it's very complex, and it's also changing and fluid. Something that is difficult to understand is probably there on purpose and he doesn't necessarily want anyone to understand. The job of an actor is different. As I see it, the writ-er has written this; my job is (a) to be 'real', I'm trying to work out how the author wants me to do this character; and then to convey that as clearly as possible to the audience, so that I'm doing the author's speaking for him. There are areas in Stoppard that you can't possibly explain because they're not explainable, and if you did he would be very angry. Because it's not necessarily on a plate: it could be something that has to be ambiguous, or it has to be something that you will only find out later . . . It's a mind-game as well as a realistic exercise of human emotion.

There are an enormous number of buried jokes, some of which eventually emerge, some of which may not.
Yes. He's a king of loops; there'll be something here that he will

then loop into, and then he'll loop into again, and then you get the pay-off much much later: the little seed is sown, but you don't even notice it until a bush turns up in the last act.

Was Annie perhaps already written with you in mind?
I really don't think I was to do with his writing Annie at that point. I was part of the *group* probably quite soon; very much as Roger Rees, if he hadn't gone to live in America, would probably have been part of many of Tom's plays. I think he hears a kind of tune in his head, and there are some actors that, rather than getting it right, don't balls it up. That could be because of my rather old-fashioned training as an actor: say the lines and let the audience hear them, and the author will do the work for them; don't start mumbling away thinking it's all to do with your emotions . . . My instinct is to say the lines and let him get the jokes; I think that is probably why I became part of the group. And also I worked very well with Peter Wood. We understood the same thing, in the same way that Diana [*Rigg*] did: she has the same ability. Often Tom would say, 'Don't try and make that funny; just say it, and I'll do the work for you.' He has a way of writing that will do it; he knows how to lay the groundwork and to feed a line, so it isn't the line that's funny, it's the bit before. If you get the bit before right, and then deliver the line, he will get the laugh for you, because he's put it together in that way. If you start thinking, 'I have to make this funny,' you'll obviously ruin the bit before and you'll never get the laugh.

John Wood said to me: 'The funniest things may come earlier on, but the laugh comes at the end. The last thing may not be the funniest, but that's the way it's shaped.'
Yes. And the rhythm, he will write the rhythm for you. You have to get the music right, otherwise the whole thing won't work. For me, the things that come first are the words; the thing that comes first is the writer. The difference between putting an 'and' or a comma there, or just running it right

through, is the difference between it being ordinary and superb. I've always loved that and noticed it; again and again if a job has excited me, it's because of the writing. Every night you're reminded of this extraordinary writing. I think in that way Tom and I think the same: not, gosh, that was such a real interpretation of a love affair, or a scene in the university, or a poet being abandoned, or whatever, but it was also *the way the people spoke*. It's marvellous, marvellous language for the theatre.

Then you did the revival of Jumpers, *with Paul Eddington. That was going back to an earlier period of Stoppard. Did you feel any sense of stepping back a bit?*
Not really. I loved the play so much; to me the play was so glorious that I just wanted to be in it. I knew Paul very well, because we'd worked together a lot; and by then I really enjoyed working with Peter and Tom – and also Carl Toms, who always designed for them. So to me it was a carrying-on, in one sense, of the family tradition that you work with the people. It's like a company: you don't always say, 'Well, that's not a big enough part'; that's the next thing they're doing and of course I'll do it, if I'm free and they offer it to me. It became a kind of natural thing.

You were much more consciously in the writer's mind by the time Hapgood *was being written. It was written for you.*
I wouldn't say actually *for* me. I think *Indian Ink* certainly was written for me to play; but *Hapgood* I think was written just because by then he was writing that sort of part.

Did you get any sort of hint, did you know what sort of work was being –
No, never. Not the slightest. I don't know even if he talked to Peter or anybody about it. Once it's *there*, the discussions are endless and open; as soon as it's complete, then I would read it. But never before, not even a . . . it was a very closed bubble.

When you read Hapgood, *that must have set you back a bit?*
No; not really! One's reaction as an actor to a play is really totally selfish: you think, 'Oh, is this a play I'm going to be in? Will I like it?' I thought it was very confusing: it was difficult to watch, but to *read* the first fifteen minutes . . . you don't know who is what, and he comes in here and *he* goes into the next loo – and I mean I'm not good at left to right anyway! But all that wasn't my problem; that's not something you bother with, as an actor: that's for the director to sort out!

A big part for you, a dominant part.
A very dominant part . . . The production was put off. We were actually going to do it, with Codron, it was scheduled; and then I got pregnant with Jacob and I remember saying, 'Ros [*agent*] I'm really sorry but life's taken over. Pity I can't, but please ring them up and say what a shame.' And then they came back and said: no, they'd wait. So they did. Which actually put a bit of a pressure on it, because one of the things that happens – hasn't happened to me too often but happened soon after Jacob was born – was that you can't actually remember things. So the rehearsals for that were not as easy, and as much fun, as for all the others before and after. With a tiny baby, I remember finding the rehearsal period very difficult. But that was not the play's fault.

You've mentioned Indian Ink; *but the radio play*, In the Native State, *came first, and was very much written for you.*
Yes, absolutely. No doubt about that.

That therefore might have been 'leaked' to you?
No. No. He did say, 'I'm writing a play about India.' But he would never have said, 'I'm writing a play for you, or about you.' He didn't; and I don't imagine that he would ever say that to anyone. A play is something that is so his own world – his own child – until it gets out, that it's nothing to do with anyone else. Whatever *influences* the play, maybe from different people

or for different reasons, it's very much his own precious thing. Until it's 'there'; and then that's something opened. Like when he translates something, he's very open, totally approachable. [*The actor says*] 'Why do I have to say this? Can I not say that? I don't understand that.' He's open: 'Come to me, discuss it.' But in the end, 'If that's what I want, then you're going to have to do it; but on the other hand I might change it.'

Hapgood was rewritten a lot; more than any other play, I'd think. More difficult, more complicated; and I think it had a bumpier beginning; we opened in the wrong place, in Wimbledon – for some reason or other it had a bumpy start, and he was rewriting all the time.

Radio plays by comparison are relatively easy to put on? A two-week job?
Yes.

Had you done much radio?
Lots . . . But I hadn't worked with Peggy Ashcroft, which was a joy, definitely the most extraordinary thing. And it was her last work. That was a play where there was not that much change or rewriting. He did change it a bit; and when it went to the theatre there was some.

There were quite a few changes, in the stage version.
But not because nobody could understand it. He was just adapting and embellishing, rather than altering.

I get the sense of wanting to make it more obviously funny; this time the American biographer is brought onstage.
Well, it had to be longer. I think to me they are two plays; the same story, but two plays. The radio play is a jewel, it really is, a little jewel in his crown, and perfectly constructed for that medium, especially since it's poetry and a painter. In your head you've got the painter painting and you imagine it, it's perfect; whereas a painter on a stage is always a bit of a problem,

because you can't see what he's doing and if you do it'll never be as extraordinary as that particular thing would be if you saw it in real life. When it became a stage play it was slightly enlarged and so it lost a little bit of its delicacy; but I think it's still one of my favourite plays.

The stage play inevitably gets compared with all his other stage plays, and does perhaps look a bit minor in comparison. And in between the two came Arcadia.

Well, that was amazing. There are very few writers who have done this extraordinary journey; it's like the Himalayas, there you've got Kanchenjunga, there you've got the smaller hills, there you've got Mount Everest, and it just goes on and on, up and down. It's a very unusual career for a writer, to be able quite frankly to do the delicate plays and then go up and do *Arcadia*, with all the other plays in between, and then come down and then go up again. *Arcadia* was going up to the sort of 'Ta-ra!' area, and perfectly placed in that theatre and beautifully directed. In the same way that *The Real Thing* was just perfect, and so was *On the Razzle*. They're not all the same, you see; they change. That's what he likes to do.

Hannah, in Arcadia, *is a bit of an enigma: not wanting to join the party. We don't learn why.*

That's her secret. There's none of that 'How did the character get to this point?' in any of his characters, actually.

Flora Crewe?

Flora Crewe, yes, because you've got her past; because that's what it's about.

It's a purely realistic play.

Purely realistic, and obviously you've got her history there on the stage. But Hannah, no. With most of the characters, sometimes you see a little bit of what happened before – in *The Real Thing* you see a bit of the marriage before. But usually it's like

257

meeting somebody for the first time and you become best friends and then you follow them through and you go on; you don't actually have to take their baggage with them: they are what they are, and that's what he presents. In some plays like the Ayckbourn, the more realistic plays, when someone comes on you can sort of place how they got there, because they're of a type. But Tom writes about unusual people, you see; he doesn't write about ordinary people, because ordinary people wouldn't think in the way that he thinks.

They wouldn't speak *in that way!*
They have to be slightly unusual, in one sense or another, either by circumstances or ambition. They're always his voice, whether they're men or women; always the thing they love to do is to think about things and work something out, and verbalise it. With some writers you cannot exchange characters' lines; but in Stoppard there are probably times when you could, and still get away with it.

Some see that as a criticism, certainly in psychological realist drama.
It is a bit, yet on the other hand when it's 'real' it seems totally real!

I wondered myself many years ago whether there was some way in which Stoppard might approach Chekhov. I think he found translating The Seagull *a satisfying thing to do.*
I think so. I think what he was trying to do was to serve Chekhov, and see what he thought. Instead of doing his interpretation and letting it become a Stoppard, though of course there were some things that he couldn't resist –

With Nestroy that would be fine, but not with Chekhov.
Exactly. I think he was asking himself, 'How would Chekhov have written this in English now? Was this where he meant to be funny, is this where he meant –' and that's how he set about

translating it. Also, Tom isn't that English, and in a way I loved his interpretation because it wasn't English. The way the people spoke was not English. His people aren't. Even in *Jumpers*, there's something extraordinary and eccentric, so they could be Bengali, you could translate that into Bengali. What I'm saying is it's not Frayn or even Pinter, very very English to me; or Ayckbourn. I've always liked the slightly exotic way he has with language.

You feel that partly because of what you know about his upbringing.
And he's got an accent. And he's not like an Englishman. I never think of him as an Englishman, as say Peter Wood is.

Yet so much of the time he's celebrating things that are English. Perhaps an English person wouldn't have celebrated them so much.
Could be. He cherishes it, in a way, possibly that some people have forgotten. But other writers also cherish the language; Pinter does, so does Simon Gray.

Is this some fellow recognition on your part, having been brought up outside England yourself?
Oh yes. I don't feel remotely English . . . I suppose I do now more; this is now my country, this is where I am, of course, my theatre; I'm not in a foreign country. But I don't feel very English.

Perhaps you're saying you don't feel too limited *by it. You and Tom have both got something extra; in his case to call it central-European would be artificial –*
Yes, exactly; that wouldn't be right either. It's sort of more – that it isn't really relevant, actually. You're not coming from that particular angle. It's actually more *neutral*.

Working on The Seagull *may have helped him towards* The

Coast of Utopia. *Was there any talk of you being in that?*
No. That was always something completely separate. That was
a long time in the making. Agony, I believe, some of the time.

*Looking back, do you share the common view that in the later
plays this is someone who's not so much wearing his own heart
on his sleeve, but who is allowing more emotion into his plays?*
I don't think he does wear his heart on his sleeve. I don't think
he is or ever will be a writer that shares in that way. He shares
his considerable brain-power, his intellect, he shares his wit, he
shares this extraordinary joy in the English language. He shares
the jokes and the wickedness of playing games with his audience, loving them and challenging them to understand everything he's researched – he researches and researches and
researches; it's not all invented. So it's very deliberate: 'I shall
research this till I know everything, and I'm going to put that
in: you will understand this, you will have read about this, and
you'll understand this; *this* bit, you won't know what I'm talking about, but it is there on purpose – you will, probably, the
second time you see the play; and other people might know dif-
ferently.' And it makes you feel wonderful; it's like a magician
– now you see it, now you don't – and when you see it, you feel
wonderful: God, it makes an audience feel incredibly clever! 'I
recognise that quote'; and then you're bewildered and you feel
you're a bloody idiot; and then suddenly he'll give you something else, and the whole audience will get it, and celebrate. It's
brilliant; and that is what he shares, that is the way he writes.
What he doesn't share are private personal things. I mean, with
every writer in the world, any kind of artist, things come from
your understanding that are quite personal, but they're not
necessarily private.

And not autobiographical.
They're not autobiographical; but still you understand that it's
personal. Like Kipling, there couldn't be anyone more private
than that, and yet a lot more in his poems comes out if you

actually know about his life, and read about it now, you can see how it's a mirror-image. But he's not *writing about* his life. And I think there are probably different times in the life of an artist where he actually feels the need to release some of that, and other times when it's not interesting – you want to play another tune, you know.

He also doesn't let his plays go. He returns to see them, he cherishes them; very few people do that. Some do: Peter Brook goes every night and two or three other directors are continually there. If something's opening in Huddersfield or Australia Tom will fly to see it, because it's his work; and in that way he is linked to his work, so it's all alive for him. I think he can do that because he hasn't used the play as a relief for his own emotions, to which then he couldn't return, he'd have to go on, because that's a journey that he wouldn't want to go down any more. Instead it's very much 'up here'.

That's a striking point. A certain sort of writer might well come back after thirty years and feel the need to stand more separately, further off from the work.
As I said, I don't think there's an artist in the world whose work is not affected by their life; but there are some who use it more as a channel.

In The Real Thing *we have a dramatist called Henry, who is making remarks about drama; but they're not the same man.*
Henry is talking about writing in the way that Tom thinks about writing, no question about that. That's where that character is. And I think in plays, not just his, there's always one character they love more; there's always a character, male or female, small or large – usually large, usually the lead part – that the author loves more than another, and who will be speaking for the author. And it's obviously Henry. But in *Arcadia* there's no single voice; arguments are going on all the time, and his voice is coming in and out of a lot of people. That's him really flying . . . it's what he really likes to do. But,

you know, it's like everything: you do that, you then can't do that again. You've got to do something else. And he doesn't say, well, that type of comedy worked well so let's write another. Which a lot of writers do; they have a Blue period, and then a Green period, you know what I mean; and he doesn't do that.

Would you have any thoughts for young actors? The next generation? Are they going to turn their noses up at Stoppard as being too middle-class, too intellectual, too metropolitan?
Bollocks, is what I'd say to that. Absolutely not! You might as well say that about any of the great writers; and he is one of the great writers. As for saying something to young people, it always sounds pompous, I think . . . Just read the play! The only advice I would give is: you must let him do the work; you must trust his script. Don't try and embellish it, and don't try and *naturalise* it. If you say his lines in the rhythm that works for the speech, which hopefully the director and you will instinctively come to, and the audience can hear the lines in the rhythm that he wants it, it will work for you and it will work for the audience, and you'll have a great time. He is an old-fashioned writer in one sense, in that you need to be able to project. The dialogue is real, but it's not realistic.

It's not method acting remotely.
No. But in the second *The Real Thing*, with Jennifer Ehle and Stephen Dillane: Stephen was totally real – and so was Roger Rees . . . I mean so of course was John Wood, but that's going back a bit and it's a different kind of character, that wasn't realistic; *Travesties* was very extraordinary 'Ta-ra!' and *Jumpers* is a bit 'Ta-ra!', but *The Real Thing* is not; it's a very realistic piece in its modern structure and production. Stephen hardly raises his voice and is totally and utterly real; and yet he looks after the lines. Simon Russell Beale is another one; he is totally real, Simon; he doesn't appear to be acting, but his technique is so superb. And so my advice would be: you have to have technique; and if you don't, learn it fast! It's like a dance routine

that's very complicated: if you get it right, it seems effortless and it seems natural.

The thing about playing Stoppard is that he attracts an extraordinary audience; more so at the National at the moment because it's cheaper, but I've never been in a play of his that hasn't had the students, the theatre-goers, the people that want a night out, the people that don't normally go to the theatre but know it'll be good so they go: every sort of group of theatre-goers, they all go. And the young people. He does that, he opens the doors to the theatre. When we did *Indian Ink* there were more Indians in the audience than had ever before been to the Aldwych, and they loved it. That's what he does: he opens these doors for people – it's quite the opposite of him being difficult. All over the world, they flock to his plays. To be clever and have a sense of humour, you can't really top it.

Select Bibliography

Stoppard's personal papers are held at the Harry J. Ransom Humanities Research Center at the University of Texas, Austin. A catalogue is viewable on line at:
http://www.hrc.utexas.edu/research/fa/stoppard.hp.html

Works by Tom Stoppard

The screenplay *Galileo* appeared in issue eleven (Spring/Summer 2003) of *Areté* magazine, 8 New College Lane, Oxford OX1 3BN (*www.aretemagazine.com*).

All the following are published by Faber and Faber.

COLLECTIONS OF PLAYS

Tom Stoppard: Plays One (*The Real Inspector Hound, After Magritte, Dirty Linen, New-Found-Land, Dogg's Hamlet, Cahoot's Macbeth*)

Tom Stoppard: Plays Two [plays for radio] (*The Dissolution of Dominic Boot, 'M' is for Moon Among Other Things, If You're Glad I'll Be Frank, Albert's Bridge, Where Are They Now?, Artist Descending a Staircase, The Dog It Was That Died, In the Native State*)

Tom Stoppard: Plays Three [television plays] (*A Separate Peace, Teeth, Another Moon Called Earth, Neutral Ground, Professional Foul, Squaring the Circle*)

Tom Stoppard: Plays Four [adaptations] (*Dalliance*, a version of Arthur Schnitzler's *Liebelei*; *Undiscovered Country*, a version of Schnitzler's *Das weite Land*; *Rough Crossing*, adapted from Ferenc Molnar's *Play at the Castle*; *On the Razzle*, adapted from Johann Nestroy's *Einen Jux will er sich machen*; and *The Seagull*, a version of Anton Chekhov's play)

Tom Stoppard: Plays Five (*Arcadia, The Real Thing, Night and Day, Indian Ink, Hapgood*)

SINGLE TITLES (in alphabetical order)
Arcadia
Enter a Free Man
Every Good Boy Deserves Favour (with *Professional Foul*)
Hapgood
Henry IV (a version of Pirandello's play)
Indian Ink
The Invention of Love
Jumpers
Lord Malquist and Mr Moon (novel)
The Real Thing
Rosencrantz and Guildenstern Are Dead
Salvage, Part III of *The Coast of Utopia*
Shakespeare in Love (screenplay, with Marc Norman)
Shipwreck, Part II of *The Coast of Utopia*
The Coast of Utopia (trilogy in one volume)
Travesties
Voyage, Part I of *The Coast of Utopia*

Articles (in alphabetical order)

'Another Country', *Sunday Telegraph Magazine*, 10 October 1999 (first published in the USA as 'On Turning Out to be Jewish', *Talk*, September 1999)
'But for the Middle Classes' [review of Paul Johnson's *Enemies of Promise*], *Times Literary Supplement*, 3 June 1977
'The Definite Maybe', *The Author*, issue 78, Spring 1967
'Going Back' [to Darjeeling], *Independent Magazine*, 23 March 1991
'Looking-Glass World' [trial of Charter 77 activists in Prague], *New Statesman*, 28 October 1977
'Making It' [conceptual art], *Times Literary Supplement*, 15 June 2001

'Orghast', *Times Literary Supplement*, 1 October 1971
   [*Orghast* was an experimental play by Ted Hughes, staged
   by Peter Brook 'in the cliffs above Persepolis', in Iran.
   Stoppard saw a rehearsal on site and interviewed Hughes,
   primarily about the play's attempt to create a new language.]
'Playwrights and Professors', *Times Literary Supplement*, 13
   October 1972 [Literary criticism 'has nothing to do' with
   writing, seeing or acting in plays.]
'Pragmatic Theater', *New York Review of Books*, 23
   September 1999
'Prague: the Story of the Chartists', *New York Review of
   Books*, 4 August 1977
'Something to Declare', *Sunday Times*, 25 February 1968
'The Face at the Window' [Moscow visit to Russian dissi-
   dents], *Sunday Times*, 27 February 1977
Untitled, a review of *A Supplement to the Oxford English
   Dictionary, volume 1, A–G*, *Punch*, 13 December 1972
   ['I'm a traditionalist myself.']

Collected interviews

Conversations with Stoppard, ed. Mel Gussow, Nick Hern
   Books, 1995
Tom Stoppard in Conversation, ed. Paul Delaney, University
   of Michigan Press, 1997

Biography

Nadel, Ira, *Double Act, A Life of Tom Stoppard*, Methuen,
   2002 [This biography was unauthorised.]

Critical studies

Billington, Michael, *Stoppard: the playwright*, Methuen, 1987
Brassell, Tim, *Tom Stoppard: an assessment*, Macmillan, 1985
Cahn, Victor L., *Beyond Absurdity: the plays of Tom
   Stoppard*, Farleigh Dickinson University Press, 1979

Corballis, Richard, *Stoppard: the mystery and the clockwork*, Methuen, 1984

Dean, Joan Fitzpatrick, *Tom Stoppard: comedy as a moral matrix*, University of Missouri, 1981

Delaney, Paul, *Tom Stoppard: the moral vision of the major plays,* Macmillan, 1990

Fleming, John, *Tom Stoppard: front and center*, University of Texas, 2000

Harty, John, III (ed.), *Tom Stoppard: a casebook*, Garland, 1988

Hayman, Ronald, *Tom Stoppard*, Contemporary Playwrights, Heinemann, 1982

Hunter, Jim, *Tom Stoppard's Plays*, Faber, 1982

Hunter, Jim, *Tom Stoppard*, Faber Critical Guide, 2000. [A detailed study of four plays: *Rosencrantz, Jumpers, Travesties* and *Arcadia*.]

Jenkins, Anthony, *The Theatre of Tom Stoppard*, Cambridge University Press, 1989

Jenkins, Anthony (ed.), *Critical Essays on Tom Stoppard*, Boston, G. K. Hall, 1990

Kelly, Katherine E., *Tom Stoppard and the Craft of Comedy*, University of Michigan Press, 1991

Kelly, Katherine E. (ed.), *The Cambridge Companion to Tom Stoppard*, Cambridge University Press, 2001 [Particularly recommended are Paul Edwards on 'Science in *Hapgood* and *Arcadia*' and Hersh Zeifman on 'The comedy of Eros: Stoppard in Love'.]

Londré, Felicia Hardison, *Tom Stoppard*, New York, Frederick Unger, 1981

Page, Malcolm, *File on Stoppard*, Methuen, 1986

Sales, Roger, *Rosencrantz and Guildenstern Are Dead*, Penguin, 1988

Sammells, Neil, *Tom Stoppard: the artist as critic*, Macmillan, 1988

Whitaker, Thomas R., *Tom Stoppard*, Grove Press, 1983

Other sources

Berlin, Isaiah, *Russian Thinkers*, Penguin, 1994

Eyre, Richard, *National Service: diary of a decade*, Bloomsbury, 2003

Eyre, Richard and Wright, Nicholas, *Changing Stages*, Bloomsbury, 2001

Gleick, James, *Chaos: making a new science*, Sphere Books, 1989

Gribbin, John, *In Search of Schrödinger's Cat: quantum physics and reality*, Corgi Books, 1993

Tynan, Kenneth, *Show People*, Weidenfeld and Nicolson, 1979

Acknowledgements

Twenty-five years ago Frank Pike, Stoppard's editor at Faber, invited me first to write about his plays, and I shall always be grateful for having been set on a course which has given so much enjoyment.

For this book, my particular thanks go to Simon Russell Beale, Essie Davis, Stephen Dillane, Sir Richard Eyre, David Hersey, Felicity Kendal, Vicki Mortimer, Sir Trevor Nunn, John Tydeman, John Wood and Peter Wood for their generosity in giving the interviews that appear here. Jacky Matthews, Stoppard's secretary, has been repeatedly helpful. Above all I thank Sir Tom Stoppard himself, for his interview with me, for checking and commenting kindly on my 'Life and Views' chapter – and, of course, for lighting up our lives.

For permission to reprint copyright material the publishers gratefully acknowledge the following:

Lucy Davies, David Leveaux and Tom Stoppard: extracts from 'David Leveaux and Tom Stoppard in Conversation' by Lucy Davies; programme notes for Donmar Warehouse production of *The Real Thing*, May 1999, reproduced with the permission of Lucy Davies, David Leveaux and Tom Stoppard; Shusha Guppy and Tom Stoppard: extracts from 'Tom Stoppard: The Art of Theatre VII' © 1988 by *The Paris Review*, reprinted with permission of The Wylie Agency; Tom Stoppard: extract from 'The Event and the Text': the Whidden Lecture, McMaster University, Hamilton, Ontario, 24 October 1988, transcribed for Ta Panta (McMaster University Faculty Association), 6,

Index

Abbe, James, 227
Absurdism, 2, 39, 40, 49, 190–2
Aldwych theatre, 181, 185, 197–8, 201
Amnesty International, 15
Areté magazine, 45, 176
Ashcroft, Peggy, 195–6, 249, 256
Auden, W. H., 125, 128, 169
Ayckbourn, Alan, 192–3, 257, 259
Ayer, A. J., 31, 67, 143

Barber, Noel, 9
Barbican theatre, 202
Bata shoe company, 4, 5, 17
BBC, 9, 29, 40–41, 66, 117, 212
Beale, Simon Russell, 238–46, 262
Beckett, Samuel, 19, 27, 33–4, 36–40, 42,
    51–2, 107, 111–12, 222, 243–4
Bell, Tom, 184–5
Benchley, Robert, 55
Benken, David, 227
Bennett, Alan, 78
Berlin, Isaiah, 100, 102, 105, 166, 248
Berman, Ed, 42, 55, 64, 71
Billington, Michael, 242
Bohn, Irene, 228
Bond, Edward, 121, 128
Brahms, Caryl and S. J. Simon (*No Bed
    for Bacon*), 228
Brater, Enoch, 42
Brecht, Bertolt, 34–5, 177, 222
Brook, Peter, 111, 261
Brooks, Jeremy, 199
Browning, Robert, 107
Bryden, Ronald, 11, 199

Carroll, Lewis, 83
Charter 77, 15, 17, 216
Chekhov, Anton, 35, 87, 105–6, 168,

    210, 235, 214, 250, 258–9
Chetwyn, Robert, 130
Christie, Agatha, 54
Clarke, Charles, 220
Close, Glenn, 243
Codron, Michael, 42, 68, 83–4, 88, 255
Congreve, William, 214
Constable, Paule, 224, 229
Crowden, Graham, 134
Crowley, Bob, 174
Crudup, Billy, 206
Cubism, 27
Czechoslovakia, 3, 14–15, 17–19, 32,
    66–7, 159, 168

Dada-ism, 27
Darjeeling, 5, 7
Davies, Lucy, 156–9
Davis, Essie, 59, 242–5
Delaney, Paul, xv
Delmer, Sefton, 9
Dillane, Stephen, 43, 100, 197, 246–9, 262
Donne, John, 64
Donmar Warehouse (theatre), 156, 223, 225
Dudley, William, 37, 104, 171, 212, 231

Eddington, Paul, 254
Eden, Emily, 85
Ehle, Jennifer, 262
Eliot, T. S., 26–7
Ellmann, Richard, 184, 187
Ewing, Kenneth, 51
Eyre, Richard, 34, 36, 203–5, 213–223,
    237, 239–40

Farmer, Doyne, 93
Fermat, Pierre de, 92
Fielding, Emma, 206

Fletcher, John, 33
Ford, John ('Tis Pity She's A Whore), 39, 74–6
Frayn, Michael, 251, 259
Fry, Christopher, 137
Fugard, Athol, 121, 125–6

Galsworthy, John, 68
Gambon, Michael, 249
Gilbert, W. S., 51
Gleick, James, 93
Goon Show, The, 40, 215
Gordon, Giles, 52
Gorky, Maxim, 168, 210
Gray, Simon, 259
Gribbin, John, 28, 80
Griffiths, Trevor, 121, 215
Guppy, Shusha, 59, 130–44
Gussow, Mel, 20

Hall, Peter, 197–8
Hampton, Christopher, 121, 126
Hare, David, 121, 127–8, 186, 215
Harris, Frank, 97
Havel, Vaclav, 14–15, 65–6, 169, 177
Haymarket theatre, 185, 206
Henderson, Mark, 223
Hersey, David, 188, 229–31
Hogg, Christopher, 13
Hopkins, Anthony, 249
Hordern, Michael, 182, 244
Housman, A.E., 95–9, 189, 218

Imison, Richard, 177
Ibsen, Henrik, 35, 106, 215, 235
Index on Censorship, 15, 216
India, 4, 7, 32, 84, 195, 263
Ionesco, Eugene, 39, 190

Jerome, Jerome K., 97, 196
Johnson, Paul, 21, 71
Joyce, James, 25, 27, 61–3, 184, 187, 201

Kendal, Felicity, 13–14, 39, 42, 73, 84, 88, 93, 195, 203, 249–63
Kohout, Pavel, 15, 71
Kundera, Milan, 246

Landovsky, Pavel, 15
Lean, David, 133
le Carré, John, 134, 188
Lenin, V. I., 26, 61–3, 101, 122–3, 152, 175
Lerner, Laurence, 67
Leveaux, David, 156–9, 223–6, 240, 244–5
Lloyd, Robert, 198
Lloyd Webber, Andrew, 37
Logical Positivism, 31, 143

Macaulay, Alistair, 95
McEwan, Geraldine, 249
McKellen, Ian, 66, 202, 220
Magritte, Rene, 1
Marx Brothers, 56
Marx, Karl, 21, 53, 63, 101–2, 105, 123
Marxism, 21–2, 101, 122–3
Miller, Jonathan, 180
Modernism, 25–8, 60–61
Molnar, Ferenc, 73
Monty Python's Flying Circus, 39
Moore, G. E., 29, 59
Mortimer, Vicki, 223–9
Mozart, Wolfgang Amadeus, 88
Mrozek, Slawomir, 11, 198–9

Nadel, Ira, xv, 20, 88
National Theatre, 11, 13, 16, 41, 56, 104, 138, 148, 154–5, 163, 170, 180–81, 189, 197, 203–5, 210–11, 213, 216–8, 221, 227–8, 231, 263
National Union of Journalists, 20, 69
Nestroy, Johann, 73, 154–5, 258
New Statesman, 21
Newton, Isaac, 28, 34
New York, 11, 81, 135–6, 174, 181, 183, 203, 206, 217, 224, 228–9, 235, 238, 242, 252
Nichols, Mike, 142
Norman, Marc, 99
Nunn, Trevor, 11, 37, 42, 65, 99, 107, 150, 168, 171, 173–4, 184, 188, 197–214, 216–17, 221, 237, 248

O'Brien, Jack, 174
O'Donnell, Paddy, 180

Old Vic theatre, 185
Olivier, Laurence, 134, 183, 249
Osborne, John, 34, 111, 249
O'Toole, Peter, 10

Paris Review, 130–44
Phoenix theatre, 186
Pike, Frank, 85
Pinter, Harold, 11, 34, 39, 143, 151–2,
    176, 179, 201, 249, 259
Pirandello, Luigi, 25–6, 35, 51, 55
Pocklington, 8
Postmodernism, 33–4
Poussin, Nicolas, 90
Prague, 17, 67, 72
Previn, André, 3, 36, 65–6, 202, 236
Pullman, Philip, 176

Radio, 40–42, 46–7, 55–6, 84–9, 162,
    177, 190–97, 256
Raine, Craig, 176
Raphael, Adam, 125
Rattigan, Terence, 137–8
Realism, 34–6, 54
Rees, Roger, 251, 253, 262
Richardson, Ralph, 249
Rigg, Diana, 71, 186, 244, 253
Rogers, Paul, 198
Royal Academy, 23
RSC (Royal Shakespeare Company),
    10–11, 41, 53, 118, 197, 200, 202–3,
    206
Rudman, Michael, 14
Russia, 15–16, 18, 20, 64–5, 69,
    100–101, 113, 122–3, 164, 174–5

Sartre, Jean-Paul, 48
Schiff, Stephen, 11, 12
Schnitzler, Arthur, 73, 148
Scene magazine, 10
Scofield, Paul, 151, 249
Sewell, Rufus, 206
Shaffer, Peter, 133, 180–81, 235
Shakespeare, William, 8, 13, 25–6, 31–8,
    51–3, 61, 72, 99–100, 104, 144–5,
    147–8, 150–51, 153–4, 156, 206,
    222, 250
Shaw, G. B., 68, 203, 214, 250

Sheridan, R. B., 206, 214
Simpson, N. F., 39
Singapore, 4–5, 32, 87
Smith, Maggie, 186, 249
Snow, C.P., 28
'Solidarity' (Polish political movement),
    79
Spielberg, Stephen, 37
Stalin, Josef, 101
Stewart, Patrick, 201–2
Stoppard, Jose (nee Ingle), 10
Stoppard, Kenneth (stepfather), 6–8, 10,
    12, 16–19, 160
Stoppard, Martha (mother), 3–8, 16–17,
    19
Stoppard, Miriam, 11–12, 14, 39
Stoppard, Peter, 3, 5, 9–10, 17
Stoppard, Tom
    boots and moons (joke-obsessions), 46,
        49, 54, 57, 83, 192
    conceptual art, on, 23
    conservatism, 6, 19–23, 110
    determinism, on, 6, 93, 102–3
    early childhood, 3–7, 32, 110
    education, 5–9
    female characters in, 50–51, 58–9,
        63–4, 83, 98, 141
    Jewishness, 3, 8, 14, 16–18, 177–8
    language in, 30–33, 47, 53, 64, 71–2,
        106, 110–1, 160–62, 167, 169, 191,
        233–4, 239, 253–4, 260, 262
    marriages and children, 10–13
    Marxist relativism, on, 21–2
    mathematics, in, 2, 28–9, 92–3, 132
    moral concerns, in, 2, 18, 22, 30–31,
        34, 67–8, 76–7, 79, 94, 122, 125–6,
        143–4, 166–9, 203, 248–9
    names, in, 19, 38, 51, 66, 69, 97, 110
    philosophy, in, 29–32, 51, 56, 58, 143
    physics, in, 28, 80–82, 92, 132–3, 188
    works
    – *A Separate Peace*, 48
    – *After Magritte*, 1, 26, 42, 54–5, 58,
        65, 115–7
    – *Albert's Bridge*, 47–8, 117, 191
    – *Another Moon Called Earth*, 54, 57,
        232
    – *Arcadia*, 2, 28, 36–7, 42, 45, 70,

88–96, 98, 100, 171–2, 178, 189, 203, 205–8, 216–18, 222, 239, 246, 257, 261
– *Artist Descending a Staircase*, 23, 26, 59–61, 98, 115, 193–4
– *A Walk on the Water / Enter A Free Man*, 46, 116
– *Dalliance* (Schnitzler), 73
– *Dirty Linen / New-Found-Land*, 32, 42, 63–4
– *Dogg's Hamlet, Cahoot's Macbeth*, 15, 42, 55, 58, 71–2
– *Every Good Boy Deserves Favour*, 3, 33, 36–7, 65–6, 72, 101, 202–3, 236–7
– *Galileo*, 43, 45, 58, 176–7
– *Hapgood*, 11, 41, 70, 72, 76, 80–84, 92, 95, 130–34, 138–9, 141, 174, 188, 206, 230, 254–6
– *If You're Glad I'll Be Frank*, 47, 65, 117, 192–3
– *Indian Ink*, 13, 42, 88–9, 98, 188–9, 254, 256–7
– *In the Native State*, 13, 42, 84–90, 95, 98, 177, 194–6, 255–7
– *Jumpers*, 1, 13, 22, 29–33, 36, 41, 53–4, 56–9, 60–61, 65, 76, 94–5, 116, 118, 120–22, 124, 129–30, 136, 143, 170–71, 179–84, 188–7, 190, 192, 206, 215, 223–30, 233, 238–46, 254, 262
– *Lord Malquist and Mr Moon*, 31, 48–51, 96
– *M is for Moon among Other Things*, 46, 191
– *Neutral Ground*, 54, 81
– *Night and Day*, 21, 32, 36, 42, 64, 68–72, 75–6, 88, 105, 138, 141, 172, 182, 186
– *On the Razzle* (Nestroy), 73, 154–5, 181, 250
– *Professional Foul*, 2, 22, 31, 66–9, 87, 101, 168–9, 196, 203, 215
– *Rosencrantz and Guildenstern Are Dead*, 10–12, 25, 38, 40–2, 51–6, 61, 65, 70, 87, 90, 113–5, 120, 129, 134, 136, 152, 179–8, 196, 198–200, 215, 230–32, 238–9, 246, 249
– *Rough Crossing* (Molnar), 73

– *Shakespeare in Love*, 43, 99–100
– *Squaring the Circle*, 79–80
– *Teeth*, 54, 132
– *The Coast of Utopia*, 20, 36, 45, 53, 85, 100–108, 159, 166–9, 171, 173–5, 178, 190, 210–13, 221–2, 230–31, 246, 248–9, 260
– *The Dissolution of Dominic Boot*, 46, 191
– *The Dog It Was That Died*, 45, 81
– *The Invention of Love*, 36, 70, 80, 95–100, 164, 174, 178, 189–90, 196–7, 203–5, 215, 218–22, 231, 237, 239–40
– *The Real Inspector Hound*, 35, 38, 42, 54–5, 115–7, 120, 135, 196
– *The Real Thing*, 32–3, 38–9, 42–3, 73–9, 88, 105, 152, 142, 156–8, 167, 172, 182, 186–7, 203, 223, 225, 228–9, 243, 246–8, 251–3, 257, 261–2
– *The Seagull* (Chekhov), 210, 258
– *Travesties*, 26, 33, 38, 41–2, 53, 61–3, 65, 83, 94, 101–2, 107, 113, 116, 121–2, 128–9, 152–3, 172, 184–6, 196, 200–202, 220, 231–7, 262
– *Undiscovered Country* (Schnitzler), 73, 148–50
– *Where Are They Now?*, 7, 55, 69, 98, 192

Straussler, Eugen (Stoppard's father), 3–5, 17, 19, 87, 159
Strindberg, August, 75, 244
Sunday Telegraph, 3
Sunday Times, 19, 109–113
Suzman, Janet, 198

Thatcher, Margaret, 20
Theatre of the Absurd, 1, 39–40
Theatre Quarterly, 9, 29, 57, 63, 101, 113–30
thermodynamics, 92
Thompson, Mark
Times Literary Supplement, 21, 23
Toms, Carl, 42, 73, 88, 133, 179, 230, 235, 254
Tusa, John, 14, 159–70
Tydeman, John, 42, 177, 190–97
Tynan, Kenneth, 8, 11, 36, 41, 137–8,

161–2, 183, 199–200
Tzara, Tristan, 27, 61, 63

Vanity Fair, 11
Vienna, 73, 181, 250
Virgil, 89, 95

Warner, David, 198
Waugh, Evelyn, 46, 130
Wesker, Arnold, 34
Western Daily Press, 9–10
Whitelaw, Billie, 249
Wilde, Oscar, 49, 96–7, 214
   The Importance of Being Earnest, 33,
      38, 61–3, 201
Williams, Michael, 198

Williams, Raymond, 26
Wittgenstein, Ludwig, 55, 58, 71, 241,
   243
Wood, John, 42, 51, 54, 73, 83, 96, 179,
   185–6, 201–2, 220–1, 231–8, 253,
   262
Wood, Peter, 6, 42, 73, 81, 88, 130–1,
   133, 139, 141–2, 148–9, 179–90,
   202, 206, 216, 224, 230, 235–6, 242,
   250–1, 253–4, 259
Woolf, Virginia, 27
Wright, Nicholas, 214
Wycherley, William, 214

Zlin, 3–4, 17